The Cold War Begins in Asia

Contemporary American History Series
William E. Leuchtenburg, General Editor

The Cold War Begins in Asia

American East Asian Policy and the Fall of the Japanese Empire

Marc S. Gallicchio

Columbia University Press
New York   1988

Library of Congress Cataloging-in-Publication Data

Gallicchio, Marc S.
    The Cold War begins in Asia.

    (Contemporary American history series)
    Bibliography: p.
    Includes index.
    1. East Asia—Foreign relations—United States.
 2. United States—Foreign relations—East Asia.
 3. United States—Foreign relations—1945–1953.
 I. Title. II. Series.
 DS518.8.G33   1988   327.7305   87-23917
 ISBN 0-231-06502-7

Columbia University Press
New York   Guildford, Surrey
Copyright © 1988 Columbia University Press
All rights reserved
Printed in the United States of America

Clothbound Columbia University Press editions are Smyth-
sewn and printed on permanent and durable acid-free paper

Book design by Ken Venezio

To Lisa Ann Ross

Contemporary American History Series
William E. Leuchtenburg, General Editor

Contents

Abbreviations of Terms Used
in the Text and Notes

CA	Division of Chinese Affairs
CAD	Civil Affairs Division
CCP	Chinese Communist Party
CCS	Combined Chiefs of Staff
CGUSFCT	Commanding General U.S. Forces China Theater
CINCAFPAC	Commander in Chief Army Forces in the Pacific
CINCPAC	Commander in Chief Naval Forces in the Pacific
DB	Diplomatic Branch
DSB	Department of State Bulletin
EUR	Office of European Affairs
FE	Office of Far Eastern Affairs
FRUS	Foreign Relations of the United States
HST	Harry S. Truman Library
HUSAFIK	History of United States Army Forces in Korea
IDACFE	Interdivisional Area Committee for the Far East
JCS	Joint Chiefs of Staff
JSP	Joint Staff Planners
JSSC	Joint Strategic Survey Committee
JWPC	Joint War Plans Committee
KMT	Kuomintang
MAG	Military Advisory Group
MHI	Military History Institute
MMRB	Modern Military Records Branch
NA	National Archives
NHC	Naval Historical Center
NOA	Navy Operational Archives

OANB	Old Army and Navy Branch
OPD	Operations and Plans Division
OSS	Office of Strategic Services
RG	Record Group
SEA	Division of Southeast Asian Affairs
SEAC	Southeast Asian Command
S&P	Strategy and Policy Group
SWNCC	State War Navy Coordinating Committee

Preface

THIS IS A STUDY of the Truman administration's efforts to create and implement a policy for East Asia amid the turmoil created by the collapse of the Japanese empire. In the last nine months of 1945, American–East Asian relations underwent a sudden and dramatic transformation. In this brief span of time, World War II came to a close in the Pacific and the Cold War in Asia began. From President Franklin D. Roosevelt's death in April onward, events seemed to outrun the ability of American officials to control them. In early May, Germany surrendered, leaving the United States free to concentrate the full weight of its military power against Japan. By the end of June, the United States had broken through the inner defenses of Japan's Pacific empire, captured Okinawa, and begun preparations for the last stage of the war, the invasion of Japan's home islands. Even though victory seemed assured, American officials expected the war to last for at least another year. According to this timetable, American political and military leaders were under little pressure to prepare for the problems that might arise when Japan surrendered and was finally stripped of its Asian possessions.

Less than two months after the fall of Okinawa, the United States exploded atomic bombs over Hiroshima and Nagasaki, the Soviet Union declared war against Japan, and the emperor ordered his troops to surrender. Suddenly, all of Manchuria, north China, and Korea lay open before the advance of Russian troops.

As the Red Army pushed into Northeast Asia it appeared that much of the continent was about to be engulfed in a tide of revolution. In Indochina, the Communist-led Vietminh moved to fill the vacuum created by Japan's defeat. In Korea, native resistance movements seized this long-awaited opportunity to declare their independence from Japan and create their own government. Elsewhere, China lurched toward civil war as Nationalists and Communists raced to take control of the territory occupied by Japanese troops.

Before the war, the American military presence in Asia had been minimal, and as late as April 1945 the United States was reluctant to become deeply involved on the continent after Japan's defeat. In the final weeks of the war, however, American officials decided that the United States must play a decisive role in determining the future development of Korea, China, and to a lesser degree, Indochina. In the months following Japan's surrender, these officials labored to construct and implement a coherent response to the convulsive events on the Asian mainland.

Although much has been written about the end of the war in the Pacific, historians have not examined thoroughly how the sudden collapse of Japanese resistance affected American plans for East and Southeast Asia. The military histories that deal with planning during the war generally confine their analysis to American preparations for the occupation of Japan's main islands. Studies on the origins of the Cold War tend to pass over Asian issues during this period and concentrate instead on the Soviet-American conflict over Europe, the Middle East, and the atomic bomb.

In recent years the history of the American wartime and postwar experience in Korea, China, and Indochina has been described in a number of important monographs. Missing in some degree from these studies, however, is an appreciation of the sweep and pace of events in the final months of the war. This was a period of great upheaval in Asia. By focusing on American policy toward a specific country, these recent histories have taken a perspective on the frenzied events of 1945 that was not available to American officials at the time. American policy-making was not so neatly compartmentalized. Officials were forced to deal with a wide range of interconnected problems with little or no time for study.

In describing and analyzing the events of April through December 1945, I have tried to make the reader aware of the atmosphere of almost continuous crisis in which American policymakers worked. By taking a regional perspective on the events of this period, I have also attempted to show how decisions made concerning one country often affected policy toward another. Finally, in emphasizing both the chaotic pace of events and the complexity of the problems caused by Japan's collapse, I have tried to provide a clearer understanding of how the United States became involved in a Cold War in Asia.

Acknowledgments

It is with great pleasure that I am finally able to acknowledge in print the valuable assistance given to me by so many of my friends and colleagues. My greatest debt is to Waldo Heinrichs who directed the writing of this manuscript as a dissertation and who read and offered expert advice on revised sections whenever they appeared in his mailbox. Fortunately for me his patience as a teacher seems to have no limit. I was also lucky to have Russell Weigley, and the late Shumpei Okamoto as dissertation advisers and teachers. Both were unfailingly generous with their advice and encouragement. For that and other reasons too numerous to mention, they have my deepest appreciation.

I am also indebted to Warren Cohen and William Leuchtenberg, both of whom read the manuscript while it was being revised for publication. Warren Cohen sent me back to the archives one last time and got me to clarify some important points and rethink others. William Leuchtenberg made numerous suggestions concerning matters of substance, style and organization, most of which I had the good sense to follow.

Early drafts of much of this study were presented in the Dissertation Colloquium conducted by the Department of History at Temple University. I wish to thank my colleagues in that seminar for their sound advice and for helping to make the business of dissertation writing a little less dreary. I also wish to thank Richard Manser, and Robert Orr, Jr., for taking time away from their own writing to read and comment on mine. Michael Palmer also read an early draft and, fortunately for me, he made the switch from the age of sail to the modern navy in time to give me the benefit of his ample knowledge of naval strategy.

I could not have completed this study without the support of the Harry S. Truman Library Institute, which made possible a trip to Independence,

Missouri. The Department of History at Temple University also provided generous support in the form of several research assistantships, summer research fellowships and a James Barnes travel award. Despite this assistance, my work in Washington would have been impossible without the gracious hospitality of Mike and Carol Palmer, and David and Susan Reinhard. I am especially grateful to Donald Stein, who went far beyond the call of duty in assisting a fellow Abingtonian on his excursions to Washington.

Among the numerous archivists and librarians who aided my research, I wish to thank Dennis Bigler of the Truman Library, Richard Sommers of the Military History Institute and Edward Reese, Terry Hammett, and John Taylor of the Modern Military Reference Branch of the National Archives for their invaluable assistance and patient handling of my many research requests. The same holds true for Sally Marks and Kathy Nicastro of the Diplomatic Branch of the National Archives both of whom made a valiant effort to instruct me in the wonders of the State Department's filing system.

Kate Wittenberg, Executive Editor at Columbia University Press, has been a pleasure to work with. I also wish to thank Susan Hopkins, who copyedited the manuscript and Leslie Bialler for guiding it through press.

My wife, Lisa Ross, read most of the manuscript. What she did not read, I read to her, more times than she would care to remember. This time around she can stop after the dedication page.

The Cold War Begins in Asia

Weighing the Options:
Truman and the Russians

The President said this morning at his conference with us that he sat up late last night reading the Yalta agreements again. He said every time he went over them he found new meanings in them. (Eben Ayers, assistant press secretary)[1]

LATE IN THE afternoon of April 12, 1945, Vice-President Harry S. Truman was settling down for a bourbon and some conversation in the chambers of House Speaker Sam Rayburn (D–Texas) when he received word to call presidential aide Steven Early. Hanging up the phone, a startled Truman explained that he was urgently needed at the White House. "Boys, this is in the room," he said, "something must have happened."[2] Arriving at a back entrance, Truman entered the White House and quickly learned the reason for his unexpected summons to the executive mansion. A short time earlier, at approximately 5:00 P.M., Franklin D. Roosevelt had died at his retreat in Warm Springs, Georgia. Harry S. Truman, a product of Kansas City machine politics, and formerly senator from Missouri, was now President of the United States.

That evening, when Truman took the oath of office to become the thirty-third President of the United States, he was already well aware of the enormous challenges he would face. Of these, perhaps the most pressing issue Truman confronted in his first days in office was the problem of the deteriorating relationship between the United States and the Soviet Union. After more than three years of war, the Grand Alliance of the United States, Great Britain, and the Soviet Union was on the verge of defeating the German Reich. Nearly every day reports from the battlefield brought news of Allied successes. At almost the same rate cables from London and Moscow carried word of new difficulties with the Soviet Union.

From his first full day in office Truman found it difficult to keep up with the pace of events. On April 14 the Joint Chiefs of Staff (JCS) predicted that German resistance would continue until September. Four days later Field Marshal Walther Model surrendered his army of 325,000 German troops in the Ruhr pocket to American officers. Three weeks later Germany surrendered.[3]

Germany's defeat removed the principal justification for the Grand Alliance, and made it difficult to paper over the growing cracks in what had always been a marriage of convenience. Even before the war ended, Soviet leader Joseph Stalin had accused the United States of planning to negotiate a separate surrender with German troops on the western front. This incident precipitated a flurry of angry telegrams between Roosevelt and Stalin, the tone of which has caused some historians to suggest that Soviet-American relations were undergoing a sea change even before Roosevelt's death.[4]

With peace suddenly at hand, the new President was forced to confront a host of complex issues that Roosevelt had deferred during the war. Chief among these was the problem of reconciling Roosevelt's public explanations of the February 1945 Yalta agreements with the private and power-oriented understandings he had reached with Stalin.[5] Fearing a recurrence of isolationism and congressional opposition if the postwar settlement failed to live up to American expectations, Roosevelt had used idealistic Wilsonian rhetoric to disguise what were really spheres of influence agreements in Europe and the Far East. For example, at Yalta the Allies had agreed to an ambiguously worded Declaration on Liberated Europe in which they pledged to promote democratic regimes within their occupation zones. But since the Russians regarded their own political system as democratic, this statement was open to a variety of interpretations.[6] Concerning Poland, the Allies concluded a more specific agreement in which the Soviets pledged to reorganize the Moscow-sponsored provisional government to give greater representation to other groups in Poland and in exile.[7]

During their meetings the Big Three had also dealt with a number of questions regarding the disposition of territory in East Asia. As part of a secret agreement signed by Roosevelt, Churchill, and Stalin, the Soviet government pledged to enter the Pacific war within three months of Germany's surrender. In return Stalin was to regain the concessions lost by czarist Russia in the Russo-Japanese war of 1904–1905. These included control of southern Sakhalin Island and the lease of a naval base at Port Arthur on the Liaotung Peninsula. In addition, Dairen, also on the Liaotung Peninsula, was to become an international port in which the "preeminent interests of the Soviet Union" would be safeguarded.[8] The agreement also provided for joint Sino-Soviet control of the Chinese Eastern and South Manchurian railroads, "it being understood that the preeminent interests of the Soviet Union should be safeguarded and that China shall retain full sovereignty in Manchuria."[9] Finally, the United States and Great Britain agreed that the Kurile Islands would be "handed over to the Soviet Union," and that the status quo in Outer Mongolia, a Soviet client state, would be maintained.[10]

The Big Three concluded these arrangements without the approval of the Chinese Nationalist government. As part of the American obligation, Roosevelt promised to obtain Generalissimo Chiang Kai-shek's consent once Stalin was ready to enter the war. The Far Eastern agreement represented a significant reversal of the earlier Cairo Declaration in which the United States and Great Britain had promised to restore Chinese sovereignty over Manchuria and other territories taken by Japan since the Sino-Japanese war of 1895. The Soviets did, however, state their willingness to conclude a pact of friendship and alliance with the Nationalist government and to render assistance to Chiang's armed forces against the Japanese.[11] In effect, by agreeing to aid the Kuomintang (KMT), Stalin was promising to withhold support from Chiang's Chinese opponents, the strongest of which were the Communists (CCP).

At Yalta, the Allies also dealt with important colonial issues. During the war Roosevelt had repeatedly voiced his opposition to a return to the status quo antebellum in Southeast Asia. He singled out French rule in Indochina for special criticism, but he also broached the subject of restoring Chinese sovereignty over Hong Kong. FDR had also given some thought to creating an international trusteeship over Indochina as an intermediate step between dependency and outright independence. But the French, with British support, remained committed to reclaiming their empire in Southeast Asia. In early 1945, as France grew stronger, Roosevelt found it increasingly difficult to oppose a French restoration in Indochina, and by the time of the Yalta conference FDR had abandoned the trusteeship plan. Instead, he agreed that the European colonies would become part of the trusteeship system only if the colonial power consented.[12]

Earlier in the war, the President had also given his tacit approval to a State Department plan for a four-power trusteeship for Korea consisting of the United States, Great Britain, China, and the Soviet Union. The Cairo Declaration hinted at the possibility of an interim regime by stating that after it was liberated from Japan, Korea would become independent "in due course."[13] Although the Yalta agreements did not mention Korea specifically, FDR and Stalin did briefly discuss the feasibility of a four-power trusteeship. If Roosevelt had any concrete ideas about the nature of the American role in Korea, he did not reveal them at the time. In response to Stalin's queries he did say that he thought the trusteeship might last twenty or thirty years and that it probably would not be necessary to station troops in Korea during that period.[14]

Taken together, the Far Eastern agreements offer the most comprehensive blueprint of Roosevelt's postwar plans for East Asia. These plans constituted a sphere of influence arrangement in which Soviet economic and security interests were given ample consideration. That is not to say that FDR came away from the conference empty-handed. Roosevelt had, in particular, secured Stalin's promise to enter the Pacific war in time to make an important contribution. Before the conference, the JCS had advised Roosevelt that Soviet assistance would lessen American casualties and shorten the war in the Pacific. Specifically, the JCS looked to the Soviets to prevent the Japanese from transferring troops in Manchuria to reinforce the home islands.[15] The Chiefs were not consulted on the final political settlement at Yalta, but they received the news of Stalin's promise to enter the war as "the lesser of three evils."[16] Based on Stalin's pledge alone, Admiral William D. Leahy, Roosevelt's representative on the JCS, was willing to judge the conference a success.[17]

Roosevelt's intentions concerning the Sino-Soviet part of the secret protocol are more difficult to interpret than the military provisions of the agreements. Some historians have viewed Stalin's pledge to support the Nationalists as Roosevelt's way of trying to contain the Chinese Communists by depriving them of outside assistance.[18] It seems doubtful, however, that FDR thought China's problems could be solved so easily. Not long before the conference, the President had told Admiral Leahy that "from the long range point of view we can do very little at this time to keep China together."[19] Yet at the very least, the Sino-Soviet treaty did offer some hope of preventing China from becoming a site of postwar competition between the United States and the Soviet Union. With Soviet interests guaranteed and with the major powers consenting to recognize and aid only the Nationalists, China would be cordoned off from outside interference. If Stalin accepted the limits on Soviet expansion defined by the Yalta agreements, the KMT and the Communists would be able to settle their dispute without disturbing the postwar balance of power in East Asia.

Although Roosevelt's limited objectives on the mainland were consistent with the general direction of military strategy in early 1945, his concessions to Stalin in Northeast Asia conflicted with his public assurances to Chiang Kai-shek and the American people. Despite the inclusion in the agreements of a statement upholding Chinese sovereignty over Manchuria, the secret protocol did infringe on Chinese sovereign rights in the area. In addition, Roosevelt's arrangements contrasted sharply with the postwar expectations of the State Department's large planning bureaucracy. By the time of the Yalta Conference the department had begun to prepare for a significant American presence on the mainland.[20] The planners expected the United States to play a leading role in balancing Chinese, Soviet, Korean, and Japanese interests in the region. In their numerous policy papers and in the briefing book they prepared for the Yalta conference, the experts recommended that the United States mediate between the Soviets and Chinese so as to restore Chinese sovereignty over Manchuria and to protect the Open Door.[21] In Korea the planners believed that the United States would have to actively participate in the occupation so as to prevent the Chinese and the Russians from competing for control over the peninsula. Noting that the Japanese had acquired the Kuriles through peaceful negotiation, the specialists also recommended that Japan be allowed to retain at least some of the islands for economic and security purposes.[23]

Early in the war Roosevelt had sought the advice of the State Department on postwar issues, but by late 1943 he had begun to develop his plans without consulting with the diplomats or informing them of his decisions. Indeed, he completely ignored the briefing book the department compiled for Yalta. After the conference, to prevent the premature disclosure of the secret agreements, Roosevelt had the documents locked in Admiral Leahy's White House safe.

It is not clear how Roosevelt planned to deal with the discrepancy between his public pronouncements and his private arrangements. With his usual self-confidence, he continued to believe that after Yalta he could

manage whatever problems developed in American-Soviet relations. Although Roosevelt concluded that the United States could not force Soviet
compliance with the agreements, he seems to have reasoned that by
postponing discussion of American postwar aid and by withholding information about the atomic bomb project, he could induce Stalin to cooperate.[24] But as the Red Army rolled across Eastern Europe in the spring of
1945, such cooperation was nowhere in evidence.

When Truman became President he assured the nation that he would
follow the course laid out by his predecessor. During his first days in
office, however, the new chief executive appeared ready to take a radically
different approach toward Russia. Then, almost as suddenly, he steered
American-Soviet relations back onto the track established by his former
boss. In part this confusion resulted from Truman's lack of knowledge
about Roosevelt's postwar plans. When FDR died, his highly personalized
view of the postwar world perished with him. To be sure, Roosevelt's
unofficial advisers, Harry Hopkins, who had carried out a number of
missions to London and Moscow for FDR, and Joseph Davies, a former
ambassador to the Soviet Union, both understood the basic aims of their
chief's diplomacy. But their influence depended in large measure on their
personal relations with Roosevelt. Although Truman sought their advice,
Hopkins and Davies no longer belonged to the President's inner circle.[25]

In his search for information and guidance Truman also relied on the
counsel of a group of officials who had long been critical of what they
perceived to be Roosevelt's open-handed policy toward the Kremlin.
Viewing the Russian occupation of Eastern Europe with alarm, they urged
the new President to take a firmer stand against the Soviets in order to
uphold the Yalta agreements. Truman, who was by temperament uncom-
fortable with the nuances of diplomacy, acted on this advice.[26] During a
White House meeting on April 23, Truman berated Soviet Foreign Minister Vyacheslav Molotov for Russian violations of the Yalta agreement on
Poland. Shortly thereafter the President began to have second thoughts
about the correctness of his actions. After discussing the matter with his
advisers, including Joseph Davies, Truman decided to send Hopkins to
Moscow to try to reach an agreement over Poland and to reassure Stalin
that there had been no fundamental changes in American policy toward
the Soviet Union.[27]

Although Truman sought to cooperate with Stalin, he also explored
possible alternatives in the event that relations with the Kremlin deteri-

orated. Before Truman had decided to send Hopkins to Moscow, the Committee of Three (the Secretaries of the State, War, and Navy departments) had begun a review of the Yalta Far Eastern accords. The committee continued its study even after the Hopkins trip was announced. Inasmuch as the Soviets seemed ready to flaunt the Yalta agreements in Eastern Europe, American officials had started to think about what could be done to save Northeast Asia from a similar fate.

On May 10 Patrick Hurley, the American ambassador to China, cabled Washington with a request that he be allowed to tell Chiang about the Yalta accords. Rumors concerning the outcome of the conference agreements circulated freely in Chungking, and Hurley thought that it would be better to clarify the situation than to leave Chiang in the dark.[28] W. Averell Harriman, the American ambassador to Moscow, quickly seized on Hurley's request as a pretext for reviewing the American policy regarding Soviet entry into the war.

Harriman had acquired considerable experience in international affairs as a businessman and a diplomat, and his recommendations carried weight in Washington. The son of railroad magnate E. H. Harriman, he had served as director of the Union Pacific line before branching out into international banking in the 1920s. He left the Republican party in 1928 to become a Democrat, and when Roosevelt was elected he served in the New Deal's National Recovery Administration. In 1941, FDR chose his friend to serve first as an envoy to Churchill and then as ambassador to Moscow.

Harriman began his mission confident that the United States and Soviet Union could cooperate, but the unrelenting frustration of dealing with the Russian government gradually eroded his optimism. By 1944 he was growing concerned over the mounting evidence that Stalin meant to extend Soviet rule into Eastern Europe. The Russian dictator's actions in Poland particularly alarmed Harriman. The ambassador began to warn Roosevelt that Stalin regarded American generosity in the area of Lend Lease as a sign of weakness. When FDR died, Harriman flew back to the United States, taking a hazardous trans-Atlantic route, so that he could alert the new President to the dangers of what he termed a "barbarian invasion of Europe."[29]

In his memoirs Harriman explained, somewhat disingenuously, that in his last meeting with Stalin the Russian leader had asked whether the new President would honor the Far Eastern accords. The ambassador decided that "since Stalin appeared to think that the question was open I thought we might as well look at it again."[30] Under Secretary of State Joseph Grew put it more bluntly. Speaking to Secretary of State Edward Stettinius, who was in San Francisco for the founding of the United Nations Organization, Grew explained that "the whole question was being discussed about whether we were going to support what had been done at Yalta."[31]

Like Harriman, Grew was deeply disturbed by the prospect of Soviet domination in Northeast Asia. One of the "founding fathers" of the modern foreign service, Grew had risen steadily up the career ladder to become ambassador to Japan in 1932. He served in that post until the outbreak of war in 1941. On the verge of retirement, the elderly diplomat had become Under Secretary in 1944. Like most of his colleagues in the old Diplomatic Corps who had served in Europe during the upheaval caused by the Russian Revolution, Grew was a political conservative and arch-anticommunist.[32]

Harriman's warnings only intensified Grew's concerns over Soviet intentions in Europe and Asia. Early one morning during the same week that his department began its review of the Yalta agreements, Grew took to his study to draft a personal memorandum on the goals of Soviet expansionism. Regarding the Far East, he wrote, "Once Russia is in the war against Japan, then Mongolia, and Korea will gradually slip into Russia's orbit, to be followed in due course by China and eventually Japan."[33]

On May 12 Grew sent Navy Secretary James Forrestal and Secretary of War Henry Stimson identical memoranda soliciting their departments' views on American policy "in connection with the political effects of the expected Soviet entry into the Pacific war and the relationship of the Yalta agreements on this subject."[34] The memo posed three questions. Was Soviet entry into the war so vital as to preclude "any attempt by the United States to obtain Soviet agreement to certain desirable political objectives in the Far East"? Second, should the Yalta decision with regard to Soviet political desires in the Far East be reconsidered or "carried into effect in whole or part"? The third question asked if the Russians should be permitted to share in the military occupation of Japan.[35]

The State Department wanted Soviet commitments on four points. First, Stalin should use his presumed influence with the Chinese Communists to bring about the unification of China's forces under Chiang. Stalin should agree to do so before the United States approached the

Chinese about the Yalta Far Eastern accords. Second, the Russians should state their unequivocal adherence to the Cairo Declaration regarding Korea. The State Department also desired assurance from Stalin that immediately after Korea was liberated the country would be placed under a four-power trusteeship. Last, the department suggested that before giving final approval to the USSR's annexation of the Kuriles, the United States should receive emergency landing rights for its commercial aircraft on some of the islands.[36]

During the next several days Stimson discussed the State Department's memorandum with Assistant Secretary of War John J. McCloy and Army Chief of Staff General George C. Marshall. On May 15, at a meeting of the Committee of Three, Stimson recommended that action on Grew's memorandum be delayed. It was not the questions that bothered him, rather it was their timing. Specifically, he argued that "over any such tangled wave of problems the S-1 secret [atomic bomb] would be dominant."[37]

Stimson, like Grew, was approaching the end of a long and distinguished career in public service. Born in 1867, two years after the end of the civil war, Henry Lewis Stimson was the archetype of what Theodore Roosevelt had called the public man. Born into a solidly middle class family whose ancestors had arrived in America before the revolution, Stimson practiced law before taking his first government post. In 1906 he was appointed a U.S. district attorney. He followed this with a stint as Secretary of War, and later, a tour of duty in Europe as a colonel in the army during World War I. During the Republican twenties, Stimson served as a special envoy to Nicaragua, Governor General of the Philippines, and then as Secretary of State under Herbert Hoover.

In this last post Stimson watched helplessly as Japan plundered Manchuria. The Secretary's refusal to recognize the Japanese conquest, the so-called Hoover-Stimson doctrine of nonrecognition, had, his critics charged, only angered the Japanese without loosening their grip on Manchuria. Having witnessed firsthand the failure of moral suasion against a determined foe, Stimson was convinced of the need for the United States to play a more active role in world affairs.[38]

In 1940, Roosevelt appointed the Republican statesman Secretary of War to win bipartisan support for his military buildup. When he answered Roosevelt's call Stimson was already seventy-three years old. To conserve his energy, he left much of the daily business of the War Department to his assistants and concentrated on major policy decisions. One area that claimed an increasing amount of the Secretary's time in early 1945 was the atomic bomb project, which went forward under the code name of the Manhattan Project.

As Secretary of War, Stimson was responsible for overseeing the secret project from start to finish. In April he formed the Interim Committee on atomic policy that examined a wide range of questions concerning the wartime and postwar use of atomic energy. Perhaps more than any other cabinet member Stimson viewed the atomic bomb in terms of how it might increase American leverage with the Soviet Union. Even at this early date, with the bomb in its experimental stages, Stimson anticipated that the weapon would make Soviet assistance superfluous. Regarding the current reevaluation of the Yalta accords, Stimson told McCloy that "the method now to deal with Russia was to keep our mouths shut and let our actions speak for words."[39] The best time to negotiate with the Russians would be when they were no longer needed to defeat Japan.

The Committee of Three accepted Stimson's advice to hold Harriman over for a few days until the matter could be given more thought. Later on the 15th, however, Grew and Harriman met with Truman to argue for an early meeting with Stalin and to recommend that a reassessment of the Far Eastern agreements be completed before Harriman returned to Moscow. Truman appeared to agree. But the following day Stimson convinced the President that it would be better to delay a meeting of the Big Three and to postpone discussion of Far Eastern problems until later. "We shall probably hold more cards in our hands later, than now," Stimson explained.[40] This advice had obvious appeal to Truman. As one historian has noted, "Harriman and Grew were telling him to be bold and take risks; Stimson was asking him to be cautious and do nothing for the moment."[41]

On May 21 Stimson transmitted a formal report in answer to Grew's memorandum. Produced by the Strategy and Policy Group of the Operations Division of the general staff, the paper represented the views of General Marshall as well as Stimson. The Army planners believed that the Yalta agreements conceded little to the Soviets that they could not take by force. The United States might occupy the Kuriles and forestall a Soviet occupation there, but only at the expense of the main effort against Japan.[42] According to the report, an overall agreement with the Soviet Union on East Asian matters was desirable. It did not seem, however, that "reconsideration" of the existing accords, if such was deemed necessary by the State Department, would be particularly fruitful at the moment.[43]

Forrestal's discussions with the Chief of Naval Operations, Admiral Ernest King, revealed a similar disinclination on the Navy's part to challenge the Russians directly in East Asia. King did believe, however, that the effects of a Soviet presence in that area might be mitigated by American support for a strong China.[44] On May 21 Forrestal sent Grew a memorandum supporting Stimson's position. For the time being, any attempt to rewrite the Yalta accords would have to be postponed.

In the discussions regarding the possible revision of the Yalta agreements, Marshall's overriding fear of a bloody invasion of Japan was crucial in sustaining Stimson's position. Long concerned with the costs of invading Japan, Marshall sent Brigadier General George A. Lincoln, the head of the Strategy and Policy Group (S&P), to the Pacific to confer with General Douglas MacArthur after the Yalta conference. Lincoln reported that MacArthur believed that "we should make every effort to get Russia into the Japanese war before we go into Japan, otherwise we will take the impact of the Jap divisions and reap the losses, while the Russians in due time advance into an area free of major resistance."[45] Although the members of S&P did not know about the bomb, Marshall did. Nevertheless, Marshall was clearly unwilling to risk losing Soviet assistance by placing too much faith in the unproven potential of an untested weapon. For Marshall the major objective was to get Russia into the war in time to help pin down Japanese troops on the mainland.

While the Committee of Three was completing its discussion of the Yalta agreements, Harry Hopkins departed for Moscow and his meeting with Stalin. He arrived in Moscow on May 26 and left on June 4. During that time Hopkins, Harriman, and Soviet specialist and interpreter Charles Bohlen met six times with Stalin. Reflecting Truman's concern, Hopkins made the Polish question his top priority. During their first meeting, Hopkins unsuccessfully attempted to explain to Stalin that Truman faced increasing pressure from Congress and the American people over the Polish question. At a subsequent meeting Stalin brushed aside these appeals, saying that he would not "use Soviet public opinion as a screen."[46] Eventually Stalin conceded four places in the proposed Polish government of national unity to representatives from groups other than the Soviet-backed Lublin Poles. This gesture would have to suffice as the fig leaf of respectability with which Truman hoped to cover the reality of Soviet control in Poland.[47]

On East Asian issues Stalin appeared more agreeable. He repeated his consent for a four-power trusteeship for Korea, and pledged his support for Chiang's regime. He added that talks with the Chinese Foreign Minister, T. V. Soong, would have to begin soon so that the Crimea agreement could be extended to China before Russia entered the war on about August 8. Stalin also disavowed any intention of aiding the Chinese Communists, and agreed to allow Chiang's representatives to establish civil administration wherever Russian troops went in China.[48]

On May 30 Truman received word from Hopkins that Stalin would allow a representative group of Poles to join the Moscow commission then forming to construct the new government. The President was relieved. In a meeting with Treasury Secretary Henry Morganthau, Truman exclaimed, "I just put across the most wonderful thing without any help from Stettinius. I just finished talking with Harry Hopkins and I am the happiest man in the world over what I have been able to accomplish."[49] The rest of the news from Moscow, including Stalin's acceptance of the American voting formula in the United Nations Security Council, gave Truman further cause for hope. Assistant press secretary Eben Ayers noted that the President was "so pleased and excited that he could not refrain from telling us of the good word from Hopkins of his success in his talks with Stalin."[50]

After the Hopkins mission, revision of the Yalta accords became less pressing to Truman. Subsequently, he agreed to a meeting of the Big Three for July 15 in the Berlin suburb of Potsdam. The President's relief over the settlement of the Polish problem was enhanced by Stalin's confirmation of the Far Eastern agreements. In a conversation with Stimson, Truman said that "there was a promise in writing that Manchuria should remain fully Chinese except for a ninety-nine year lease of Port Arthur and the settlement of Dairen."[51] When Stimson warned that Russia's share in the railways would give Stalin considerable control in the area, Truman replied that he realized that "but that the promise was perfectly clear and distinct."[52] Truman did agree, however, with Stimson's recommendation that the United States should attempt to use its monopoly on atomic information as a bargaining lever to ensure Soviet compliance with American objectives in Eastern Europe and Manchuria.[53]

Ironically, Truman's discussion with Stimson came not long after the President had confided to his staff that every time he read the Yalta accords he "found new meanings in them."[54] Actually, Truman's comment could have been made by almost anyone in the administration. With the only copy of the agreements in the White House safe, Grew, Stimson, and Forrestal were relying on Harriman's recollection of the actual text when they made their review of American Far Eastern policy.[55] They did not learn the precise language of the document until the second week of June. On June 10 McCloy visited the White House Map Room to read the cables from the Hopkins mission. While there he also read the copy of the Yalta agreements. Later that day he prepared a memorandum for Stimson and Forrestal alerting them that "the only thing I noted which had not been mentioned at the Committee of Three meetings was the recurrence of the phrase 'the preeminent interests of the Soviet Union being safeguarded.' "[56]

McCloy's discovery came too late to have an impact on the Committee of Three's reevaluation of the Yalta agreements. It seems likely, however, that the news of the actual wording of the agreements did nothing to allay the apprehensions shared by Grew, Stimson, and Forrestal. The open-ended language of the accords seemed to invite Soviet domination of Manchuria. For the time being, however, little could be done to change the agreements. Unless the United States could find some way of quickly defeating Japan and securing the surrender of Japanese armed forces on the mainland, the United States would require Soviet assistance to end the war. The atomic bomb offered one way out of this dilemma. Its viability as a weapon would not be known, however, until after the first test scheduled for mid-July.

As long as the military picture remained uncertain, American strategists had to continue to plan for the invasion of Japan. "I have to decide Japanese strategy," Truman wrote in his diary. "Shall we invade Japan proper or shall we bomb and blockade? That is my hardest decision to date. But I'll make it when I have all the facts."[57] Ever since the devastating fire bombings of Japan had begun in March, the JCS had been debating the best means of defeating Japan. The Navy and the Army Air Force believed that a combination of blockade and strategic bombing could bring Japan to its knees without risking an invasion. Marshall disagreed. He argued that an invasion would be necessary to force Japan's unconditional surrender within a year of Germany's defeat. The general feared that if the war lasted much longer the American public might settle for a negotiated peace.[58]

By the time Truman called together his top military and civilian advisers the JCS had reached a compromise, thus making the President's decision somewhat easier. During a White House meeting on June 18, the Chiefs agreed that the invasion of Kyushu (code-named OLYMPIC), the southernmost of Japan's main islands, would be the next logical step in the war against Japan. The Navy and Air Force agreed that possession of Kyushu would provide them with the necessary anchorages and air bases to intensify their operations against Japan.[59] Truman approved the invasion date for early November. He also instructed the Chiefs to continue planning for the invasion of Honshu (CORONET) in early 1946, but he withheld his formal approval of the operation. Finally, the President told his advisers that "one of his objectives in connection with the coming conference would be to get from Russia all the assistance in the war that was possible."[60]

As the meeting was breaking up, Truman stopped the previously silent McCloy and told him, "No one gets out of here without committing himself." McCloy replied that he thought there might be a political solution to the war that would obviate the hazards of a direct assault on Japan and at the same time reduce American reliance on the Red Army. "I think we ought to have our heads examined," he recalled saying, "if we don't let them keep the emperor." He added that the United States should also tell Japan about the atomic bomb.[61] McCloy believed that Japan was already beaten. What was needed now was a way to induce the Japanese to surrender without compromising American war aims. If this could be accomplished, hundreds of thousands of American lives would be spared. Moreover, a sudden Japanese surrender would make American concessions in Northeast Asia unnecessary.[62]

The policy of unconditional surrender was first announced by FDR at Casablanca in January 1943. During the next two years some Allied officials questioned whether or not such a policy would prolong the war by convincing the enemy that he had nothing to gain by an early surrender. Roosevelt, however, was determined to avoid a repetition of the events surrounding Germany's defeat in World War I. In 1918 the government had surrendered before Allied troops had actually set foot on German soil. Following the war, Hitler had been able to gain a huge following by claiming that a victorious German army had really been betrayed by a Jewish-Communist conspiracy. This time there would be no room for doubt. In addition, Roosevelt was also greatly concerned with the need to convince the Soviets, who were then bearing the burden of the war against Germany, that the United States would not negotiate a separate peace that would leave the Germans free to destroy Russia.[63]

By early 1945, as Germany neared defeat, support was gathering within the American government for finding some way to clarify the meaning of unconditional surrender so as to convey to the Japanese that the United States sought to destroy Japanese militarism without destroying Japanese civilization. Among those favoring this approach were Grew, Marshall, Stimson, McCloy, and Forrestal. Grew believed that once the Japanese knew that they could retain the imperial institution and that Hirohito would not be tried as a war criminal, they would surrender. The former ambassador to Japan argued that the emperor's power was symbolic rather than real. Japan's militarists, not the emperor, had been responsible for the Pacific war. Moreover, as a symbol of national unity the emperor would play an important role during the occupation in ensuring Japanese cooperation with American objectives.[64] Grew's arguments were enough to sway McCloy, and to an extent they influenced Stimson and Forrestal. Moreover, Grew's analysis seemed confirmed by American intelligence reports that indicated that Japanese officials in Switzerland were trying to negotiate a surrender providing the emperor remained untouched.[65]

After receiving Lincoln's report in early March, Marshall also favored clarification of unconditional surrender. Marshall believed that an imperial rescript to Japan's military commanders would greatly reduce the difficulties of securing the surrender of millions of Japanese soldiers and sailors scattered throughout East Asia.[66]

The opponents of modifying unconditional surrender contended that the emperor was an archaic and undemocratic institution that was easily manipulated by whoever held power in Japan. To preserve the emperor, it was argued, would be to undermine any chance of achieving democratic reform in Japan. Within the State Department, Grew's opponents tended to be political liberals who supported a thorough reconstruction of Japanese society. To these proponents of a Japanese New Deal, the conservative Japan hands like Grew and the former counselor of the Tokyo embassy, Eugene Dooman, were "emperor worshipers." Although Grew received similar treatment from the press, Assistant Secretary of State Dean Acheson went the journalists one better by dubbing his colleague the "prince of appeasers."[67]

Despite these criticisms, Grew took his case to the new President. Truman, however, was unwilling to make such a drastic departure from Roosevelt's wartime policy. On the day Germany surrendered, Truman, in an address to the Congress, did state that unconditional surrender did not mean the "extermination or enslavement" of the Japanese people, but he said nothing about the emperor.[68] Grew tried once more in late May, only to encounter unexpected opposition from the JCS, Forrestal, and Stimson. The military, especially the Navy, believed that no statement should be made until the battle of Okinawa, then under way, was won. Even then, they feared that in light of the heavy losses the United States suffered, the Japanese might counter any proposal with warnings that more Okinawas awaited the Americans unless they softened their terms.[69]

For his part, Stimson was already thinking of coupling the proposed statement with the "shock action" of the atomic bomb.[70] As Brian Villa has written, "The schedule almost seemed to impose itself: a demand for a surrender late in July, and an atomic attack in early August, and finally Soviet entry. The invasion could be kept as a last resort. Between June and the end of July, no crushing blow was expected to offset the psychological advantage Japan had gained by her resistance on Okinawa. A surrender demand would have to wait until then."[71]

That was how matters stood when Truman asked for McCloy's opinion on June 18. After hearing McCloy's views, Truman authorized Grew, Stimson, Forrestal, and McCloy to prepare the proposed statement. The actual proclamation was drafted by a subcommittee chaired by McCloy. Energetic and strong willed, "Jack" McCloy was not one to shrink from controversy. As Assistant Secretary of War he had overseen the forced relocation of Japanese-Americans living on the West Coast, and refused requests from Jewish leaders to bomb rail lines leading to the Nazi death camps on the grounds that the raids would accomplish little to save the prisoners. In both of these cases he was carrying out the policy of others, but he strongly defended both decisions.[72]

McCloy's stormy tenure as Assistant Secretary of War marked the beginning of a long career as an official and unofficial adviser to eight Presidents. This "chairman of the American establishment," as he was later called, was born into a Philadelphia family of modest means. Raised by his mother, who sent him to private schools by working as a beautician, McCloy worked his way through Amherst College, graduating in 1916, a year before the United States entered World War I. During the war, he served with distinction as an artillery captain. After the armistice, he refused an officer's commission in the regular army and attended Harvard Law School. Following graduation he became a successful corporate lawyer in New York. In the 1930s McCloy impressed then Secretary of State Stimson by his determination in pursuing a lawsuit against the German government. When Stimson joined Roosevelt's administration in 1940 he brought McCloy along as a consultant and soon afterward made him an Assistant Secretary. Years younger than his chief (he was not yet fifty), McCloy was involved in the full range of War Department business. "I was a leg man," he recalled. "My job was getting things done."[73]

In June 1945 "getting things done" meant modifying unconditional surrender. After several sessions, McCloy's committee approved a tersely worded proclamation to the Japanese. The final document was largely the work of the Strategy and Policy Group, an elite cadre of politically sophisticated staff officers within the Operations Division of the Army's general staff. Under the leadership of Brigadier General George A. ("Abe") Lincoln, later the head of West Point's social sciences department, S&P had a strongly academic atmosphere. In addition to Lincoln, S&P boasted a number of Rhodes scholars, including Colonel Charles Bonesteel, who took primary responsibility for drafting the proclamation, and Colonel Dean Rusk, a future Secretary of State. These officers evaluated strategy in terms of its consistency with political objectives in the war. As the war entered its final year and political and military policy no longer seemed as separable as they once had, S&P assumed greater importance in the general staff. McCloy counted on S&P to draft papers for his meetings with the recently formed State-War-Navy Coordinating Committee (SWNCC), and Marshall depended on it to prepare his replies to queries from the State Department and the White House.[74]

The proclamation drafted by S&P, and approved by McCloy's committee, contained an explicit statement on the future of the emperor. Point twelve declared that Allied occupation forces would withdraw from Japan after their objectives were achieved and a peacefully inclined government was established. This could include a constitutional monarchy under the present dynasty, "if it be shown to the complete satisfaction of the world that such a government will never again aspire to aggression." In the letter of transmittal, McCloy noted that this wording might "cause repercussions at home, but without it those who seem to know most about Japan feel there would be very little likelihood of acceptance."[75] Grew made several slight revisions on this draft and returned it to the committee, which sent it to Stimson on July 1.

The next day Stimson presented the proposed announcement to Truman, explaining that neither the JCS, the Secretary of the Navy, nor the Secretary of State had cleared the paper. Stimson had been unable to confer with his counterpart in State because as of June 27 Stettinius no longer headed the department. Truman had announced that James F. Byrnes, a former Senate colleague of Truman's and recently Roosevelt's Director of War Mobilization, would be his new Secretary of State. The formal swearing in was not to take place until July 3.

Shortly before Byrnes took office, a *Washington Post* poll showed that 33 percent of those polled favored executing Hirohito and a little more than a third favored putting him on trial, imprisoning him for life, or sending him into exile.[76] Given the politically sensitive nature of the emperor question, Byrnes chose to make a thorough canvass of government opinion before he exposed himself and the department to charges of appeasement. Although Byrnes agreed to take the proclamation with him to Potsdam, Grew feared that it would be "ditched on the way over."[77]

During his first months in office, Truman had grappled with the related problems of holding the Alliance together, ending the war with Japan, and protecting Northeast Asia from Soviet encroachment. The possibility of inducing the Japanese government to surrender was one of several options open to policymakers. The atomic bomb was another. For the time being, however, Truman and his advisers agreed that the United States would do nothing to jeopardize Soviet assistance against Japan. There were simply too many unanswered questions for them to decide otherwise. If the Soviets entered Manchuria, would they adhere to the Far Eastern agreements? Would the atomic bomb work? Could the Japanese be forced or persuaded to surrender without an invasion and before the Soviets entered the conflict? In one way or another all of these questions hinged on the larger question of ends and means. In short, what were Truman's postwar goals for Asia, and by what means did he hope to achieve them?

2

Ends and Means: Postwar Policy and Military Strategy on the Eve of Potsdam

It appears to the Joint War Plans Committee that there is a lack of coordination in examining and reporting upon the implications of [our] various Far Eastern policies.[1]

W HEN HARRY TRUMAN took office in April 1945, he inherited from his predecessor only the faintest outline of a postwar policy for East Asia. Among a mélange of public statements and private agreements Truman found a confusing assortment of contradictory policies and unfinished business. Regarding China, the new President faced the difficult task of reconciling American support for a free and democratic China, which included Manchuria, with the provisions of the Yalta Far Eastern accords. On Korea, Roosevelt's preparations seemed little better. The United States was committed to the restoration of Korean independence in "due course," but although the possibility of a quadripartite trusteeship had been discussed with the British and the Chinese, no final agreement had been reached. Moreover, the fourth power, Russia, would not agree to a formal discussion of the matter until it was ready to enter the Pacific war. Finally, Truman learned that despite Roosevelt's numerous anticolonial pronouncements, despite his well-known contempt for France's role in Indochina and his frequent comments to Churchill about Hong Kong, FDR had done almost nothing to advance the cause of colonial independence in Southeast Asia.

In attempting to sort through Roosevelt's bewildering legacy and come to some understanding of American interests in East Asia, Truman relied heavily on the State Department to formulate policy. The result was a movement away from FDR's cautious diplomacy in Northeast Asia and the complete abandonment of the last remnants of his anticolonialism. To protect American interests Truman adopted a policy that came to include aid to British and French imperialism, increased support for Chiang Kai-shek, defense of the Open Door in Manchuria, and maintenance of a controlling interest in Korea's occupation. But although Truman looked to the State Department for a definition of American postwar policy, he allowed the compartmentalization of political and military planning that had begun under Roosevelt to continue. As a consequence, a disjunction between postwar policy and military strategy developed in the final weeks of the war.

Despite his desire to carry out Roosevelt's policies, Truman quickly ran into problems. Roosevelt's China policy was largely symbolic. Substituting gestures for action, Roosevelt sent envoys, not armies, to Chungking. Nor was his policy static. After Nationalist forces were thrown back by Japan's 1944 offensive, FDR concluded that Chiang would not unite China anytime soon.[2] His major concern became ensuring that the anticipated chaos in postwar China did not fuel another international crisis. Reflecting this changing perception of China's importance, the Yalta agreements provided for accommodation with the strongest power in the region. Russian interests in Northeast Asia would be served, but in return, Stalin agreed to conclude a treaty of alliance and friendship with the Nationalist regime, thereby recognizing Chiang's as the only legitimate government of China. Together the United States and the Soviet Union would continue to recognize the Nationalists, while refraining from interference in China's internal problems.

Truman's objectives were more ambitious. The new President hoped to use Stalin's pledge not to aid the CCP as a means of achieving what he perceived to be the major objective of American policy—the creation of a free and friendly China. Four frustrating years of involvement in China's politics had led Roosevelt to abandon his hopes for China as a stabilizing force in East Asia. Truman would have benefited from greater knowledge of FDR's experience. "I think one of the difficulties with us was—one of the difficulties with me—" he observed years later, "was that I thought that Chiang Kai-shek had a government that was established and sound and could stand up to conditions as they developed."[3]

In part, Truman's early optimism concerning Chiang was the result of the declining quality of reporting from Chungking. In April 1945 Ambassador Hurley purged a group of dissenting China hands from his embassy staff, thereby hindering the coverage of CCP activities for the remainder of the war. In replacing these veteran foreign service officers, Hurley placed more emphasis on loyalty than initiative. But this was not enough to satisfy him. As a rule, Hurley cleared every report out of Chungking. In his own cables he habitually offered promising reports on Chiang's efforts to liberalize his regime and reach an agreement with the Communists.[4] In one peculiar instance Hurley did forward a report describing a number of KMT-CCP clashes in which Chiang's forces suffered surprising losses. Hurley released the report to show that he was giving "full freedom to my reporting officers even though I may not concur in their reports."[5] He then went on to belittle the reporting officers and discredit their story. Hurley concluded his cable with the observation that "the communist controversy can be settled satisfactorily and without civil war if some of our American ideological crusaders will permit the American policy to become more effective."[6] The entire report was passed on to Truman.

The China specialists in the State Department remained unconvinced by Hurley's reports. Within the Division of Chinese Affairs (CA), two schools of thought had developed on how to deal with what was believed to be an impending clash between the Communists and Nationalists. Heading CA was John Carter Vincent, a career diplomat with fourteen years experience in China. Vincent's tour in Chungking during the war had convinced him that the United States should not support Chiang to the exclusion of other groups, particularly the Communists, who would be effective in fighting the Japanese. Roosevelt had explored this idea, sending an observer group, the so-called Dixie mission, to the Communist headquarters in Yenan. After Yalta, however, Roosevelt had decided against aiding the Communists. To do so might lead to Chiang's overthrow and relieve Stalin of his obligations under the Yalta agreements.[7] Nevertheless, Vincent continued to believe that the United States should pressure Chiang into reaching an agreement with the CCP. Vincent feared that unless Chiang reformed his regime the Communists would eventually defeat the Nationalists.[8]

Within CA the most vigorous champion of American support for Chiang's regime was Everett F. Drumright. Like Vincent, Drumright believed that the United States had an obligation to help unify China. Unlike Vincent, however, Drumright believed that the creation of a friendly and unified China could take place only under Chiang's leadership. Vincent argued that if the United States pressured Chiang into liberalizing his regime, and thereby eliminated the source of peasant discontent, the Communists would lose support. Drumright rejected this notion. Pressuring Chiang, either by withholding aid or arming the Communists, would only weaken the one Chinese leader capable of unifying China along lines acceptable to the United States. A Communist China, Drumright argued, would be neither democratic nor friendly.[9] Drumright was especially concerned that the Communists would turn to Moscow in their battle against Chiang. In one meeting of the department's Interdivisional Area Committee for the Far East, Drumright argued that if American troops landed in Manchuria they should "remain until the Central Government was ready to take over even though this might lead to war with Russia."[10]

Given the division of opinion within CA and the lack of strong leadership from either Stettinius or Grew, the State Department could do no better than to inform the new President that American policy sought to promote the "establishment of a broadly representative government in China."[11] The United States would continue to support the recognized government of Chiang Kai-shek while maintaining a "degree of flexibility to permit cooperation with any other leadership in China which may give greater promise of achieving unity and contributing to peace and security in east Asia."[12] Since the Communists were not expected to contribute to stability and security in East Asia, this policy statement put the United States squarely, if unenthusiastically, behind Chiang.

Given Truman's desire to follow FDR's policies, it seems doubtful that in the spring of 1945 he could have been convinced to follow the advice of Vincent and the purged China hands in Chungking. Under the circumstances, with Hurley reporting that China's internal situation "seems definitely improved," and Stalin's reaffirmation of his promise to support Chiang and recognize Chinese sovereignty in Manchuria, Truman had no reason to even consider an alternative policy.[13] A Sino-Soviet agreement with terms acceptable to the United States now seemed likely. Once an agreement was reached, the Communists, deprived of Soviet support, would be more willing to settle with the Nationalists. After a rocky start in his first few weeks in office, Truman now seemed close to securing the keystone of his East Asian policy.

On June 9 Truman met with Chinese Foreign Minister T. V. Soong to discuss the secret Yalta agreements prior to Soong's leaving for Moscow.

Although Soong already had some idea of the contents of the agreement, this was the first time the Chinese government was permitted to see the entire text. Truman carefully explained that Stalin had disavowed any connection with the CCP and that the Russians promised to respect Chinese sovereignty in Manchuria.[14] Stalin's assurance notwithstanding, Soong was greatly concerned by the ambiguity of the agreements. The Chinese Foreign Minister spent the next several days talking with anyone who could help in explaining Roosevelt's intentions at Yalta. His efforts were unavailing, however, and to Joseph Grew's comment that the United States would stand by the agreements, Soong could only reply that "the question arises as to what you have agreed to support."[15]

During a second meeting with Truman, Soong was told that the minutes of the Hopkins mission revealed Stalin's pledge to be even more categorical than the President had first believed. Soong seemed cheered by the news, but subsequent requests by the Chinese to have the United States participate in the lease arrangements for Dairen indicated that Truman's assurances had not produced their intended effect. Although Truman resisted this and other attempts to draw the United States into the negotiations, he did allow Harriman to act as Soong's unofficial adviser in Moscow.[16]

The negotiations began in mid-June with Stalin making increased demands on the Chinese. Harriman notified Truman that Stalin had opened negotiations by pressing for concessions from China that went well beyond the American understanding of the Yalta agreements. Harriman learned from Soong that Stalin interpreted the clause referring to the maintenance of the status quo in Outer Mongolia as requiring China to recognize the independence of that territory. Stalin was unmoved by Soong's explanation that, although Chiang did not expect to exercise suzerainty over Outer Mongolia, he could not surrender China's claims to nominal sovereignty and remain in power. Harriman also reported that Stalin interpreted "internationalization of Dairen as meaning Russia would have a preeminent interest in the port as against China and there should be a Russian management."[17]

On July 4 James F. Byrnes, newly sworn in as Secretary of State, instructed Harriman that he and Truman expected to be consulted before the conclusion of any arrangements between the Chinese and Soviets. He then provided an explanation for this heightened interest on the part of the administration. Although the United States would not participate in the administration of Dairen, Byrnes said he and Truman expected that

"the principle of non-discrimination in international commercial inter-
course will be respected in relation to Dairen, as well as any other areas
which may be the subject of special arrangements between the Soviet
Union and China."[18]

American efforts to stiffen Soong's resolve might yet bring Stalin into
line. But as Truman and his advisers prepared for the Potsdam conference,
their previous optimism regarding a Sino-Soviet agreement was being
tempered by a growing anxiety over Stalin's demands on China. A similar
concern was evident in American planning for Korea.

In the spring of 1945, as Soviet participation in the Pacific war became
likely, American policymakers approached the Korean question with a
new sense of urgency. Like most Americans, Truman knew little about
the postwar plans for Korea.[19] Roosevelt's desire to bring the Soviets into
the war and his apparent refusal to involve American troops on the mainland meant that the Russians would have the dominant voice in Korea's
future.[20] In this sense there was a similarity between Roosevelt's postwar
policy for Eastern Europe and his plans for Korea. Once again, Roosevelt
had raised public expectations by promoting the trusteeship plan as an
example of great-power respect for the rights of smaller nations. In reality,
he seemed to be conceding the peninsula to the Soviets, depending once
more on Soviet discretion in dealing with Korea as an open sphere of
interest.[21]

Because Roosevelt had failed to discuss foreign policy with his Vice-
President, Truman turned to the State Department for guidance. In contrast to FDR's policy, the department's planners believed that significant
American participation in a trusteeship was essential to the development
of a free and democratic Korea. First envisaged as a means of balancing
competing interests on the peninsula, American participation in a four-
power trusteeship gradually evolved into a means of preventing Soviet
hegemony in Korea.

An awareness of Korea's internal conditions increased American concern
over Soviet influence on the peninsula. Most Koreans eked out an existence as tenant farmers on small plots of land. They lost most of their
produce to taxes and rent and lived under the constant threat of starvation.
During the course of Korea's forty-year occupation most landowners and
merchants had come to collaborate with the Japanese. Under these circumstances it seemed likely that liberation would lead many Koreans to
seek revolutionary changes in their country's political and social structure.

State Department specialists recognized the explosiveness of the situation, and they watched with increasing concern the activities of Soviet and CCP-sponsored Korean liberation groups.[22]

In a memorandum sent to the Secretaries of the State, War, and Navy departments, as well as to the President, the Office of Strategic Services (OSS) reported that Soviet seamen in San Francisco were saying that Korea would be a Far Eastern Poland. According to the report, the Soviets boasted that they had "100,000 Koreans in Central Asia ready to go back."[23] Harriman also warned that Stalin would not support the trusteeship plan if he could control the peninsula with Soviet-trained proxies.[24] On the eve of Potsdam the success of the department's policy depended on the United States' ability to check Russian expansion and control the revolutionary situation in Korea. Toward this end the department's planners urged that "none of the interested parties alone . . . invade Korea, particularly the Soviet Union."[25]

In contrast to Northeast Asia, where the new administration's policies seemed to be drawing the United States into deeper involvement on the mainland, Truman's policy in Southeast Asia aimed at minimizing the American role in the region. In part this was the result of the changing focus of American military operations in preparation for the invasion of Japan. But American difficulties with the Soviet Union also played a part in the formulation of colonial policy. As the United States prepared for the charter meeting of the United Nations Organization, American officials sought to enlist British and French support in opposing the Soviet Union in Europe. "When perhaps the inevitable struggle came between Russia and ourselves," observed Isaiah Bowman, a member of the State Department's postwar planning staff, "the question would be, who are our friends."[26] Self-government for colonial peoples remained the ultimate aim of American policy, both out of fear that the Soviets would exploit nationalist aspirations to their own ends, and because the American public appeared to oppose a return to the status quo antebellum in Southeast Asia. But the United States would rely on moral suasion rather than direct political pressure to move the colonial powers toward these goals.[27]

The State Department was itself divided over the issue of colonial policy. The members of the Division of Southeast Asian Affairs (SEA) were acutely aware of the rising tide of nationalism in the region. The Asianists repeatedly warned that the Europeans could not hope to restore their former empires after the war. The members of the Office of European Affairs

(EUR), however, discounted reports of Asian nationalism as Japanese propaganda. Instead they insisted that stability in Western Europe depended in part on the restoration of the colonial powers to their former stature. Inasmuch as the two offices were instructed to reach agreement on issues before passing them up to a higher level, the Europeanists exercised *de facto* control over department planning on colonial policy.[28]

Although the Yalta agreements had virtually ended the possibility of developing a strong anticolonial policy, Roosevelt had indicated that he might use France's military dependence on the United States to exact some concessions from the French government.[29] During Truman's first months in office, however, the members of EUR consolidated their position within the department and used their influence to pave the way for France's return to Indochina with no strings attached.[30] Led by James C. Dunn, a veteran of numerous bureaucratic battles, the Europeanists quickly seized control of the issue. On Truman's first full day in office he received a memorandum that included several observations on the state of Franco-American relations. France's defeat, it noted, had left that country's leaders preoccupied with questions of national prestige. In particular, the French suspected American motives in Indochina. To remedy this situation and smooth relations between the two countries, the department prescribed a therapeutic policy that would take account of this "psychological factor in the French mind."[31] Before long Stettinius was telling the French that "the record is entirely innocent of any official statement of this government questioning, even by implication, French sovereignty over Indochina."[32]

Despite the apparent agreement by both governments on colonial policy, a number of obstacles stood in the way of a successful French restoration in Indochina, the most important being the existence of indigenous opposition to any form of French rule. By the early summer of 1945 the State Department knew enough about the strength of the Indochinese liberation movement to realize that the reestablishment of French control would be met with stiff resistance.[33] Officially, American policy encouraged some measure of self-government for Indochina. Only by making concessions toward self-rule could the French hope to avoid a fight in Indochina. Given France's obsession with matters of prestige, however, concessions seemed doubtful. Although some conflict between the French and Indochinese seemed likely, the State Department remained primarily concerned with avoiding public criticism for aiding French imperialism.[34]

The decision to support France in Indochina was made easier by what was seen as the absence of viable alternatives to French rule. Even some of the specialists in the Office of Far Eastern Affairs (FE) conceded that Indochinese independence could not be maintained in the presence of French and Chinese pressure. In determining the future of Hong Kong, however, the United States was forced to choose between two allies. Chiang, as he made clear in his book *China's Destiny*, planned to pursue the retrocession of Hong Kong at the "proper moment." As part of his China policy, Roosevelt had encouraged the Chinese along these lines, even going so far as to broach the subject with Churchill. Roosevelt hoped that a settlement could be arranged where Chinese sovereignty would be restored and Hong Kong would become a free port.[35] Churchill would have none of it, however, and in the summer of 1945 the British were as determined as ever to retain control of their possessions.[36] British officers were already undergoing training in preparation for a resumption of imperial administration in the colony.[37]

The Truman administration did not question British sovereignty over Hong Kong, although it could not state its position so forthrightly. That is to say, the United States recognized British claims to the colony but also took note of China's interest in its eventual retrocession. The administration sought to find some middle course by offering its assistance "at the proper time" in the mutually satisfactory settlement of the dispute.[38] This policy seemed workable as long as the United States did not become directly involved in the region. But by early summer Chinese troops, trained, armed, and supervised by Americans, began preparing for operations in the Hong Kong–Canton area. American officials realized that if Chinese troops liberated Hong Kong, Chiang might decide that the "proper moment" to reclaim the colony had arrived. China's first major offensive of the war threatened to embroil the United States in a showdown over Hong Kong.

To head off a possible crisis, the State Department prepared a statement of policy to be delivered to the British and Chinese governments. Briefly put, the message explained that the coming operations were under the generalissimo's direction. Participation by American troops would be kept to a minimum. The United States would not take part in the administration of civil affairs in Hong Kong. The Allies were to be informed that the operations were strictly military in nature and did not prejudice the future status of Hong Kong.[39]

During Truman's first months in office a significant shift had taken place in American policy for China (including Manchuria), Korea, Indochina, and Hong Kong. Despite his occasional criticism of the foreign service's "smart boys," Truman allowed the State Department to define the range of American interests in the East Asia.[40] To be sure, Truman believed that he was following Roosevelt's policy, especially with respect to China. Yet ever since the Tehran conference FDR had excluded the department from the policy process. The advice Truman received on American interests in East Asia was more the product of the peculiarities of the department's bureaucracy than it was an accurate picture of Roosevelt's policies.

Southeast Asian policy reflected the administrative supremacy of the Europeanists over their colleagues in FE. American China policy also underwent a subtle change during Truman's apprenticeship. After three years of frustration, FDR viewed the China problem as nearly insolvable. The Yalta agreements were a recognition of the limits of American influence. The China hands continued to believe, however, that the United States had to play a leading role in the unification of China. Even those foreign service officers who had lost faith in Chiang's leadership could agree with their colleagues on this point. Thus, on the eve of Potsdam, Truman edged the United States toward a more activist policy in China. Given the administration's increased concern over Soviet intentions in Manchuria and the deterioration of KMT-CCP relations, this reevaluation of American interests increased the potential for deeper involvement on the mainland. Likewise, the State Department's emphasis on having the United States exercise a controlling influence in the occupation of Korea also increased the likelihood that there would be a sizable American presence in Northeast Asia at the end of the war.

In the summer of 1945, however, American military planners were preoccupied with preparations for the invasion of Japan. Although the State Department and some of Truman's advisers were growing wary of Soviet intentions in Northeast Asia, the JCS continued to rely on Soviet cooperation to defeat Japan. In this respect the JCS, particularly the Army general staff, had become the custodians of Roosevelt's Soviet policy.

For Marshall, three years of having to deal with the political-military intrigues in Chungking had given him all the reason he needed to avoid involving American troops in a land campaign in Asia. By June the JCS had decided against any major landings on the China coast. A smaller operation to open communications in the Port Bayard area was under consideration. But this would not take place until after the Kyushu invasion in the fall. As planned, the operation did not call for the introduction of large numbers of American troops in China to fight the Japanese. The port was to be opened to provide Chiang with a more direct supply route and nothing more.[41]

This amounted to another disappointment for Chiang, although Stimson saw things somewhat differently. The Chinese, he believed, were planning to let the United States take on the bulk of the Japanese in China. Upon hearing that T. V. Soong was lobbying for a strong American presence in China, Stimson warned the President that the American public would not tolerate a land war in Asia.[42]

Military expediency also guided the general staff's handling of problems relating to China's internal situation. In the spring of 1945, while landings on the China coast were still under consideration, Army planners had begun preparations for civil affairs administration in the projected areas of American occupation. The possibility that foreign troops might enter a part of China not under KMT control greatly concerned Chiang. Accordingly, Soong pressed the Americans for an agreement that would allow for the speedy transfer of civil authority to representatives of the Kuomintang. The War Department, primarily concerned with facilitating its operations in China, advised against making any such agreement. Assistant Secretary of War McCloy informed the State Department that "such a commitment would not be in accord with either our military or political interests."[43] The United States would work with the *de facto* power in the area of operations.

By mid-June, the members of the Army's general staff had begun to perceive a widening gap between ends and means in American China policy. These doubts about the direction of American policy surfaced in a briefing paper written in S&P for General Marshall's use at Potsdam. "The U.S.," it stated, "as a matter of public will, positively supports the integrity of China as a nation. U.S. formal policy at present formally favors a united China. Whether the future will bring a different definition of what constitutes China proper cannot now be said with certainty."[44] The authors believed that a Sino-Soviet treaty recognizing Russia's economic and security interests in Manchuria was desirable. If, however, the Soviet demands exceeded China's willingness to meet them, it was not believed that "U.S. military force could be effectively employed to further our objective."[45]

A similar caution was evident in American military planning for Korea. Prior to the June 18 White House meeting of the JCS, Marshall was advised by his staff that military operations against Korea would be more costly than the assault on Kyushu. "With reference to the clean-up of the Asiatic mainland," the planners wrote, "our objectives should be to get the Russians to deal with the Japs in Manchuria (and Korea if necessary) and to vitalize the Chinese to a point where, with assistance of American air power and some supplies, they can mop out their own country."[46] If Russia entered the war on schedule, Soviet troops would overrun Korea.

In analyzing this situation the members of S&P emphasized the importance of obtaining Soviet approval of a trusteeship plan prior to an invasion of Korea. Because American landings in Korea were unlikely, it appeared doubtful that American troops would be able to fulfill the role envisioned for them by the State Department. The military planners warned that "the U.S. will not be in a position to force the independence of Korea."[47] It was believed that even after Japan's defeat commitments to the occupation of Japan and possible assistance to China would preclude the effective use of American forces in the region. "The U.S. can bring little military pressure on the Russians in the Far East," the planners concluded. "U.S. aims on the northern Asian mainland must be negotiated."[48]

Not surprisingly, the Civil Affairs Division of the general staff (CAD) recommended that American participation.in the administration be kept to a minimum. A control council on the Austrian model seemed acceptable in that American authority would be "more than nominal but . . . something less than predominant."[49] The CAD planners observed that the long-range status of Korea was of more importance to China and Russia than it was to either the United States or Great Britain.[50] Moreover, the internal affairs of Korea did not pose a serious problem for the civil affairs planners. They simply did not expect the United States to play a leading role in the administration of the country.

By early July there existed a divergence of views between the JCS and the State Department on the use of American forces in East Asia. In Southeast Asia, however, American policy was characterized by consensus at the highest levels. The generals and the diplomats agreed that responsibility for the region belonged to the European powers. Of course, without a strong American presence in the area the probability of Britain and France accepting a trusteeship system in the region became almost nil. The Joint Chiefs acknowledged this point, and in fact they favored a full restoration of British and French rule. In part the Chiefs were motivated by a desire to lay claim to Japan's former mandates for security purposes. They could hardly challenge France's claims to Indochina while making a grab for island bases in the Pacific.[51] More significant, however, was their decision that American security in Europe required the full cooperation of England and France.[52] This last point was, of course, the major argument of the Europeanists in the State Department.

This shift in American policy coincided with stepped-up efforts on the part of the French to participate in the Pacific war. American representatives soon found themselves set upon by a seemingly endless procession of French officials requesting aid and equipment. The JCS agreed to permit French troops into the Far East with the provision that the new forces receive supplies from aid already earmarked for France.[53] Although the French managed to draw needed supplies from the British and Americans, they could not secure enough shipping to move their troops into the Pacific. Here they encountered an insuperable obstacle. Allied shipping could not be spared from existing operations.[54]

Nevertheless, the French accused the Americans of duplicity. They argued, with some validity, that despite recent assurances, American officials continued to frustrate French efforts to reclaim their colony. In fact, because word of the administration's new position was slow in reaching the field, General Albert Wedemeyer, the American commander in China, continued what he believed to be American policy by refusing to aid French covert operations in Indochina. OSS operatives in the area also continued their collaboration with Vietnamese guerrillas, much to the dismay of the French. Wedemeyer eventually brought his activities into line with Washington's policies, although for years afterward French officials believed that the United States had tried to prevent their return to Indochina.[55]

American indifference to the coming struggle in Indochina can be attributed in large part to the tendency of most State Department officials to deprecate the strength of Asian nationalism. The warnings emanating from the Division of Southeast Asian Affairs simply were not heeded. Preparations were under way to bring the French back into the region. Armed and assisted by the United States and Britain, France's Corps Leger d' Intervention (comprised of all-white troops) was expected to throw the Japanese out of Indochina and overawe their former subjects.[56]

Although the JCS did not deliberately obstruct France's efforts to reclaim Indochina, they did seem ambivalent about the prospect of actual French military participation in the Pacific. Previous difficulties with de Gaulle's troops in Europe, where the French tried to occupy a portion of the Val d' Aosta region in northern Italy, and in the Levant, where the French tried to force their way back into their former mandates of Syria and Lebanon, had created little enthusiasm for French involvement in the Pacific.[57] In short, the American attitude seemed to be one of favoring a French return to Indochina, providing it did not interfere with American military planning or arouse American public opinion. With JCS attention focused on Japan, the planners had little time or inclination to concern themselves with the problems France might face in reimposing its authority over Indochina.

The single-minded concentration on Japan that characterized American strategic planning was only slightly less evident in the preparations the JCS made for the sudden collapse of Japanese resistance. Although the Joint Chiefs anticipated the need for surrender planning as early as August 1944, staff work on the problem had not progressed very far by the following spring. The possibility that Japan might capitulate soon after Germany's defeat increased interest in the project, and by late May preliminary staff papers began to circulate through the joint staff committees.

Prepared by a drafting committee known as the Joint War Plans Committee (JWPC), these papers tended to list problems without proposing concrete solutions. Most papers were then reviewed by a higher-level committee, the Joint Staff Planners (JSP), on which General Lincoln served as the Army's representative. In the early stages of developing staff papers the JSP would discuss the report of the drafting committee, recommend revisions, and return the paper to the JWPC. In some cases, however, the JSP would circulate the working paper for informal comments from other sectors such as theater planners or the Far Eastern subcommittee of the State-War-Navy Coordinating Committee. (SWNCC, an interdepartmental committee at the Assistant Secretary level, was created in late 1944). All this was prefatory to submitting the staff paper to the JCS for their approval.[58]

The JWPC emphasized the need for Allied cooperation in its recommendations for specific operations in the event of a Japanese collapse. Designating the home islands as the primary responsibility for United States forces, the planners all but excluded American troops from initial participation in surrender operations outside of Japan.[59] In criticizing this oversight Colonel Max C. Johnson, the head of the Strategy Section of the Army general staff, warned that a sudden surrender would be followed by a "land-grab stampede by the British, French, Chinese, Russians, and possibly other states insofar as they were humanly capable of doing."[60] Johnson agreed that Japan took precedence in any operation, but he argued that it was not acceptable to focus American efforts on the home islands while "small forces of our Allies have meanwhile seized everything else of strategic value."[61] Taking note of Johnson's criticism, Lincoln recommended at a meeting of the JSP that the paper be redrafted in such a way as to acknowledge that American forces might be employed beyond the home islands.[62]

In the last week of June another JWPC paper was ready for review. Titled "Occupation of Japan and Japanese-Held Territories After the Collapse or Defeat of Japan," this study emphasized the need for international agreement on long-term postwar occupation policies. Initial occupation would conform to areas of assigned military operations. Since this would be the case even if Japan suddenly surrendered, the JWPC recommended that agreements defining these areas of *initial* responsibility be concluded at the forthcoming conference.[63]

This paper met with criticism from Lt. Gen. John E. Hull, the head of the Operations Division, whose staff officers were preparing a briefing book for the conference. Disturbed by the lack of an overall plan for postwar occupation zones such as had existed for Germany, Hull urged the JWPC to prepare a list of recommendations. Believing that the planners should do more than urge consultation, Hull wanted the JCS to arrive in Potsdam with a list of basic aims and objectives for the post-hostilities era. Significantly, Hull slighted the importance of reaching agreement on preliminary occupation operations. Implicit in Hull's comments was the assumption that there would be no danger of Allied troops conducting operations in the same area. "Generally," he wrote, "initial occupation will be by military operations, and hence the initial occupation is not a real problem requiring governmental agreement."[64]

Despite these criticisms the JWPC's papers remained, by their own admission, vague and indistinct. Planning lagged in part because of the perceived improbability of Japan's immediate surrender. But planning also suffered from a lack of political direction, and it is difficult to see how the staff's proposals could have been sharpened without first receiving a clearer picture of American objectives. Numerous questions remained unanswered. Were postwar arrangements, as General Hull suggested, more important than specific understandings on initial occupation responsibilities? More specifically, would the United States participate in the postwar occupation of such mainland areas as Manchuria and Thailand? Would American troops be involved in the initial occupation of Korea and north China? If, as Hull suggested, initial occupations were the result of military operations, this was not likely. What arrangements were to be made for the four-power trusteeship of Korea? Opinions on all of these questions varied. Despite the views of some of his subordinates, Lincoln doubted the need for American troops on the mainland. He continued to think that if Japan surrendered, Russian and Chinese troops could disarm the Japanese on the continent.[65]

The awareness of American limitations that colored the planners' preparations for a sudden surrender was also evident in their recommendations regarding the best time to issue an ultimatum to Japan. In the course of preparing the draft surrender proclamation, General Lincoln and the members of S&P had also produced a memorandum advising McCloy on the best possible time to issue the ultimatum. They concluded that the most favorable period would be just before the actual invasion when the pressure on Japan would be at its height. A convergence of factors made late August or early September seem like the optimum moment. By that time the American bombardment of Japan would reach a new intensity with the arrival in the Pacific of eight heavy bomber groups. About the same time, the Chinese would be beginning their drive on the Canton–Hong Kong area and the British would be launching an operation against Port Sweetenham–Dickson off Malaya. Finally, the Soviets would also be in the war by then.[66]

The planners concluded that the announcement would be most effective if it were delivered immediately after Russian entry into the war, meaning sometime between August 15 and early September. Time for negotiations would be available because army intelligence (G-2) expected the Japanese to put up stiff resistance in Manchuria during the first thirty days before the Red Army began to "roll."[67] In the meantime, American forces would be moved into position to occupy Japan after the surrender. This was an important point. One of the reasons the planners rejected making an immediate surrender demand was that American forces were not yet able to accept a surrender should one be offered. "Our forces," read the report, "must be concentrated, rested, reequipped and brought up to strength.

Further, the redeployment program is not sufficiently advanced to give us in the Pacific the strength necessary to garrison all the strategic positions in Japan."[68]

Citing the "affair Wolfe in northern Italy" when a German general of that name had sought to negotiate a surrender, the planners predicted that it would take some time for Japan to capitulate after the proclamation was released. The hiatus between the release of the ultimatum and the actual surrender would provide additional time to move troops into the Pacific. Simply put, the United States would not be prepared to accept a Japanese surrender before early September. It should be noted that Lincoln's staff based their calculations on a conservative estimate of American objectives. The possibility of placing American forces onto the mainland was not even considered in this paper.

In confirming their attention to an American occupation of Japan, the planners were concerned with coordinating the surrender operations with the Allies, especially the Soviet Union. This is not to say that the JCS were naive about the implications of a Soviet occupation in Northeast Asia. One of their studies noted that since the Soviets were expected to occupy Manchuria and northern Korea, any agreements concerning the occupation responsibilities of the Allies would have to take into account the Soviet Union's "methods and her interpretation of 'cooperation,' witness Berlin, Rumania, Bulgaria, etc."[69]

Nevertheless, the JCS believed that American power could most effectively be put to use by occupying Japan and controlling the central Pacific islands. In what was undoubtedly a reference to the Soviet Union, the officers of S&P recognized that "Japan is not the sole threat against peace in the Pacific in perpetuity."[70] Korea, Manchuria, and Japan, if controlled by any one power, would pose a threat to American security. Therefore the planners recommended that it was in American interests "to insure in so far as possible that the combination is not reformed under the guidance of *any* power."[71] In general, the planners saw the American role as a preclusive one. The purpose of American bases in the region was "to keep the rest of the world militarily out of the Pacific, rather than to commit us irrevocably and in perpetuity to affairs in the Sea of Japan."[72]

The military planners also seemed well aware of the political complications that would arise if China remained divided at the end of the war. According to Admiral Charles Cooke, head of the Navy's War Plans Division, by the time of the Yalta conference Navy planners were becoming "increasingly concerned with the strategic vacuum that would result in East Asia and the Western Pacific following the complete elimination of Japanese power."[73] As a possible solution to that problem Admiral King suggested that it might be necessary to build China up as a counterbalance to the Soviet Union in the Far East.[74] General Lincoln was likewise concerned that if the United States failed to unify China, American "political policy and military expenditures might go for naught."[75]

The military planners were also interested in China's postwar future for reasons more closely related to securing their share of postwar military budgets than to matters of national security. During the war the Navy, through its Naval Group China, an advisory team headed by Admiral Milton Miles, had developed substantial ties with the Nationalist government. Enjoying the full support of Chiang, Miles' group collaborated closely with Tai Li, the notorious head of the KMT's secret police. Although officials in Washington blanched at rumors of Miles' participation in Tai's Gestapo-like activities, the Navy looked forward to a continuation of the mission in some form in the postwar era.[76]

The Army Air Force was also pushing for a role in the modernization of Chiang's armed forces. As early as February 1945, Robert Lovett, Assistant Secretary of War for Air, warned that the United States would need armaments markets to aid "our over expanded aviation industry."[77] Advocates of a postwar military mission also argued that continued aid to China would help sustain the close ties that had developed between the two countries during the war. The Army Air Force already had an advisory team in China, and they looked forward to its enlargement in peacetime.[78]

All of this maneuvering for position in the postwar China arms market had little direct impact on the conduct of the war against Japan. The JCS were aware of the havoc the Soviets could create in Northeast Asia. They also understood the political importance of unifying China. Nevertheless, military planning proceeded on the assumption that for the next six months at least, American resources would be devoted entirely to the defeat of Japan. The JCS believed that American security interests would best be served by a successful occupation of Japan, retention of the former mandates, and bases on Okinawa and the Philippines. The JCS could feel reasonably sure that even if the Soviets dominated Northeast Asia and China sank into prolonged civil war, the United States could be protected by these outposts in the Pacific. Thus, despite growing concern over Soviet expansion, the JCS continued to focus their attention on the invasion of

Japan. Only after Japan was defeated and occupied would it be possible to take another look at the situation on the mainland.

On the eve of the Potsdam conference the Truman administration's plans for Northeast Asia and China appeared to be drawing the United States toward deeper involvement on the continent. At the same time, however, the JCS continued to pursue a strategy that would leave the Russians unchallenged in Northeast Asia. This disjunction between political and military policy was not irreversible. Truman and his advisers still had time to bring about a closer correspondence between ends and means. Much, however, would depend on the outcome of the Potsdam conference.

3

Potsdam: Truman Takes Charge

[Stalin] doesn't know it but I have an ace in the hole and another one showing.
(Harry Truman, July 31, 1945)[1]

W ISH I DIDN'T HAVE TO GO," wrote Truman on the eve of his departure
for Potsdam, "but I do and it can't be stopped now."[2] Truman had cause
to be apprehensive about the coming conference. A welter of important
postwar problems awaited him at Berlin, the prospect of which was made
even less inviting by the knowledge that his first performance on the world
stage inevitably would be measured against that of the two veterans,
Churchill and Stalin.[3] It is perhaps indicative of how Truman's inexperi-
ence shaped public perceptions that, as he later noted, although the
President was several inches taller than Stalin or Churchill, the press
described only him as short.[4]

Truman planned to meet the challenges of this conference the way he
had met other difficult challenges in his life, with careful preparation, hard
work, and good counsel. To provide the latter he was bringing with him
the newly appointed Secretary of State, James F. Byrnes. Crossing the
Atlantic on the USS *Augusta*, the two men met frequently to map out
strategy for the conference with Admiral Leahy, Byrnes' assistant Ben
Cohen, H. Freeman Matthews, the head of EUR, and Charles Bohlen.[5]
In this group, Truman's closest advisers were Leahy and Byrnes.

As Roosevelt's White House chief of staff and the chairman of the Joint
Chiefs, William D. Leahy advised the President on military questions and
presided over meetings of the JCS. Leahy did not make policy, but his
control of the flow of information (he ran the Map Room, the White House
communications center) and his proximity to the President gave him
considerable influence over how that policy was carried out.

Raised in a small town in Wisconsin, Leahy, like Stimson, had been imbued with a strong sense of patriotism and devotion to public service. His long and varied public career began with his graduation from Annapolis in 1897. This was followed by participation in the Spanish-American War, and a steady rise up the career ladder to the topmost rung, Chief of Naval Operations. During this ascent he had the good fortune to command the dispatch boat *Dolphin* which, among other things, functioned occasionally as a pleasure yacht for then Assistant Secretary of the Navy Franklin Roosevelt.

Following the admiral's mandatory retirement in 1939, FDR made Leahy Governor of Puerto Rico and later appointed him ambassador to Vichy France. Leahy handled this sensitive mission with tact and skill, and in 1942 the President brought him into the White House. He had traveled widely throughout his career, but as his biographer has noted, Leahy associated primarily with fellow officers and government officials. As a result, he never had much understanding of what were referred to at the time as the backward countries of the world.[6] Strongly anticommunist and suspicious of change in general, he was also somewhat out of touch with what he called the "proletariat" of his own country.[7]

Truman respected the crusty old admiral, and Leahy reciprocated that feeling. Leahy's loyalty to the new President was unquestionable, and Truman soon learned to trust his chief of staff with a wide range of responsibilities. Truman's decision to keep Leahy as his principal White House aide guaranteed a degree of continuity in the management of that office. He was more willing, however, to make changes in his cabinet. One of his earliest decisions was to accept the resignation of Treasury Secretary Henry Morgenthau, whom he regarded as something of a nuisance. Even before that, however, Truman had decided to make James Byrnes his Secretary of State.[8]

Truman seems to have had a number of reasons for appointing Byrnes to this post. Byrnes, a former senator from South Carolina, Supreme Court justice, and head of the War Mobilization Board, was a highly respected Washington insider. Moreover, when Truman had been a fledgling senator, Byrnes had taken him under his wing. Truman also felt he owed a larger debt to Byrnes. During the 1944 Democratic convention, Truman had agreed to nominate Byrnes for Vice-President, only to discover at the last moment that FDR had dumped the South Carolinian in favor of Truman. Byrnes could not help but think that he belonged in the office that Truman now occupied. Thus Truman may have hoped to lessen Byrnes' sense of injury by appointing him to the most important office in his cabinet.

According to his own account, Truman also chose Byrnes because, according to the law at that time, the Secretary of State was next in the line of presidential succession, there being no Vice-President. Truman believed that the position should be filled by an experienced politician who was familiar with government and the responsibilities of elective office.[9] This aspect of Truman's reasoning was tactlessly revealed in a *Time* magazine article announcing that if Byrnes and Truman did any flying on the way to the conference they would take separate planes, "so as not to hand the presidency over to retiring Treasury Secretary Henry Morgenthau in the event of a fatal accident."[10]

Historian Robert Messer has shown, however, that Truman may also have had other motives for making the appointment. Byrnes had been to Yalta with Roosevelt, and, as Truman knew, he had kept a stenographic record of the conference proceedings. Truman may have reasoned that Byrnes could give him the full story on Yalta. Consultation with Byrnes offered Truman the advantage of learning about FDR's policies from a man he trusted, a man like himself, a self-educated veteran of the pragmatic world of party politics.[11] At first neither man realized that Byrnes had not been privy to the most important transactions of the conference. Messer has shown, however, that Roosevelt deliberately groomed Byrnes to help him sell the Yalta agreements to the Senate. The less Byrnes knew about the concessions Roosevelt made to the Russians, the more willingly he would encourage his former colleagues in the Senate to support FDR's postwar plans. Byrnes saw only the harmonious side of the conference. He did not attend the meeting at which the final agreement on Poland was reached, nor did he know about the secret Far Eastern accords.[12]

Exactly when both men read the Far Eastern protocol has become a matter of controversy. Years later when Republican politicians turned the "betrayal" at Yalta into a political issue, Byrnes and Truman tried to distance themselves from the agreement. Byrnes later wrote that he did not see the actual text of the accords until December 1945. But this story is hard to credit. George Elsey, the naval aide responsible for the White House safe in which the document was kept, has insisted that he showed Byrnes the official text in April 1945. According to Elsey, Leahy told him to show Byrnes the agreements to "get him up to speed," it being understood that Byrnes would be the new Secretary of State. Elsey brought the document to Byrnes' suite at the Shoreham Hotel, where it was studied by Byrnes and Ben Cohen. When the two men were finished Elsey returned the only copy of the top secret agreement to his safe.[13]

Truman claimed that he had not seen the document until he began preparing for the Potsdam conference. It seems doubtful, however, that Leahy, who knew of the agreement, would not have immediately shown it to the new President. Moreover, as we have seen, Truman knew that the Far Eastern agreement was being reviewed by the Committee of Three as early as mid-May. It is difficult to imagine that, at a time when Truman is known to have been devouring anything he could read on FDR's foreign policy, he would not have wanted to see the text of the Yalta agreements. Thus, it would seem that whatever difficulties Truman and his new Secretary of State had to overcome in their first summit meeting, incomplete knowledge of the Yalta agreements was not one of them.[14]

After a safe and uneventful trip across the Atlantic, the President arrived in the Berlin suburb of Potsdam on July 15. The following evening Stimson brought him news of the successful test of an atomic device at Alamogordo. Truman had been anxiously awaiting word on the test, and efforts by the project scientists to postpone the experiment for several days had been overruled.[15] That night Joseph Davies recorded that the President had told him that the news had taken a great load off his mind.[16] The first reports reaching Berlin gave little indication of the bomb's true power, however, and Truman's relief may have resulted from the simple realization that the entire project was not a failure.[17]

The next morning, the seventeenth, Stalin paid a visit to the "Little White House" and accepted Truman's invitation to a potluck lunch of bacon and liver. That evening Truman wrote in his diary, "He'll be in the Jap war on August 15. Fini Japs when that comes about."[18] Truman's notes for the seventeenth also suggest that he was satisfied that Stalin would adhere to the American interpretation of the Yalta agreements. After the meeting he told Stimson that he had "clinched the Open Door in Manchuria."[19] To his wife, to whom he wrote with surprising openness about highly secret matters, Truman confided, "I've gotten what I came for— Stalin goes to war August 15th with no strings on it. He wanted a Chinese settlement and it is practically made—in better form than I expected."[20]

There is, however, reason to question whether Truman believed the situation was as bright as he described it. Shortly after his luncheon with Stalin, Truman and Byrnes told Leahy that they thought a Sino-Soviet agreement could be reached only through "radical concessions by China." Truman and Byrnes also told the admiral that they thought Russia would enter the war whether or not such concessions were granted, and thereafter "satisfy Soviet demands regardless of what the Chinese attitude might be."[21]

It is difficult to reconcile these apparent contradictions in Truman's perception of Soviet aims in the Far East. Perhaps he had not made up his mind as to how he should view the Russians. Perhaps he hid his own uncertainty by telling people what they wanted to hear. It is also possible that Truman's diary was not a completely frank description of his private thoughts. Truman often sprinkled his journal entries with little asides to the reader, which suggests that he expected his papers to be read at some future date.[22] Having recently averted a near break with the Soviets, Truman may have wanted to make it abundantly clear for the record that he was going into the conference prepared to cooperate with the Russians.

In any event, few of the members of the American delegation would have agreed with Truman's statement that the Sino-Soviet agreement was practically made in better form than expected. Certainly Harriman did not. In his last message to Truman before leaving Moscow for Potsdam, the ambassador explained that Stalin's demands for Soviet supervision of the Manchurian railways and inclusion of Dairen in the Russian military zone would effectively close off any outside commerce with Manchuria.[23] Harriman warned Stimson that the Open Door was in jeopardy, and the Secretary of War took the matter directly to Truman. Even after Truman informed him that he had "clinched the Open Door," Stimson continued to advise the President to get Stalin to commit his promises to paper. Harriman and Stimson also thought that Truman should get Stalin to agree formally to a detailed trusteeship arrangement for Korea before Soviet troops occupied the area.[24]

On the morning of the eighteenth, Stimson delivered a second report on the test at Alamogordo. This contained more details than the previous report, but it still did not give a full description of the bomb's power. Stimson did observe, however, that the President was "very greatly reinforced over the message."[25] That night while reflecting on the day's events

Truman appeared to reassess the import of the second message on the bomb. "Believe the Japs will fold up before Russia comes in," he wrote. "I am sure they will when Manhattan appears over their homeland."[26]

During the next several days little progress was made in the meetings of the Big Three. Stalin met Truman's proposal to consider an interim regime for Italy with a counterproposal to include Rumania, Hungary, Bulgaria, and Finland in any softening of the surrender terms. Truman refused, arguing that the Eastern European states had not been open to American inspection and that their regimes did not live up to the standards of the Declaration on Liberated Europe. Neither side gave any ground on this point. It was during one of these meetings that Churchill declared that an iron curtain had fallen around British representatives in Rumania. "All fairy tales," answered Stalin.[27]

On July 21 Truman received the first full report on the test at Alamogordo. "The test was successful beyond the most optimistic expectations of anyone," wrote Manhattan Project director General Leslie Groves. The general conservatively estimated the energy generated by the blast to exceed that of 20,000 tons of TNT. According to Groves, the explosion was so powerful that among the unauthorized witnesses who caught a glimpse of the blast was "a blind woman who saw the light."[28] Stimson delivered the message to Truman's residence and noted that the President was "tremendously pepped up by it."[29] The following day, a Sunday, Stimson told Truman that the bomb would be ready for use against Japan sooner than expected.[30]

On Monday, July 23, Stimson met again with Truman. That morning Stimson had learned from Ambassador Harriman that during the plenary sessions Stalin had expanded Russian demands to include a base in the Black Sea Straits and an interest in Italy's former colonies. Harriman and Stimson were also concerned that Stalin would use Britain's and France's refusal to discuss trusteeships for Hong Kong and Indochina as a justification to abandon the trusteeship plan for Korea.[31] Truman confirmed all this, but he added that the United States was standing firm. Truman thought most of Stalin's claims were bluff and that the Russians would settle for less than they were demanding. Stimson inferred from Truman's remarks that the President was counting on the information from Groves in formulating his response to the Soviets.[32]

Before Truman called Stalin's bluff, he had to be sure about the strength of his own hand. Toward this end he asked Stimson to find out if Marshall believed the Russians were still needed in the war.[33] Although Marshall was circumspect in answering, Stimson concluded that Soviet assistance was no longer needed and he so informed Truman on the twenty-fourth. That day Stimson told Truman the first bomb would be ready between August 1 and 6.

The following morning Truman met with Marshall and Admiral Lord Louis Mountbatten, head of the Southeast Asian Command (SEAC). Truman's diary contains the vague notation that "at 10:15 I had General Marshall come in and discuss with me the tactical and political situation."[34] According to Mountbatten's recollection, Truman discussed the atomic bomb at the meeting. Following the meeting Churchill told Mountbatten to notify his staff to prepare for an early Japanese surrender.[35] Truman must have given Marshall similar instructions, for that afternoon the general sent a message to MacArthur requesting information regarding plans for the rapid occupation of Japan *and* Korea.[36]

The awesome power of the atomic bomb was very much on Truman's mind that day. "We have discovered the most terrible bomb in the history of the world," he wrote. "It may be the fire destruction prophesied in the Euphrates Valley Era, after Noah and his fabulous Ark."[37] After noting that the bomb would be used only on military targets and not before Japan received a warning, Truman added that "it seems to be the most terrible thing ever discovered, but it can be made the most useful."[38] Truman may have been referring to the long-range potential of atomic energy when he described the bomb as being "most useful." His actions on the twenty-fifth, however, suggest that he was also thinking about more immediate benefits.

The success of the Manhattan Project offered Truman a chance to avoid a repetition of events in Eastern Europe. Convinced that a Japanese surrender could be achieved without Soviet assistance, Truman sought to steal the march on the Russians by landing troops in Korea. Although it seems clear that Truman wanted to prevent a unilateral occupation of the peninsula by the Russians, his long-range objectives can be stated with less certainty. James Matray has argued that "Truman and his advisors decided to abandon trusteeship in anticipation of a rapid end to the Pacific war that would forestall Soviet occupation."[39] To support his argument, Matray shows that despite the urgings of Molotov and American advisers to conclude a detailed agreement before the Soviets entered the war, Byrnes and Truman avoided any discussion of the Korean trusteeship issue at the conference. Other historians have argued that Truman's goals were more limited. To expect the Red Army to sit idly by while the war ended was wishful thinking. Moreover, Marshall must have told Truman that the United States could not occupy the entire peninsula on such short notice. Instead of hoping to keep the Soviets out of the war altogether, Truman seems to have been hoping to minimize Russian influence in Northeast Asia by having American troops occupy as much territory as possible.[40]

Byrnes' thinking seems also to have moved along these lines. At first he hoped that he might prevent Soviet entry into the war by having Soong drag out the negotiations with Moscow. Stalin had told Truman and Byrnes that the Soviets would not enter the war until they had a firm agreement with the Chinese. To prolong the talks, Byrnes sent a cable to Chiang over Truman's signature in which he advised the Chinese not to make any concessions in excess of the Yalta agreements.[41] By the twenty-fifth, however, Byrnes' aide reported that the Secretary had lowered his expectations: "JFB still hoping for time, believing after atomic bomb Japan will surrender and Russia will not *get in so much* on the kill, thereby being in a position to press for claims against China."[42] Three days later Byrnes told Forrestal that he was "most anxious to get the Japanese affair over with before the Russians got in, with particular reference to Dairen and Port Arthur. Once in there he felt, it would not be easy to get them out."[43]

As part of their effort to end the war without the Russians, Truman and Byrnes released a warning to the Japanese people on July 26. After receiving Chinese and British approval for the broadcast, Byrnes issued the proclamation to the press, and then, after it was too late to revise the document, he showed it to Molotov. The Russians asked for several days to study the proclamation, but it had already gone to the newspapers. Byrnes explained rather weakly that he had not discussed the proclamation with the Soviets because he did not want to involve them in anything that could be construed by the Japanese as an unneutral act.[44]

The Potsdam Proclamation, as the warning was called, was the product of a number of small dramas that had been played out at different levels in the government. It will be recalled that although Byrnes had agreed to bring the draft proclamation to Potsdam, he had witheld his approval from the document until he had a chance to study it further. Before making his decision Byrnes sought the advice of Cordell Hull. Roosevelt's former Secretary of State still wielded influence in Washington, and Byrnes could count on Hull to provide him with an accurate sense of how the proclamation would be received in congressional circles.

Hull's reply reached Potsdam on July 16. The former Secretary found the proclamation deficient on two counts. First he questioned the need to include a public assurance regarding the preservation of the monarchy. Second, he questioned the desirability of releasing the proclamation from Potsdam. If it failed, "the Japs would be encouraged while terrible political repercussions would follow in the U.S. Would it be well to await the climax of allied bombing and Russia's entry into the war?"[45] Clearly, Hull was thinking of the need to demonstrate Allied determination before approaching the Japanese. Because he had not learned of the successful test of the bomb, he thought that the best time to make any overtures was after the Soviets entered the war.

By the evening of the sixteenth, however, Byrnes knew of the bomb's success. Nevertheless, Hull's warning about the political repercussions of making any concessions on the emperor, especially if the Japanese rejected them, carried great weight with Byrnes. On the seventeenth he wired Hull, saying, "I agree that the issuance of statement should be delayed and, when made, should not contain commitment to which your refer."[46] That morning a disappointed Stimson left the "Little White House" after learning that Byrnes, and apparently Truman, opposed giving Japan an early warning.[47]

The communications between Hull and Byrnes were relayed through the State Department office of Joseph Grew, who then telephoned Hull to tell him that Byrnes had decided to strike out the provision regarding the emperor and to delay issuing the warning.[48] Grew's sense of frustration must have been palpable. During the spring, Grew had loyally represented the views of his colleagues on the emperor question in interdepartmental meetings. By late June, however, he appears to have grown somewhat tired of the resistance he faced from within the department. On June 30 Grew sent Truman an agenda for the coming conference along with several briefing papers, all of which were identified as representing "the carefully considered recommendations of the Department of State."[49] Included among the documents was a position paper that recommended giving the Japanese assurances that would "eliminate the most serious single obstacle to Japanese unconditional surrender, namely, concern over the fate of the throne."[50]

Such was not, however, the view of the majority of Grew's colleagues in the Secretary's staff committee. In the course of two meetings held on July 7 and 9, Grew was forced to accept a watered-down version of the controversial clause referring to the emperor. On the ninth the committee approved a revised version promising that "when the people of Japan have convinced the peace loving nations of the world that they are going to follow peaceful lives they shall be given an opportunity to control their destiny along peaceful lines."[51] This revision was carried to Potsdam and given to Byrnes by James Dunn.

Hull and the State Department were now on record as opposing any explicit reference to the emperor in the proclamation. Hull's advice alone was enough to convince Byrnes to excise the controversial clause. The proposed proclamation had a strong bearing on American military policy, however, and Truman's reluctance to interfere in military planning meant that the views of the JCS would not be ignored.

The Chiefs had been given a chance to review the proclamation when Forrestal referred a copy of the original draft to Admiral King during the first week of July. From there it traveled a circuitous route, arriving before the JCS at Potsdam on the seventeenth. In the interim the proclamation was reviewed by the Joint Strategic Survey Committee (JSSC), a group of elderly high-ranking officers empowered to think broadly about the future of American security.[52] The JSSC recommended several revisions, the most important having to do with the assurance in paragraph twelve that the Japanese could keep the emperor. Citing the phrase allowing Japan to keep a "constitutional monarchy under the present dynasty," the JSSC argued that this reference might lead the Japanese to believe that the current emperor would be deposed and replaced by another member of the ruling family. They also believed that paragraph twelve might be interpreted by Japanese leftists as a commitment to maintain the imperial institution against the wishes of the Japanese people.[53] In place of the original wording, the JSSC suggested informing the Japanese people that "subject to suitable guarantees against further acts of aggression, the Japanese people will be free to choose their own form of government."[54] These revisions were dispatched to Potsdam.

A copy of the JSSC's recommendations also found its way into the office of the Strategy and Policy Group, where it provoked an immediate protest. These authors of the original proclamation were willing to make some concessions on the JSSC's first point by changing the reference to the emperor so as to make it unmistakably clear that nothing would happen to Hirohito. The staff officers completely rejected the JSSC's second argument. They could see no logical reason for worrying how the Japanese Left would interpret the agreement. The radical element in Japan was at present too small to have any influence on the government's decision to surrender. Noting that the consensus in the McCloy committee was agreed that "we should not beat around the bush but should state unequivocally what we intend to do with the Emperor," they dispatched their own memo to Potsdam containing a revision of the JSSC report. If accepted, the new proclamation would read, "The Japanese people will be free to choose whether they shall retain their Emperor as a constitutional monarch."[55]

Despite this spirited last-minute opposition from S&P, the Chiefs approved the JSSC report on July 17. General Marshall insisted, however, that the report include a recommendation that nothing be done "prior to the termination of hostilities that would indicate the removal of the Emperor of Japan, since his continuation in office might influence the cessation of hostilities in areas outside of Japan proper."[56]

Unfortunately for historians, the JCS minutes do not provide a clear explanation as to why Marshall accepted the views of the JSSC over those of his own staff officers in S&P. In his personal diary, the secretary of the JCS, Charles H. Donnelly, wrote only that "the Chiefs spent considerable time discussing the application of the unconditional surrender formula to Japan. General Marshall cautioned against any move to oust the Emperor because it would lead to a last-ditch defense by the Japanese."[57]

The minutes do, however, provide one possible explanation for Marshall's decision. Before the Chiefs discussed the JSSC paper, Admiral Leahy mentioned the proposed revision in paragraph twelve and noted that "the matter had been considered on a political level and consideration had been given to the removal of the sentence in question."[58] Thus it seems that Leahy informed the Chiefs that Truman and Byrnes were opposed to making any promise regarding the emperor. Given these circumstances Marshall may have thought that there was no point in trying to persuade Truman and Byrnes to retain the reference to the emperor. If this was Marshall's reasoning, then what the JCS gave Truman was simply an echo of his own thoughts, as opposed to their own independent judgment on an important question.

It also possible that Marshall no longer believed that a proclamation, regardless of what it said about the emperor, would be very effective. Ever since Germany's defeat American OSS operatives in Europe had been in contact with Japanese officials stationed in Berne, Switzerland. These early meetings had been tentative at first, but by July both sides were speaking more openly about how the war could be ended. In one set of talks, Dr. Per Jacobsson, a former officer of the Bank of International Settlements, and Kitamura Kojiro, also an officer of the bank, met to discuss the meaning of unconditional surrender. Jacobsson was acting as a representative of Allen Dulles, the OSS chief in Europe, and Kitamura represented Kase Shunichi, Japan's minister to Switzerland.

On July 15 Jacobsson told Kitamura that Dulles believed the only way "for Japan to save anything for herself is for her to accept at once 'unconditional surrender' as defined in Grew's statement of 10 July."[59] The aforementioned statement had emphasized the goal of unconditional surrender as being the destruction of Japanese militarism, and had said nothing about the imperial institution. Jacobsson stated that Dulles had been in touch with Grew and in Dulles' judgment the omission of any reference to the emperor was a clear indication that the United States would not destroy the imperial institution.[60] Dulles, according to Jacobsson, had also said that "once Russia joins England and the United States [against Japan], it will by no means be so simple to end the war."[61]

No response was immediately forthcoming from Tokyo. Dulles notified Washington that important developments in the talks were not likely in the next few days, but he concluded that "a line is being opened which the Japanese may use when the situation in Tokyo permits Japan to accept unconditional surrender."[62] The message, dated July 18, was rerouted to Potsdam.

Through the efforts of its cryptanalysts, the United States was able to read the encoded messages of the Japanese diplomatic service, thus enabling American officials to follow both sides of the Jacobsson-Kitamura talks. The name given to this top secret operation was, appropriately enough, MAGIC. The MAGIC intercepts soon made it clear to American officials that Kase did not yet speak for the Foreign Ministry, let alone the Japanese government. Of more significance to American officials looking for some sign of the Japanese military's willingness to surrender were a series of messages regarding an attempt on the part of the military attaché in Stockholm to involve the Swedish government in a "peace maneuver." According to Japanese Foreign Minister Togo Shigenori, the war and navy ministers and the chiefs of the army and navy staffs agreed that such activity should be stopped. A subsequent message from the vice-chief of the general staff to the offending attaché reaffirmed that "Japan is firmly determined to prosecute the Greater East Asia war to the very end."[63]

Subsequent discussions between the Japanese naval attaché in Switzerland and another of Dulles' associates were not likely to encourage the JCS to think that the Japanese would surrender if they were given explicit assurances on the emperor. According to Commander Fujimura Yoshiro, Dulles, speaking through a third party, suggested that Switzerland would be a suitable place to hold a "discussion" or "talk." Fujimura quoted Dulles as saying that since Russia did not have diplomatic relations with Switzerland, there would be little "surveillance or meddling on the part of Russia."[64] If Japan wished to hold such talks, they were to send "in all haste" an admiral with a small staff of three officers to Switzerland. The requests of the Fujimura group for authorization to open negotiations fell on deaf ears. On July 22 the navy general staff instructed Fujimura to turn the matter over to Kase and remove himself from the discussions. The final paragraph of this message underscored the fruitlessness of Fujimura's efforts.

At present Japan is endeavoring to store up fighting power and in accordance with her predetermined policy is devoting all her efforts to the prosecution of the war. Since we believe recent propaganda of an enemy character and such schemes as this really indicate what difficulties the enemy is facing, naval representatives abroad should be all the more careful at this time not to act heedlessly.[65]

To the Americans reading the cable traffic between Tokyo and its representatives in Europe, Japan's military leaders gave little indication of a willingness to surrender. To those Japanese officials who urged their government to begin negotiations, the militarists seemed isolated from reality. During the second week of July, Japan's leaders demonstrated their capacity for self-delusion by attempting to seek Soviet mediation to end the war. As part of this effort the Japanese sought Russian approval to send a special representative to Moscow. The Soviets put the Japanese off until Stalin had left for Potsdam, and then explained that they would have to wait for his return. On July 18 Stalin showed the President the Japanese message. Both men agreed that the Russians should continue to stall the Japanese.[66] Despite the recommendations of their minister in Moscow to accept unconditional surrender "or terms closely approximating thereto," the Japanese government insisted that the United States and Great Britain had to recognize "Japan's honor and existence" and give up their demand for unconditional surrender.[67] The Japanese continued to hope for Soviet assistance until the Russians entered the war.

By the first week of the Potsdam conference, the JCS, the State Department, and Roosevelt's former Secretary of State had all advised Truman to avoid any mention of the emperor in the proposed warning. The MAGIC intercepts seemed to confirm this advice. Before the President departed from FDR's policy and risked being labeled an appeaser, he would have to have a clearer indication that his proposal would be accepted by the Japanese, and by the American public.

Debate in the Senate appeared to reveal some enthusiasm for an explicit warning to Japan, but the depth of this support was uncertain. On July 12 Homer Capehart (R–Indiana) announced that he did not share the view that "we must destroy Japan's form of government and then spend years in occupation and teaching a different form of government." Capehart wanted the administration to offer Japan a clear definition of unconditional surrender. He believed that the terms need not go beyond demanding that Japan disarm, surrender its conquered territories, yield its war criminals, and pay war reparations. Senate majority leader Alben Barkley (D–Kentucky) disagreed. Japan, he argued, should ask for terms rather than be induced to surrender. Otherwise Americans would find themselves accepting a compromise peace. Japan must know it had been defeated, Barkley maintained.[68] On July 23 another Republican, Kenneth Wherry (R–Nebraska), recommended that Truman spell out American war aims in precise language. "If we can end the war by stating what we want," asked Wherry, "why not do so?"[69]

These isolated incidents of congressional support fell considerably short of the ground swell that probably would have been needed to convince Truman to change his mind about including the emperor in the proclamation. It is interesting to note, however, that although Grew, Stimson, McCloy, Forrestal, and Leahy had access to either some or all of the information provided by Dulles and MAGIC, they continued to believe that it was necessary to retain the original wording of paragraph twelve. Without an explicit promise on the emperor, they believed, the peace faction in Japan did not stand a chance of ending the war.[70]

Grew and the others were also less concerned than Truman and Byrnes over the public's reaction to the proposed statement. This does not seem too surprising when one considers that the President and his Secretary of State would be held accountable for any proclamation issued by the United States. But differences in experience and political convictions also help to explain the disagreement over unconditional surrender. Those who entered the foreign policy elite through career service (Leahy and Grew) or through the more conventional avenues of corporate law and finance

(Stimson, McCloy, and Forrestal) were aligned on one side of the issue. Byrnes and Truman, the only members of the group to hold elective office, were on the other. As a result of their wartime experience Stimson and the others shared a greater appreciation for the power of a President to shape public opinion. As insiders they controlled the information on which any intelligent decision would be made. Stimson and the others believed their duty was to the national interest as they understood it, and they regarded public opinion as something of an intrusion in the policy process. Conversely, Truman and Byrnes were not only more concerned about popular sentiment, but it is likely that they also sympathized with the public's desire to punish the emperor.

There is some evidence to suggest that Stimson and his associates had begun a campaign to ensure that Truman released the proclamation while he was at Potsdam. On July 22 the *New York Times* reported that an editorial in the *Army and Navy Journal* described the contents of a draft of American surrender terms that Truman had taken with him to Potsdam. What followed was an accurate description of the proclamation drafted by McCloy's committee. The editorial went on to say that Truman was "disposed" to make the announcement from Potsdam rather than Washington. The *Journal* added that the emperor question was the source of considerable debate within the administration. Those who wanted him executed were described as "Liberals and New Dealers." Other officials, according to the editorial, blamed the warlords for Japanese aggression, and believed that the emperor did not "involve our security and that the war would only be prolonged if we should fight to destroy Japan's religious and political systems."[71]

During the same week a small storm broke over the content of a Japanese-language propaganda broadcast by Captain E. M. Zacharias, a naval intelligence officer working out of the Office of War Information. On July 21, in what was the twelfth in a series of broadcasts, Zacharias informed the Japanese people that if they surrendered immediately Japan would receive terms that were consistent with the Atlantic Charter. This was considered to be an oblique reference to the emperor question in that the charter recognized the rights of all peoples to choose their own form of government. The speech also hinted at the impending Soviet entry into the war by urging Japan to surrender before the international situation became more complicated. The *New York Times* reported that the broadcast had been made with Truman's full knowledge.[72] This seems doubtful.

Zacharias was subsequently informed that he was to drop the words "official spokesman" from his future broadcasts.[73]

All of this public speculation about American war aims may have caused Truman to wonder if he was losing control of his own government. It is doubtful, however, that the President felt pressured into issuing the proclamation.[74] The availability of the atomic bomb for actual combat use was the controlling factor in Truman's decision. On July 22 Truman learned that the bomb would be ready sooner than expected. On the twenty-third, Byrnes asked Stimson when he would know the precise date.[75] The following day Stimson was able to tell Truman that a uranium bomb would be ready soon after August 1, and a plutonium bomb (the type tested at Alamogordo) about August 6. According to Stimson, Truman replied that the schedule "gave him his cue for his warning."[76] A copy of the proclamation had just been sent to Chiang for his approval. Stimson then made one last effort to retain the reference to the emperor in the proclamation. The Secretary said he thought that it might be the one thing that "might make or mar their acceptance." He realized, however, that since the proposed ultimatum had been sent to Chiang it was now too late to change it. As a final suggestion, Stimson asked Truman to consider using diplomatic channels to reassure the Japanese that they could keep the emperor, "if it were found that they were hanging fire on that one point."[77] Truman responded vaguely that "he had that in mind, and that he would take care of it."[78]

The ultimatum was released on July 26. After warning Japan that the forces arrayed against it were far more powerful than those that destroyed the Nazis, the leaders of the United States, Great Britain, and China announced their terms. "We shall not deviate from them. There are no alternatives. We shall brook no delay."[79] Japan would be demilitarized, those who "deceived and misled the Japanese people" into following the path of aggression would be forever removed from authority, and the terms of the Cairo Declaration would be enforced. There would also be an occupation of Japan, but, on the advice of the British, the proclamation stated that "points in Japanese territory" would be occupied.[80] The proclamation also explained that the Japanese people would not be enslaved and the nation would not be destroyed. It also promised Japan "access to as distinguished from control of, raw materials" and the maintenance of a peacetime economy. Paragraph twelve read as follows: "The occupying forces of the Allies shall be withdrawn from Japan as soon as these objectives have been accomplished and there has been established in accord with the freely expressed will of the Japanese people a peacefully inclined and responsible government."[81]

On the afternoon of July 27 the Japanese cabinet met to discuss the Allied ultimatum. Foreign Minister Togo Shigenori had already decided that the government should take a "wait and see" approach to the proclamation while it attempted to solicit Soviet assistance in mediating an end to the war. He also thought that it might be possible to clarify some of the Allies' terms in a manner that would be beneficial to the Japanese. Despite opposition from the military, who wanted to make a ringing denunciation, Togo persuaded the cabinet to ignore the proclamation for the time being. An expurgated text of the proclamation was released to the press with instructions to treat it as a straight news story.[82]

Somehow, and precisely how we will probably never know for certain, when the newspapers received the censored text they were also informed that the government's attitude would be *mokusatsu*, literally to "kill it with silence." Interpreted idiomatically, however, it could also mean "take no notice," "treat with silent contempt," or "ignore it."[83] Once the papers described the government's attitude as *mokusatsu*, the military demanded a more positive rejection of the Potsdam Proclamation to steady morale among the troops. That afternoon Premier Suzuki Kantaro, in answer to a planted question at a press conference, read the following: "I consider the joint proclamation of the three powers to be a rehash of the Cairo Declaration. The government does not regard it as a thing of any great value; the government will just ignore [*mokusatsu*] it. We will press forward resolutely to carry the war to a successful conclusion."[84]

As unfortunate as the choice of the word *mokusatsu* was, it is clear that the Japanese government was simply not prepared to accept the terms laid out in the proclamation.[85] The Allies, of course, regarded Suzuki's statement as a rejection of their ultimatum. Truman had already approved the use of the atomic bomb, and preparations for its assembly and delivery were under way in the Pacific. On July 30 Stimson cabled Truman from Washington requesting permission to release a presidential announcement on the bomb should it become available for use before the President returned home. Truman gave Stimson the go-ahead, providing the bomb was not used before August 2. According to George Elsey, Truman did not want to be in Potsdam with Stalin when the bomb was dropped.[86]

Some historians have suggested that in omitting any reference to the emperor in the Potsdam Proclamation, Truman revealed that he was not concerned with ending the war before the Soviets intervened. On the one hand it is argued that Truman wanted to keep Japan in the war long enough to make a combat demonstration of the bomb as a means of intimidating the Soviets. This assumes that the President knew that if he offered to preserve the emperor institution, Japan would surrender and deprive him of his opportunity to use the bomb.[87] The reverse of this argument has it that Truman believed Japan would scoff at any offer and that seeing no way to keep the Soviets out of the war Truman sought only military cooperation with Stalin.[88] It has also been suggested that had the Americans seriously believed that the proclamation could induce Japan's surrender, they would not have treated it as a mere propaganda tool by sending it out over the airwaves.[89]

These arguments overlook several important points. First, the decision to address the proclamation to the Japanese people through a broadcast was first recommended by the McCloy committee. The committee members believed that the warning would be most effective if it were treated like the Cairo Declaration and the other major Allied pronouncements during the war.[90]

The apparent incompatibility between the omission of the emperor from the proclamation and Truman's desire to end the war quickly requires a more elaborate explanation. To begin with, it should be understood that Truman did not think that the warning alone would convince Japan to surrender. Given the intelligence available to him, it is hard to see how Truman could have been certain that the Japanese government would surrender once it received an explicit promise on the emperor. Indeed, even Sato Naotake, Japan's ambassador in Moscow, confessed at one point in his communications with Tokyo that he was "not clear about the views of the Government and of the Military with regard to the termination of the war."[91] On the day the Potsdam Proclamation was released, Admiral Leahy wrote that "some indulge in a hope that this statement will bring about an unconditional surrender by the Japanese Government before the Soviet Government joins in the war."[92] Truman, however, was not so sanguine. On July 25 he wrote in his diary that he would give the Japanese a chance to surrender and save lives. "I am sure they will not do that," he added, "but we will have given them the chance."[93] But if the warning was not sufficient by itself, it seemed to be more than adequate when followed by an atomic bomb. Possession of the bomb provided Truman a way out of a dilemma. He could avoid the political risks entailed in making any reference to the emperor, and still bring about a rapid end to the war. Truman and Byrnes expected the immense power of the atomic bomb to force the Japanese to see the reasonableness of Allied war aims as stated in the proclamation.

As for Truman's desire to cooperate militarily with the Soviets, both he and Byrnes believed strongly enough that the war could be ended quickly that they ignored the advice of their political and military advisers and left the conference without any firm understanding on the Korean trustee-ship.[94] Moreover, by encouraging the Chinese to drag out their negotiations, the Americans risked having the Red Army enter the war without any agreements to restrict their behavior in Manchuria. The Americans also left the conference without discussing either immediate or long-range occupation duties with their Russian counterparts. During one of their meetings the JCS and the Soviet high command did establish an operational boundary to prevent any clashes between the converging forces. But this line, which cut across Korea at the forty-first parallel, was for air and sea operations only.[95] The JCS had given the Russians no indication that American forces might operate on the mainland in the near future. This omission left open the possibility of a collision between American and Soviet forces as they rushed to fill the vacuum created by Japan's surrender.

Truman's strategy involved a great many risks. By mid-July, however, he had come to believe that Stalin would not live up to his agreements in the Far East any more than he had in Eastern Europe. In order to preserve the Open Door in Manchuria, support the KMT, and save the Korean trusteeship, Truman decided that he needed to counter Russian power with an American presence in Northeast Asia. The United States would be in a better position to resist Soviet pressure in Manchuria and Korea after Japan was defeated and American troops were on the mainland. The success of Truman's strategy depended on a number of factors, not the least of which was the swift movement of American forces into the areas held by Japanese troops. The President had addressed himself to this problem in his talk with Marshall and Mountbatten on the morning of the twenty-fifth. Thus, while the Big Three were meeting in Potsdam, halfway around the world American and British commanders were receiving instructions to prepare for the sudden collapse of the Japanese empire.

4

Final Preparations

When the Japanese surrendered it caught the whole goddamn administrative machinery with their [sic] pants down. (Col. Robert Wood, OPD)[1]

Aᴛ Pᴏᴛꜱᴅᴀᴍ, Truman had decided to postpone detailed discussions on Northeast Asia in the hope that an early Japanese surrender would leave the United States in a better position to influence the postwar settlement in the region. The convergence of events at Potsdam, specifically the successful test of the bomb and Stalin's increased demands, removed the uncertainty that had hovered over American policy in the first months of the Truman presidency. But although the atomic bomb made Soviet assistance superfluous, it did not eliminate the myriad problems that the United States faced in accepting the sudden surrender of Japan. Indeed, Truman's desire to project American power onto the mainland actually added to these difficulties.

By July 1945 the military situation in the Pacific had entered a period of comparative calm. The costly battle for Okinawa had ended recently, leaving American forces victorious but exhausted. The inner ring of Japan's defenses had been breached, but the United States needed time to regroup before launching the long-dreaded invasion of the home islands. Some of the troops that were scheduled to participate in the final assault were still being transferred from the European theater. Others were located on widely separated island bases throughout the Pacific. The problems posed by this dispersion of forces would be only slightly diminished by a sudden surrender. In the event of a collapse of Japanese resistance, most of the troops that were earmarked for the invasion would be needed for the rapid occupation of Japan's key areas.[2]

An early draft of General MacArthur's planned operations to occupy

Japan (BLACKLIST) clearly revealed the problems that the United States would face in rushing troops into Japan. Dated July 11, the first draft of BLACKLIST focused on the occupation of Japan's main islands. The plan called for the introduction of forces in three phases. The first called for 15⅔ divisions, 9⅔ of which would come from the Philippines, 2 from the Ryukyus (which included Okinawa), 2 from the Marianas, and 2 from as far off as Hawaii. Phase two would draw 4 divisions from the Philippines. The final phase took an additional 3 divisions from the Philippines, bringing the total to 22⅔ divisions, not counting any divisions that might be redeployed from the European theater.[3] As the Commander in Chief of Army Forces in the Pacific (CINCAFPAC), MacArthur was supposed to be ready to impose the surrender terms any time after July 15. The inclusion of 4 divisions from the Marianas and Hawaii in the initial deployment meant, however, that there would be a considerable lag between the time when Japan surrendered and American troops completed the first phase of the plan.

BLACKLIST anticipated the possibility that American troops might be needed to accept the surrender in some places on the mainland if Japan surrendered before the Soviets entered the war. MacArthur planned to keep the First Army in reserve to meet this contingency. Without instructions from the JCS, however, he could not specify where they might be used.[4] On July 22, following the arrival in Potsdam of the second report on the bomb, the JCS notified MacArthur and Admiral Chester Nimitz, Commander in Chief of Naval Forces in the Pacific (CINCPAC), that the Japanese might surrender before August 15, the expected date of Russian entry into the war. MacArthur and Nimitz were instructed to prepare accordingly and to include Korea in their plans. The message added that the administration and occupation of Korea would most likely be on a quadripartite basis.[5]

The news from Alamogordo sparked a new flurry of activity among planners at Potsdam. In preparation for a meeting with Truman, Marshall instructed General Lincoln to prepare a report on the problems that would arise from a Japanese surrender in the near future. The report was dated July 25 and may have been used by Marshall in his discussions with the President on the same day.[6] Based on the latest estimates, the report provided Marshall, and presumably Truman, with an up-to-date summary of American planning.

The report began with a brief outline of the BLACKLIST operation, noting that there might be a "time lag of perhaps three weeks" before shipping could be assembled to move an appreciable number of divisions into Japan. In the meantime, however, enough assault shipping existed to carry a sufficient number of divisions into Japan to control the key strategic areas until additional forces arrived. No numbers were provided to indicate what constituted a sufficient total of divisions.[7] As for Korea, it was believed that MacArthur would be able to land a division "within a short time on the western side of Tsushima strait at Fusan [Pusan]."[8] Although MacArthur and Nimitz had been told that Japan might surrender before the Soviets came into the war, the military planners in S&P continued to predict that the Russians eventually would overrun Manchuria, and possibly north China. A Soviet thrust into Korea was also likely, making it "desirable for the U.S. to establish early control over any areas which our political policy considers should be held by the U.S."[9]

The planners also predicted that the Chinese would require assistance in taking the surrender of Japanese forces on the mainland and Formosa. If the Chinese encountered difficulties it would be necessary to open a coastal port through which Chiang's troops could be supplied. American air power would also be called into service to help the Chinese subdue the remaining Japanese. If the situation proved to be more than the Kuomintang could handle, the United States might have to make some small landings in north China to establish supply points for Chiang's army. Even though the paper made it clear that the Chinese, for reasons of prestige, were to have the primary responsibility for driving out the Japanese, Marshall informed his staff that "he did not like very much the idea that we might make any assault on the China coast."[10]

In the event of a Japanese surrender all of the anticipated operations were expected to tie up American shipping for some time. If all went well and the Japanese obeyed the emperor's order to surrender, all of the assault shipping would be needed for at least a month to move American troops into place. The redeployment of American troops to the Pacific would continue to draw on transpacific shipping for a period of three months.

In addition to the problems posed by the need to move large numbers of troops into the occupation zones, the planners anticipated that the scarcity of shipping would hinder the rapid repatriation of American forces from East Asia. To prevent any unnecessary delays in returning the troops home, the planners recommended that the United States continue to convert Victory ships into transports, and insist on the use of British and captured German ships.[11] Added to this was the possibility that American shipping would be needed to transport Chinese and Russian troops into Japan as part of the occupation force. Finally, American vessels would be required to repatriate the nearly three million Japanese living outside the main islands.[12]

As a general summary of American planning, Lincoln's report was a useful study. It touched on most of the major issues related to Japan's surrender, and where political guidance was lacking, as in the case of American objectives in Korea, it raised important questions. The report was, however, short on specifics. How many divisions would be needed for Korea? For China? When could they reach their destinations? The answers to these questions would have a strong bearing on the success of Truman's plans to counter Soviet power in Northeast Asia.

Following Marshall's meeting with Truman on the twenty-fifth, the chief of staff sent MacArthur a message requesting his views on matters relating to the surrender of Japan. "It appears likely," MacArthur was told, "that decisions may be reached in the near future on the occupation, control, and treatment of Japan after Japanese capitulation."[13] Marshall wanted to know MacArthur's views on the size of the occupation forces, the extent to which Japanese government offices would be used by the occupying forces, the organization of the Allied occupation force, and the priorities in which parts of Japan and Korea would be entered. "It would be helpful to have your views on the foregoing," Marshall added, "to assist in the discussions which are certain to arise shortly on the matter."[14] Although the message does not identify who was expected to participate in these discussions, subsequent events show that Marshall was requesting this information for use in upcoming meetings with the JCS.

The JCS met the next day, July 26, to discuss further the appropriate procedures in the event of a Japanese surrender. Although MacArthur's response to Marshall's queries had yet to reach Potsdam, the Chiefs did have a copy of Nimitz's proposed plan of action. Code-named CAMPUS, the Navy's plan called for the rapid movement of naval forces into strategic areas such as Tokyo Bay and, where possible, the occupation of key points ashore by Marines. The JCS tentatively accepted Nimitz's plan on the grounds that it promised the quickest means of introducing American forces into Japan. Following their meeting the Chiefs notified MacArthur and Nimitz of their decision.[15]

The JCS also informed the theater commanders that they favored operations on the CAMPUS model to occupy key areas on the mainland in the following order of priority: Shanghai, Pusan, Chefoo on the Shantung Peninsula, and Chinwangtao on the Manchurian border. The JCS believed that it would be "highly desirable" to occupy these Chinese ports so as to facilitate the reoccupation of north and central China by Chiang's troops. The Chiefs added, however, that they did not want American forces to become involved in a land campaign in China.[16]

At this point preparations snagged on the problem of interservice rivalry. Long a source of tension between MacArthur and Nimitz, the contest over headlines and service recognition intensified as Japan's surrender drew near. The prospect of seeing naval forces make the first triumphant entry into Tokyo Bay was more than MacArthur could tolerate. "It would be psychologically offensive to ground and air forces of the Pacific Theater," MacArthur argued, "to be relegated from their proper missions at the hour of victory."[17] He warned the Joint Chiefs that naval forces were by themselves insufficient for occupation operations as long as a large enemy army remained in being. MacArthur also disapproved of having Marines under Nimitz's control land on the China coast.[18]

For his part, Nimitz's representatives had refused to discuss surrender planning with MacArthur's staff during a conference at Guam. This unseemly bickering provoked a sharply worded response from Marshall. The chief of staff informed MacArthur that the Navy's plan was designed to meet an emergency situation. It was important that once Japan surrendered American forces arrive before the Japanese had time to reconsider their action. Marshall also questioned MacArthur's judgment on the use of Marines to occupy the China ports. "I do not understand the tenor of your comments," he told MacArthur. "You have not the Army troops available . . . therefore the Marine divisions appear to be the logical troops to be employed for China or Korea ports as they are available." A frustrated Marshall concluded the message on a rare note of sarcasm. "We are trying to end the war with Japan," he reminded MacArthur.[19]

By the time Marshall received MacArthur's criticisms, the meeting at Potsdam had ended and the JCS, Truman, and other important members of the American delegation were making their separate ways back home. Resolution of the MacArthur-Nimitz controversy had to be delayed until the key policymakers assembled once again in Washington.[20]

While MacArthur and Nimitz argued over the best means of occupying

Japan, the JCS received a third opinion on the proposed surrender operations from General Albert C. Wedemeyer, Commanding General United States Forces China Theater (CGUSFCT), and chief of staff to Chiang Kai-shek. After receiving instructions to prepare for a sudden end of the war, Wedemeyer had met with Chiang to discuss the reoccupation of Japanese-held territories in China. The outlook was not bright. "Frankly, if peace should come within the next few weeks," he told Marshall, "we will be woefully unprepared in China."[21]

During the first months of summer the military situation in China had begun to improve. The Japanese were withdrawing from south China to consolidate their forces for defensive purposes in the north. Although the Chinese had been unable to turn this orderly retreat into a rout, Chiang's newly trained troops had begun to demonstrate both a desire to fight and an ability to do so successfully. As of late July operations to capture Port Bayard on the southern coast of China were under way and proceeding smoothly.[22]

As encouraging as these developments were, however, the Nationalists were still a long way off from being able to throw the Japanese out of China. In order to create an effective Chinese army, Wedemeyer had embarked on an ambitious training and educational program supported by an elaborate system of liaison teams and staff schools. Wedemeyer feared that if Japan suddenly surrendered, the whole program would be disrupted as Chinese officers and troops were reassigned for occupation duties.[23] The lack of any civil affairs training for Chinese troops also worried Wedemeyer. The nonmilitary problems the Nationalists would face in the event of a Japanese surrender were staggering. Wedemeyer reported that the Chinese had "no plan for rehabilitation, prevention of epidemics, restoration of utilities, establishment of a balanced economy, and redistribution of millions of refugees." Widespread "confusion and disorder" could be expected.[24]

The situation in China was further complicated by the continuing conflict between the Nationalists and the CCP. On his last visit to Washington in March 1945, Wedemeyer had told the JCS that, with a small amount of support from the United States, the KMT would be able to subdue the Communists, should actual fighting break out.[25] These calculations were apparently based on the assumption that the KMT would gradually retake most of China from the Japanese. Five months later, with the end of the war in sight and Nationalist troops trapped in southwestern China, the CCP loomed as a more serious obstacle to a reassertion of KMT authority in the north. Wedemeyer feared that if Japan suddenly surrendered, the Communists would greatly expand the area under their control. Although he believed that Nationalist forces would eventually drive out the Communists, the ensuing chaos would seriously hinder efforts to disarm and repatriate the estimated two million Japanese forces in China. If Chiang's troops could not disarm the Japanese, Wedemeyer warned, the situation might "require intervention in China by outside powers."[26]

To prevent CCP efforts to expand their control over north China, Wedemeyer recommended that upon their capitulation, all Japanese troops be ordered to surrender to Chiang's representatives. In effect, Japanese troops would be used to prevent CCP control from spreading into areas beyond the reach of Nationalist forces.[27] Wedemeyer and Chiang were also counting on American assistance to keep the situation in China under control. In making his plans known to the JCS, Wedemeyer reversed the occupation priorities established by the Chiefs. Writing from his position in Chungking, Wedemeyer assigned first priority to key areas in China, as opposed to Japan. These included, in order of importance, Shanghai, Peking-Tientsin, Canton, and Hong Kong. Hainan, Formosa, and the Pescadores were second in importance. Manchuria, Korea (which Chiang wanted to enter to forestall a Soviet occupation), and Indochina were third. Inasmuch as civil disturbances in Japan were unlikely owing to the existence of recognized government, Wedemeyer believed that the home islands did not need to be occupied immediately.[28] Although Wedemeyer asked for "limited" assistance, his plan actually called for the use of eight American divisions in China.[29]

Like their American and Chinese allies, the British also found themselves poorly positioned should Japan suddenly surrender. While at Potsdam, the Combined Chiefs of Staff (CCS) reached several important decisions regarding the future of British participation in the war against Japan. As part of the final Anglo-American agreement, the CCS placed all of Thailand and Indochina below the sixteenth parallel in the SEAC. The Chinese were to retain operational responsibility for the northern portion of Indochina so Wedemeyer could have better control over his right flank during his forthcoming offensive. Mountbatten consented to this division in principle, but he added that the "French might find the proposition a little less agreeable."[30] The final agreement included an important provision stating that all or part of Indochina might come under British control at a later date.[31]

During the conference the CCS also agreed to expand the boundary of

Mountbatten's command in the southwest Pacific to include Borneo, Java, and the Celebes. This placed an additional one-half million square miles under his authority.[32] Although the British were being given a free hand in Southeast Asia, their efforts to assume a greater role in the operations against Japan's main islands were rebuffed by the JCS.[33]

Generally speaking, these decisions were aimed at facilitating American and British access to those areas that each country thought vital to its own interests. The problem for the British was that their area of interest took in over a million and a half square miles, much of which was occupied by undefeated Japanese armies. Although the British were making inroads into Burma, 60,000 Japanese soldiers were still in the field. In addition, there were 55,000 Japanese troops in Thailand, 110,000 in Indochina, 116,000 in Malaya, and nearly 500,000 in the Netherlands East Indies.[34] It was with this situation in mind that Mountbatten later observed that the decision to enlarge the area under his command "was not as flattering as it may sound."[35]

The British originally hoped to reconquer Southeast Asia in stages, thereby ensuring an orderly transfer of power from the Japanese to British representatives. Mountbatten's scheduled operations included an assault on the Port Sweetenham–Dickson area in the early fall, followed by an attack on Singapore in December, and a campaign to recapture Hong Kong a few months after that.[36] The success of the test at Alamogordo upset these calculations and presented the British commander with a new dilemma. After telling Mountbatten about the atomic bomb, Churchill instructed the admiral to warn his staff to begin planning for a Japanese surrender, but to say nothing about the bomb. The British commander protested that his officers would think he was losing his senses if he ordered them to prepare for a surrender without any explanation. As Mountbatten recalled, "Churchill insisted and so my SEAC staff had to rush forward all our plans for landing in Malaya and Singapore, and just take my word for it that there would be no opposition."[37]

While the Americans, British, and Chinese were planning to meet the problems that would accompany peace in East Asia, the Soviets were preparing for war. Throughout the spring and summer the Soviets transported supplies in vast quantities to the Far Eastern front. Japanese consular officials kept track of the Russian buildup, counting nearly two hundred supply trains in a three-day period on the trans-Siberian railway.[38]

The Soviet offensive was to be an elaborate and extensive series of operations drawing on one and a half million men, five and a half thousand tanks, and equally impressive numbers of artillery pieces and aircraft. To conduct the campaign the Kremlin created a special High Command for the Far East headed by former Chief of the General Staff Marshal Aleksandr Vasilevskii.[39] In his instructions to the general staff, Stalin emphasized the need for a swift and decisive campaign. A quick victory would serve his political objectives by bringing the maximum amount of territory under Soviet control before Japan surrendered. It was also deemed advisable to isolate quickly the Japanese forces and destroy them in detail before elements of the Kwantung army had time to regroup in southern Manchuria or north China.[40]

Although the Russians were prepared to enter the war even if they had not reached an agreement with the Nationalists, arrangements had been made for Soong to return to Moscow following the Potsdam conference. Before Soong's arrival, Harriman requested permission from Byrnes to inform Stalin that the United States believed his insistence on placing Dairen in the Soviet military zone exceeded the terms of the Yalta accords.[41] On August 5 the Secretary cabled his approval to Harriman. Byrnes instructed the ambassador to tell Stalin that the United States believed that Soong had already met the requirements of the Yalta agreements. In addition, Byrnes advised Harriman that the United States desired a written reaffirmation of Stalin's pledge to respect the Open Door. As a final suggestion, the Secretary informed Harriman that if Stalin did not accept Soong's offer to make Dairen a free port under Chinese control but with special commercial and transit rights for the Soviets, the United States and possibly Great Britain would be willing to participate in a four-power international commission to operate the port.[42]

Byrnes' instructions to Harriman represented a marked departure from the administration's earlier position concerning the Sino-Soviet negotiations. Before the Potsdam conference Truman had been unwilling to have the United States become directly involved in the talks. He was now proposing American participation in the operation of Dairen if Stalin did not accept the administration's interpretation of the agreements. Confident that the Soviets were no longer needed to end the war, Truman and Byrnes had become more assertive in their effort to protect the Open Door. It remained to be seen, however, if Stalin would permit the United States to determine the limits of Russian influence in Manchuria.

Following Japan's apparent rejection of the Potsdam Proclamation, it may have seemed to the public that the war in the Pacific had entered a momentary lull. Behind the scenes, of course, all of the Allies were feverishly preparing to protect their interests in the event of a Japanese surrender. But to the uninformed observer, little in the way of new developments was expected until the heads of state returned to their respective capitals. On August 6 this illusory calm was shattered by the explosion of the first atomic bomb over Hiroshima.

The extent of the damage was at first unknown to officials in Tokyo. Reports filtered in from the city during the day, but it was not until dawn on the seventh that the military received the news that "the whole city of Hiroshima was destroyed instantly by a single bomb."[43] By that time Japanese listening posts had picked up the American broadcasts describing the atomic nature of the attack. Some of the military regarded the broadcasts as propaganda, and an investigation team was dispatched to the scene. Others believed that the United States did not possess enough radioactive material to follow up on its threat to "obliterate every productive enterprise the Japanese have above ground in any city."[44] The Japanese government continued to look for some way out of the war other than unconditional surrender. On August 7 Foreign Minister Togo instructed his ambassador in Moscow to seek an immediate audience with Molotov to determine the Soviets' attitude toward acting as a mediator. The next day at 5:00 P.M. Ambassador Sato was led into Molotov's office where he was abruptly informed that the Soviet Union had declared war on Japan, effective on August 9. Two hours later, slightly after midnight in East Asia, Russian armored divisions smashed through the Japanese lines and began their conquest of Manchuria.[45]

American intelligence reports had predicted that it would take at least thirty days before the Soviets began to roll into Manchuria. Although the Americans knew that much of the crack Kwantung army had been withdrawn from Manchuria during the war, they were uncertain as to the number and quality of troops that remained.[46] Moreover, the suddenness of the Soviet offensive had caught the Japanese completely off guard. To begin with, Japanese intelligence officers did not believe that the Russians would be able to stage an attack before September. Thus the Soviet offensive caught the Japanese in the midst of a military reorganization. Although the Japanese expected the Soviets to launch an attack from Outer Mongolia, they were surprised by the size of the force that the Russians were able to assemble in that extremely inhospitable region. Finally, after years of fighting the Americans, the Japanese had come to expect a sustained artillery barrage before the opening of any campaign. Instead, the Soviet attack began at night, in a driving rainstorm, without a preparatory bombardment.[47] In less than thirty *hours* the Soviets had driven deeply behind Japanese lines.

The unequivocal success of the Soviet offensive provided a bleak backdrop for the continuation of the Stalin-Soong talks. The negotiations resumed on August 7 with Stalin refusing to moderate his demands concerning Dairen. In addition, Stalin now also asserted the right to remove some of the Japanese industries from Manchuria as "war trophies."[48] Inasmuch as the United States considered the industrial capacity of Manchuria as vital to China's postwar recovery, Stalin's demand seemed especially dangerous. Byrnes immediately instructed Harriman to advise the Russians of the American position on this important point.[49]

By this time, however, Harriman believed stronger measures were needed to bring the Soviets into line. On August 10 he wired Byrnes and Truman to recommend that the United States land troops on the Kwantung Peninsula and in Korea to accept the surrender of Japanese troops. "I cannot see that we are under any obligation to the Soviets," he concluded, "to respect any zone of Soviet military operation."[50]

By the time Harriman concluded that the United States would have to match Russian power on the mainland, the course of the Pacific war had finally reached the point where a Japanese surrender was all but assured. On August 9 a second atomic bomb was dropped, this time over Nagasaki. The news of the blast reached Tokyo while the Supreme Council for the Direction of the War was in session. Even after the fate of that city was known, those seeking an immediate acceptance of unconditional surrender, providing the imperial structure as preserved, were stymied by the military's insistence that the final terms permit the Japanese to disarm themselves and try their own war criminals.[51] In an attempt to break the deadlock, members of the peace faction took the unprecedented step of calling an Imperial Conference for the purpose of enlisting the emperor's direct intervention into the decision-making process. Late in the evening Hirohito used his special influence to end the debate. After questioning the military's ability to repel the invaders and lamenting the many sacrifices made by those who loyally served their emperor, Hirohito concluded that "the time has come when we must bear the unbearable."[52]

While the Japanese government moved tortuously toward the inevitable, American policymakers raced against the clock in order to be prepared when that moment finally arrived. Following the Potsdam conference, American military planners in Washington and in the Pacific had begun to work on the assumption that Japan might surrender in the next few weeks. Since they did not know about the atomic bomb, Japan's rejection of the Potsdam Proclamation had led many planners to conclude that Japan would not surrender before the main islands were invaded.[53]

Following the attack on Hiroshima, the planners tackled their work with new vigor. Whatever doubts may have remained were quickly wiped away by the Soviet declaration of war and the destruction of Nagasaki. Writing to his wife, Lt. Gen. Robert Eichelberger described the mood at MacArthur's headquarters. "You can imagine what is going around in our minds now," he wrote, "because most of us believe Japan is going to quit soon and this is the first time we have really believed it."[54] The following day Eichelberger noted that the dramatic turn of events had surprised MacArthur's planners, or, as he put it, they had been "caught partially with their panties down . . . but not entirely so."[55]

The same held true for the planning staff in Washington, although other factors beyond their control had hindered their work. On August 9 Colonel Bonesteel summarized the planning situation in a memo to General Lincoln. Under the heading of "Policy Directives to Theater Commanders" for the period after Japan's surrender, Bonesteel noted that none of these important orders had been approved. A draft directive for MacArthur had been produced but it was awaiting approval from SWNCC. Nothing, however, had been written for Admiral Nimitz. This seemed especially important to Bonesteel because it was still possible that the admiral would be given command of the forces used to land in Korea and perhaps China. Bonesteel added that a draft directive was being written for Wedemeyer. The China situation particularly troubled Bonesteel. "*China, to my mind, is an area of much greater fundamental concern to us than Japan. . . .* The interim action of 'keeping Wedemeyer talking' is, to my mind, unlikely to produce any positive results."[56]

Aside from the problem of getting usable orders into the hands of the theater commanders in the event of a surrender, the planners were experiencing difficulty in obtaining political guidance on a number of important issues related to the use of American military forces in Japan and on the mainland. Under the heading "Basic Policies Required in Connection with Surrender of Japan," Bonesteel explained that a list of twenty-five basic policy questions was being typed for presentation to SWNCC. Included on this list were questions concerning the objectives of United States forces in Korea, Manchuria, Formosa, and the Kuriles. The planners also needed to know what American policy would be toward the Chinese Communists. Bonesteel explained that the list, by itself, did nothing to expedite action by the State Department, the cause of the current bottleneck. As a possible course of action he recommended that Stimson discuss the list with Byrnes and "ask him [Byrnes] to turn the heat on the State Department."[57]

Under the best of circumstances the mills of the State Department bureaucracy ground slowly, but in the summer of 1945 their movement seemed especially labored. While Byrnes was in Potsdam, the department's committees were left almost completely uninformed about the policy changes that were being made at the highest levels of government. Thus, while the Japanese were attempting to interpret the meaning of the Potsdam Proclamation, a similar scene was taking place within the State Department's Interdivisional Committee for the Far East.[58] Did the provision limiting Japanese sovereignty to the main islands, and such minor islands as the Allies determined, mean that Japan would not keep southern Sakhalin, but that they would retain the Kuriles? No one knew for certain.

As for the use of American troops on the mainland, the department's planners had always expected the United States to participate in the occupation of Korea, and possibly China and Manchuria as well. Nevertheless, they were unprepared for these eventualities when the time arrived. Incredibly, Byrnes appears to have neglected to inform his subordinates that the war might suddenly come to an end and that American forces would be dispatched to the mainland as soon as possible. Thus, when the first bomb was dropped, the department's planners were still discussing the means of control that would be employed to administer Korea.[59]

The problems facing the military and political planners on the eve of Japan's surrender seemed overwhelming. These officials were being called on to compress into several days work that under normal circumstances would take weeks to complete. Even the most basic staff work had not been completed. "First and foremost," Bonesteel noted, "is the *fact* that there is *no* approved surrender document, surrender proclamation, or general orders [*sic*] No. 1 in existence."[60] The last-mentioned document,

General Order No. 1, was to be issued by the Japanese emperor to his troops telling them to whom they should surrender their arms. In short, this order would determine how the Allies divided Japan's empire during the initial period of occupation, a matter of supreme importance for the future of East Asia. After four years of war and with victory now in sight, the shape of postwar East Asia seemed less certain than ever.

5

Peace Breaks Out

Don't want to get any politics in this General Order. What we want is you military people to know when and where to act. (James Dunn to General Lincoln)[1]

Early on the morning of August 10 American radio monitors picked up a broadcast by the Japanese government announcing that Japan had decided to surrender. The message stated that Japan would accept the terms put forth in the Potsdam Proclamation with the understanding that they did not contain "any demand which prejudices the prerogatives of His Majesty as a sovereign ruler."[2] Later that evening when the broadcast became known to American troops on Okinawa the night sky was illuminated by the glow of .50-caliber tracers, rockets, and signal flares. A condition red alert was required to end the fireworks, but the celebration continued by other means throughout the night.[3] Writing from the Philippines, General Eichelberger told his wife that "Japan has accepted the terms of the Potsdam conference with minor exceptions . . . which I believe will be accepted."[4]

What Eichelberger described as a minor exception, that the surrender not prejudice the prerogatives of the emperor, was viewed as a major problem by Truman and Byrnes. Officials in Washington were surprised to learn that even after two atomic bombs had been dropped and the Soviet Union had entered the war, Japan was still unwilling to surrender without a guarantee that the imperial institution would be preserved. In deciding how to respond to Japan's offer, Truman had several alternatives to consider. He could reject the offer and continue the war, even to the point of dropping another atomic bomb if he thought it necessary. Moving to the opposite extreme, he could accept Japan's condition and thereby make the commitment he had declined to make at Potsdam. A third option, which fell somewhere between these two, would be to answer Japan's offer with a counteroffer.

Early on the morning of the tenth, Truman called together the heads of the State, War, and Navy departments. Also present were Admiral Leahy and John Snyder, a banker and close friend whom Truman had called to Washington soon after taking office. In this group only Byrnes argued against accepting Japan's offer. To do so, he warned, would lead to the political "crucifixion" of the President. Byrnes said that the American public and the Congress would not understand why the United States was accepting something less than unconditional surrender now that it had the atomic bomb and the Russians were in the war. At this point Forrestal suggested a compromise. The United States should make a positive reply to Japan but couch it in language that would be consistent with the administration's definition of unconditional surrender. Truman approved this solution, and Byrnes returned to the State Department to draft an answer.[5]

Not long after the Secretary arrived at his office he was joined by several of the department's Japan experts, including Grew and Joseph Ballantine, the head of FE, and by Ben Cohen, Byrnes' longtime adviser and currently the department's counselor. The Japan hands were afraid that Byrnes would accept the Japanese offer without realizing that if the Allies recognized the emperor's prerogatives, which were all-embracing, they would undermine the authority of the occupation before it began. Byrnes accepted their advice and incorporated a phrase prepared by Cohen into his reply. The crucial sentence stipulated that "the authority of the Emperor and the Japanese Government to rule the state shall be subject to the Supreme Commander of the Allied Powers."[6]

Byrnes presented this draft to the full cabinet in the early afternoon. According to Commerce Secretary Henry Wallace, "Byrnes stopped while reading the proposal and laid special emphasis on the top dog commander over Hirohito being an American."[7] Byrnes then said that the British had already agreed to the American draft. Suddenly Truman "interjected most fiercely" that the Russian answer probably would not be forthcoming, but that the United States would go ahead without them. Stimson added that the Soviets would want to delay the surrender while they pushed farther into Manchuria. To which Truman replied that it was in American interests that they not push too far.[8]

The Soviets approved the American draft later that day. Stalin no doubt was aware that Truman would go ahead without Russian concurrence. The Allied reply was released on the morning of the eleventh and reached Japan shortly after midnight on the twelfth.[9] Having made their reply, administration officials now had to prepare for the possibility that Japan would surrender in the next twenty-four hours.

On the night of August 10–11 the members of SWNCC and the Joint Staff Planners met in separate rooms in the Pentagon to prepare the official surrender documents. The job of writing the first draft of the General Order No. 1 went to Colonels Bonesteel and Rusk. Before they began they were informed that the Secretary of State wanted the United States to accept the surrender of Japanese troops in Korea as far north as possible.[10] Having only the wall map in General Lincoln's office for reference, Bonesteel and Rusk decided on the thirty-eighth parallel as the dividing line between the American and Soviet zones. That line would place Keijo (Seoul), the capital and communications center of Korea, in the American sector. It also gave the United States access to two ports, at Inchon and Fusan (Pusan). Bonesteel then set to work dictating the first sections of the order. In less than thirty minutes a draft was ready to be submitted to the Joint Staff Planners.[11]

When Bonesteel's handiwork reached the JSP the Navy's representative, Admiral Mathias B. Gardner, advocated moving the surrender line north to the thirty-ninth parallel. This would put Dairen in the American zone, an idea that Secretary Forrestal was known to favor. Lincoln objected, arguing that the Soviets would never accept a surrender line that kept them out of the Liaotung Peninsula. If the line were raised to include Dairen the Soviets might not feel bound by any of the order's provisions. Lincoln then telephoned Assistant Secretary of State Dunn, who was chairing the SWNCC meeting in another room. Dunn told the general that Byrnes believed that Korea was more important than Dairen. The thirty-eighth parallel remained in the draft.[12]

As of the morning of August 11, the all-important first paragraphs of the General Order read as follows:

a. The senior Japanese commanders of all ground, sea, air and auxiliary forces within China (excluding Manchuria), Formosa and French Indo-China north of 16° north latitude shall surrender to Generalissimo Chiang Kai-shek.
b. The senior Japanese commanders and all . . . forces within Manchuria, Korea north of 38° north latitude and Karafuto shall surrender to the Commander in Chief of Soviet forces in the Far East.

    c. The senior Japanese commanders and all . . . forces within the Andamans, Nicobars, Burma, Thailand, French Indo-China south of 16° north latitude, Malaya, Borneo, Netherlands Indies, New Guinea, Bismarcks, and the Solomons shall surrender to the Supreme Allied Commander Southeast Asia.

    d. The senior Japanese commanders and all . . . forces within the Japanese Mandated Islands, Ryukyus, Bonins, and other Pacific Islands shall surrender to the Commander in Chief Pacific Fleet.

    e. The Imperial General Headquarters, its senior commanders, and all . . . forces in the main islands of Japan, minor islands adjacent thereto, Korea south of 38° north latitude and the Philippines shall surrender to the Commander in Chief, U.S. Army forces in the Pacific.[13]

This was only the first draft of the General Order. Before being sent to the President it would have to be approved by SWNCC, the JCS, and the Secretaries of the State, War, and Navy departments. Normally, a paper that required this amount of politico-military consultation would take weeks to complete. Owing to the time limitations involved, however, a systematic exchange of memoranda on the subject was impractical, if not impossible. Telephone calls, hallway conversations, and hastily arranged meetings had to suffice as substitutes for what was usually a more formalized policy-making process. In this unstructured setting, with snap judgments taking the place of careful staff work, it was possible for individuals to exercise greater influence over policy decisions than they did under the normal committee system.

    Almost as soon as this review process began, it became evident that an important difference of opinion existed between the civilian and military representatives as to the nature of the General Order and the related surrender operations. Reflecting their previous concern over Soviet encroachment in Northeast Asia, Byrnes, McCloy, Forrestal, and Harriman emphasized the political importance of having the United States take the surrender of Japanese troops as far north on the mainland as possible. Although the staff officers were aware of the political implications of the General Order, they believed that the surrender lines had to reflect the present military realities or else run the risk of having one or more of the Allies reject the entire document. As General Lincoln later explained: "I knew the draft had to go to [British Prime Minister Clement] Attlee, Chiang, and Stalin for acceptance. . . . Every day's delay added increased hazards of a very grave nature. We recognized time was pressing and that a sound solution needed to be found which would also gain the acceptance of everyone. If not accepted, we might approach near chaos in East Asia."[14]

It was this emphasis on viewing the surrender as a continuation of the existing military operations that made it possible for Bonesteel to quickly draft the initial paragraphs of the General Order even though there had been no discussion of occupation responsibilities at Potsdam. With the exception of Korea, on which he received specific instructions from the State Department, Bonesteel constructed the surrender line based on what he knew to be the current operational boundaries. Although this may have been a sound procedure from the military point of view, it was fraught with political complications.

In establishing the surrender boundaries between the China theater and SEAC, Bonesteel placed two areas of interest to the British, Hong Kong and northern Indochina, in Chiang's zone. Although Mountbatten had his hands full in trying to reoccupy all the territory within his newly expanded theater, it was difficult to imagine that the British government would allow the Chinese to liberate Hong Kong. Given China's historic interest in Indochina, a fact that was known to American officials, and considering that the State Department and the Joint Chiefs both favored a restoration of French rule, the decision to divide Indochina was dubious at best. Problems also seemed destined to arise within China itself where the General Order implicitly ruled out the Communists from taking any surrenders.

Looking farther north there was, of course, the potential for disagreement with the Soviets. Having received instructions to include a portion of Korea in the American zone, Lincoln and his fellow officers settled on the thirty-eighth parallel after weighing a number of factors pro and con. As mentioned, this line would give the United States control of two important ports and the capital of Korea. Lincoln considered but rejected the idea of drawing a line through the peninsula that would correspond to Korea's provincial boundaries. Although such a line would have made the subsequent administration of the American zone somewhat simpler, Lincoln feared that "this arrangement, technically 100% military, might be taken by the USSR as implying US views as to a territorial arrangement."[15] Most important, Lincoln wanted to draw a line the Soviets would accept and actually honor. Thus he opposed raising the line to the thirty-ninth parallel.

Although Lincoln sought to make the General Order as clear as possible regarding the division of responsibilities between the United States and the Soviets, Bonesteel's draft did not stipulate who would take the surrender for the Kuriles, an area of major importance to the Russians. Lincoln later recalled that in an effort to get "clarity and concision in a hurry, we overlooked the Kuriles matter [i.e., that they were to be handed over to the Russians] and gave them initially, for surrender purposes to Nimitz under some such wording as 'other islands of the Pacific.' "[16]

The existing evidence suggests, however, that the omission of the Kuriles from the General Order was actually quite deliberate. Less than three weeks earlier Bonesteel had expressed a strong opinion regarding the relation of the islands to American security. "We should go *very* slow in giving freely to Russia all the *Kuriles*. . . . We are going to great lengths to hold all the Jap Pacific islands—which are on the route to Asia which is twice as long as the Aleutian-[Kuriles] route. Unless we kid ourselves we [k]now damn well the only Asiatic enemy we are guarding against is Russia."[17] Moreover, on August 10 the JWPC recommended that the United States occupy either Matsuwa or Paramushiro in the Kuriles "in order to assist any negotiation for post-war airfield rights therein."[18] In deciding whether or not to include the Kuriles in the General Order, Bonesteel was no doubt aware that at Potsdam the Russians and the JCS had agreed to an operational boundary that cut across the island chain and placed the area south of the Onekotan Straits (below Paramushir) in the American zone.[19] The colonel may have decided that if he omitted the Kuriles from the General Order it might be possible for Nimitz, in the course of his normal operations, to occupy at least some of the islands before the Russians could protest.

Despite the disagreements that seemed certain to arise over Hong Kong, Indochina, north China, and the Kuriles, it appears that the only provisions in Bonesteel's draft that provoked any discussion among the JSP were those that dealt with Korea and Manchuria. After approving the draft General Order sometime before daybreak on August 11 the JSP submitted it to Stimson who in turn passed it on to Byrnes. A copy was also sent to Admiral Leahy along with a copy of the directive that the Joint Chiefs planned to issue to MacArthur.[20]

In their directive the JCS made the occupation of Japan the supreme operation. The early occupation of Keijo (Seoul) was a second charge on MacArthur's resources. Despite Wedemeyer's recommendations, landings on the China coast were given third priority, subject to the progress of the first two operations.[21] In referring to the China coast, the JCS meant China proper. No mention was made of Dairen or any other Manchurian port. Sometime that morning, however, Truman instructed the JCS to begin preparations for the occupation of Dairen and a port in Korea immediately after Japan surrendered. These instructions went out to MacArthur in the form of a supplement to the original directive.[22]

Whether Truman acted on Harriman's recommendations of the previous day, Forrestal's promptings, his own inclination, or some combination of the three is not clear. What is clear is that the Dairen operation now had the full support of the President. Truman had not only given new life to the idea of landing troops in Dairen ahead of the Russians, but he had done it without revising the General Order.[23] If MacArthur succeeded in carrying out his directive, American troops would arrive at Dairen completely unannounced. The implications of Truman's directive were immediately grasped by Vice-Admiral Charles M. Cooke, the head of the Navy's War Plans Division, and General Hull, the head of OPD. Both men concluded that the decision to leave the General Order unchanged, despite the new directive to MacArthur, had been intentional.[24]

That same day the JCS received additional information, this time from the British, that seemed to indicate a need to rewrite part of the General Order. The impending surrender of Japan was creating considerable consternation at Lord Mountbatten's headquarters. It now appeared that the major British assault on Malaya-Singapore could not be mounted before Japan surrendered. Whitehall attached great political significance to this operation, believing that a peaceful restoration of British control depended on Britain's ability to impress its subjects with the inevitability of a return to imperial rule in the region.[25] If Japan suddenly surrendered, it might take weeks or even months until British troops reoccupied the entire region. Emergency measures were called for. On August 11 the British Chiefs requested JCS permission to release royal naval units from the Pacific Fleet as soon as Japan surrendered. The British informed their colleagues that these units were needed for the immediate reoccupation of Hong Kong.[26]

In view of these new developments concerning Dairen and Hong Kong, the Army's staff officers requested additional information from the State Department. As the War Department's representative on SWNCC, John McCloy assumed responsibility for these and other problems related to the General Order. Following the marathon meeting of SWNCC the previous evening, McCloy spent most of August 11 reviewing the surrender papers and seeking answers to questions that had arisen since the

General Order had been sent to the White House. Late in the afternoon, at 5:45 P.M., Byrnes called McCloy to discuss the surrender.[27]

Regarding Hong Kong, Byrnes said that the British should be urged to take the matter up with the Chinese. The United States should not be asked to participate "either in approval or in the operations without Chinese acquiescence." The conversation also touched indirectly on the problem of French Indochina. Byrnes reported that the French would not be allowed to participate in the surrender ceremonies in Tokyo, to sit at the "big table" as McCloy put it. Truman did hope, however, that arrangements would be made for French representatives to be present at the surrender of Japanese troops in Indochina.[28] Evidently there were no plans at this time to remove northern Indochina from the China theater.

Byrnes had also discussed the Dairen operation with the President. On this point McCloy wrote that "on TIENTSIN and the North China ports the President agreed with my suggestion that to make the occupation of Dairen and Port Arthur less pointed we ought also to land at one of these North China ports."[29] McCloy seems to have reasoned that if the United States occupied several ports along the coast of the Yellow Sea, it would create the appearance that the occupation of Dairen was part of a larger operation and that it was not directed specifically against the Russians. In the final analysis both the Dairen directive and the General Order remained unchanged, and at least one more port was about to be added to MacArthur's list of objectives. This was not the sort of news the Army planners were hoping to hear.

During this same conversation Byrnes told McCloy that the "Kuriles ought to be surrendered to the Russians." This was in response to a previous suggestion from McCloy. McCloy recorded that "I spoke again about the air rights there and he [Byrnes] said that we had agreed to give the Kuriles to the Russians and we couldn't go back on it."[30] McCloy reminded Byrnes that earlier in the year Harriman had been instructed to approach the Russians on this subject. The conversation ended, however, with both men agreeing to check the relevant correspondence before reaching any conclusions.[31]

The following day, August 12, SWNCC met again to discuss the General Order. According to the official minutes, Admiral Gardner recommended "that further study be given to the areas for the purpose of surrender to the various allied commanders." The minutes show that "the Kuriles, Ryukyus, the Admiralties and Korea among others were specifically discussed in this connection."[32] Although there is no record of what was said regarding Korea, the content of the discussion concerning the Kuriles can be deduced from other evidence. After the meeting adjourned, Dunn and McCloy met with Byrnes. That evening Dunn reported that Byrnes had agreed to have the United States take the Japanese surrender in the Kuriles below the operational boundary, that is, south of Paramushiro. McCloy subsequently instructed Admiral Gardner to send the necessary orders to Nimitz and to also determine which island the United States wanted for an air base.[33]

Although the Kuriles and Dairen had been added to the list of American occupation objectives, neither of these areas had been explicitly mentioned in the draft of the General Order. Given the JCS's concern that the surrender take place as orderly as possible, and considering the Chiefs' reluctance to confront the Russians in Northeast Asia, these recent developments were not at all to their liking. On August 13 the JWPC recommended that, given the directive to occupy Dairen, the United States should reach immediate agreement on the surrender zones in Northeast Asia. To this end the JWPC proposed that the United States place all of Manchuria and Korea south of the fortieth parallel in the American zone.[34]

The Joint Staff Planners, it will be recalled, had rejected a similar proposal during the all-night session of August 10–11. At that time Lincoln had opposed raising the line to include Dairen for fear that the Soviets might reject the entire General Order. Now, however, the situation had become more complicated. Truman and his civilian advisers, particularly Harriman, Forrestal, Byrnes, and McCloy, all favored having American troops land on the Kwantung Peninsula. All appeared to agree, however, that the Soviets should not receive any advance notice for fear that the Russians would either reject the American proposal, or move to occupy the region before the American forces could arrive.

The JSP were faced with a dilemma. If they recommended placing Dairen in the American zone and the Soviets rejected the entire General Order, chaos would ensure. If on the other hand they left the General Order unchanged and American troops succeeded in occupying Dairen, there was no predicting what the Soviet response would be. Under these circumstances a third alternative seemed in order.

Rather than raise the surrender line, the JSP recommended that the Joint Chiefs approve the General Order as written. The JSP handled the

Dairen problem by drafting a special memorandum which the Joint Chiefs would present to the President if it appeared that American troops were about to land in Manchuria. This memorandum contained the draft of a message from Truman to Stalin, to be delivered to the latter at the President's discretion. This message would explain to Stalin that American operations in the Yellow Sea were being carried out to prevent the sabotage of port facilities and to discourage a continuation of hostilities. Stalin would be informed that these operations were for "military purposes only" and would not "prejudice the final peace settlement."[35] The JSP also recommended notifying the Soviets of the contemplated operations in the Kuriles at the "appropriate time," so as to avoid any confusion following Japan's surrender.[36]

The following day, August 14, the JCS approved the General Order and the special memoranda prepared by the Joint Staff Planners. That afternoon SWNCC also approved the General Order. Later that day, however, McCloy recommended inserting a new paragraph into the General Order just below the sections dealing with the surrender zones. This new provision notified the Japanese that the Allied commanders listed in the preceding paragraphs were "the only representatives empowered to accept the surrender, and all surrenders of Japanese forces shall be made only to them or their designated representatives."[37] This new provision effectively ruled out Chinese Communist participation in the surrender by implicitly ordering the Japanese to resist the CCP's efforts to disarm them.[38]

In all likelihood this new section was added to the order in response to General Wedemeyer's requests. Since receiving his first postwar directive on August 10, Wedemeyer had been in frequent contact with Washington. At that time he had been instructed to assist Chiang with the reoccupation of Japanese-held areas in China but admonished to avoid participation in a "fratricidal war." Wedemeyer was also told that at some future date American troops might land on the China coast to aid in the movement of KMT troops.[39] On reading these instructions Wedemeyer decided that the Joint Chiefs did not understand the situation he was facing in China. It would take weeks for KMT forces to reach northern China, by which time the Communists would have greatly expanded their control over the region. Nothing short of making China MacArthur's first priority following Japan's surrender would prevent an outbreak of civil war.[40]

On August 14, after soliciting MacArthur's advice, the JCS rejected

Wedemeyer's request. To soften the blow, General Marshall informed Wedemeyer that the JCS were preparing to recommend to the President that Lend Lease to China be continued in the immediate postwar period. Wedemeyer was clearly frustrated by his failure to convince the JCS of the explosiveness of the situation in China. He tried once more to make his point. "I view Asia as an enormous pot," he wrote, "seething and boiling the fumes of which may readily snuff out the advancement gained by the Allies the past several years."[41] To save the situation Wedemeyer suggested that the General Order clearly stipulate that Japanese forces must surrender only to KMT or Soviet representatives. This provision was inserted by McCloy, and the completed General Order was submitted to Truman on the fifteenth. It was not a moment too soon.

At 7:00 P.M. on August 14 Truman called reporters into his office to announce that Japan had surrendered unconditionally. It now became necessary to issue the General Order to the Allies as quickly as possible and to begin arranging for the armistice. It was also necessary for the JCS to take care of some unfinished business so that the American theater commanders had a clear idea of their responsibilities in the coming weeks.

The members of the Joint Staffs appear to have been particularly concerned by the way in which MacArthur's responsibilities were being expanded to include new objectives on the mainland. First there had been Korea, and then Dairen, and most recently a port in north China had been added to the list. This last directive was received on August 14 and it quickly became the source of considerable confusion among the planners. The idea of landing in north China was, of course, first broached by McCloy in his conversation with Byrnes. The Joint Chiefs, however, appear to have been unaware of the origin of this directive. On the fourteenth they received a message from Admiral Leahy in the White House informing them that "it is now considered wise from a political point of view to also occupy as soon as possible some other mainland ports that definitely are not in the area of Soviet operations."[42]

Following the receipt of this message Marshall spoke with Byrnes about the priorities on the mainland. Marshall came away from this discussion with the impression that Byrnes wanted American forces to occupy some other port on the Liaotung Peninsula in addition to Dairen. Puzzled by the apparent discrepancy between the message from the White House and Byrnes' statement, Marshall instructed General Lincoln to find out what Byrnes was talking about. On the morning of the fifteenth Lincoln telephoned James Dunn, with whom he had been working in drawing up the surrender papers, and asked about Byrnes' comments. Dunn's initial responses were not encouraging.

D: Is Tsingtao in the Liaotung Peninsula?
L: No, that's in the Shantung Peninsula.
D: Well, where is the Liaotung Peninsula?
[Later]
L: You see the predicament I'm in is—rises from the Chief of Staff understanding that Mr. Byrnes said, when he was talking about something additional beyond Dairen he meant something else in the Liaotung Peninsula.
D: No you can assure the Chief of Staff that isn't what he meant. I know that. At least I'm perfectly safe and I'll take responsibility for assuring him that what he meant was, if possible, a couple of places over on the China coast. I mean on the south—that's the China Sea there isn't it?
L: That's the Yellow Sea.
[Later]
D: Tell him [Marshall] that I did it with Mr. Byrnes on a map. So I know just exactly what he was pointing to.
L: I see. Well, that clears it up very much.[43]

Once Lincoln had cleared up this problem to his own satisfaction he and Admiral Gardner took another look at the problem of allocating forces for all of the objectives on the mainland. Even after they rejected Wedemeyer's calls for the immediate deployment of troops in China, the planners doubted that MacArthur would have enough resources to carry out these other assignments. "I feel that if we are going to do any business at Dairen we've got to give it a concurrent priority with Tokyo," Gardner said. "Otherwise we may not get there. We may not get there anyhow. It may be all washed out anyhow." Ignoring Gardner's comments about upgrading Dairen, Lincoln confided that he thought American troops did not have "much chance of getting there."[44]

This was also the view of Lincoln's and Gardner's immediate superiors, General Hull and Admiral Cooke. The latter two discussed the Dairen situation just before 11:00 the same morning. Referring to the Dairen directive, Cooke said, "I don't think we are going to make it." Hull agreed. "I don't think there is very much attempt [*sic*] we are going to make," Cooke added, "but we can arrange to get a ship in there with our people pretty soon."[45]

On August 15 the JCS issued a comprehensive directive to MacArthur. The message informed him that the priorities established in the previous directive of August 11 would not be changed. Japan remained a first charge on MacArthur's resources. Dairen and Keijo were second priorities. China was a distant third. The JCS did inform MacArthur, however, that they desired that "every effort be made to expedite the movement of U.S. forces into key ports on the China coast."[46]

As part of their final preparations for Japan's surrender the Joint Chiefs also needed to make the necessary arrangements with the British regarding Hong Kong. In keeping with the policy outlined by Byrnes in his conversation with McCloy, the Chiefs agreed to release the ships in question but urged the British to coordinate their operations with the Chinese. The JCS message also carried a disclaimer stating that "the release of British ships is viewed by the U.S. Chiefs of Staff as being unrelated to any proposals of the British Chiefs of Staff concerning Hong Kong."[47]

In essence the United States had decided to treat the problem of who would receive the surrender of Hong Kong as though it were none of the administration's concern. What Truman and Byrnes failed to realize, however, was that Chiang would cite the General Order as proof of American support for his position. Admiral Cooke recognized this point, but by the time he mentioned it to General Hull the General Order had already been released.[48]

On the afternoon of the fifteenth Truman sent the General Order to the Allies. Apart from the provision added by McCloy on the fourteenth, the principal paragraphs of the General Order remained unchanged from Bonesteel's draft. Despite a report from Ambassador Hurley in China that the French were predicting "grave consequences" if Chinese troops entered Indochina, the northern portion of the country remained in the area of Chinese responsibility.[49] Although the United States had been given advance notice that the British were planning to reoccupy Hong Kong, that territory was not removed from the Chinese occupation zone. Finally, although American troops had been directed to occupy Dairen, Korea, and the Kuriles, only Korea was mentioned in the General Order. Given these circumstances it is not surprising that American officials waited in suspense for the Allies' response to the General Order.

The Soviets replied to the General Order on the sixteenth. "I have no objection against the contents of the order," answered Stalin, "keeping in view that the Liaotung Peninsula is a composite part of Manchuria."[50] Stalin also wanted to make several "corrections" in the order. These included placing all the Kuriles and the northern half of Hokkaido (the northernmost of Japan's main islands) in the Soviet zone. In explaining the reasons for these changes Stalin reminded Truman that the Kuriles "have to come into the possession of the Soviet Union." Stalin also explained that the occupation of Hokkaido held special meaning for the Russian people because of Japan's earlier occupation of Siberia during the Russian Revolution. Implicit in Stalin's reply was Soviet acceptance of the surrender line in Korea.[51]

If the Truman administration accepted all of Stalin's "corrections" it would have to share postwar control of Japan with the Soviets and abandon the Kurile and Dairen operations. It is impossible to know whether or not Stalin expected the United States to agree to a Russian occupation of Hokkaido. The Americans had already refused Molotov's request to name a Soviet Supreme Commander to share power with MacArthur.[52] At this point Stalin may have been trying to learn exactly what role the Soviets would be allowed to play in Japan's occupation.[53]

The answer to that question would not have pleased him. American policymakers had already decided that there would not be a zonal occupation of Japan. Other United Nations forces would be employed in Japan's occupation, partly to reduce American troop commitments, but also to serve as a symbol of Allied unity. The preponderance of troops would be American, however, as would be the Supreme Commander.[54] Concerning Stalin's request, therefore, the only question for American policymakers was deciding how firmly their reply should be worded to convey the determination of the Truman administration on this point.

American officials were pleased, and not a little surprised, that Stalin accepted the thirty-eighth parallel in Korea. It is possible that, as Lincoln feared, Stalin may have interpreted this part of the General Order as a proposal for an old-fashioned spheres of influence arrangement on the peninsula. Unknown to Lincoln and Colonels Rusk and Bonesteel, the Japanese and Russians had discussed a similar division of Korea earlier in the century. Stalin may have also decided to exercise some restraint in the hope that the Soviets would be given a voice in the control of Japan.[55] One thing is certain, however: the Red Army could easily have occupied the entire peninsula before American troops arrived.

Stalin's request that the Kuriles be included in the Soviet zone created problems for the United States, as did his reminder that the Liaotung Peninsula was part of Manchuria and thus in the Soviet zone. The Soviets may well have anticipated American efforts to occupy these areas. At the very least they were unwilling to leave any room for doubt as to how the General Order would be interpreted on these important points.

Truman, Leahy, and Byrnes met to discuss their reply to Stalin on the morning of August 18. Later that afternoon Byrnes called the War Department to find out the estimated arrival time of Russian and American forces in Dairen.[56] In preparing a reply for Byrnes, Lincoln called Gardner for the Navy's estimate. Gardner thought the Russians would reach Dairen first. He explained that the Navy had no plans for sending ships into Dairen for the purpose of obstructing the Soviets or showing the flag. He added, however, that "of course we could throw naval forces into Dairen any time we wanted to, we got them and it's just a matter of steaming up there."[57] Gardner concluded that a naval operation would not be of much use as long as the Russians controlled the area around the port.

When one considers that Admiral Nimitz had been prepared to steam into Tokyo Bay to accept the Japanese surrender, Gardner's reluctance to send ships into Dairen, or to even mention the possibility to Byrnes, is revealing. Clearly the Joint Chiefs were not prepared to challenge the Russians in Northeast Asia. Later in the day, the eighteenth, the War Department informed Byrnes that Russian troops would reach Dairen by the nineteenth. Byrnes then canceled the mission.[58]

Truman's reply to Stalin went out later that day. Stalin's request to occupy Hokkaido was denied. Truman explained that MacArthur would take the surrender in the four main islands. The occupation would employ "token Allied forces." The message did not mention the Liaotung Peninsula. Truman did agree to change the operational boundaries in the Kuriles and to place all the islands in the Soviet zone. He informed Stalin, however, that the United States desired "air base rights for land and sea aircraft on some one of the Kurile Islands, preferably in the central group, for military purposes and commercial use."[59] The details were to be worked out by specially appointed representatives of the two governments.

The American request for air base rights was open to a number of interpretations. It could easily be construed as a request for a permanent air base under American control, although this does not appear to have been its intent. Admiral Cooke regarded the American request as sweeping, the Russians considered it an insult. Stalin did not reply to Truman's message until August 22. He expressed disappointment at being excluded from the occupation of Hokkaido, but said no more on the subject. Stalin was openly hostile, however, to Truman's request for air base rights in the Kuriles. Stalin interpreted this as a demand for a permanent American aviation base on what was to become Soviet territory. A claim of this kind was usually made against a conquered state or a weak ally. Stalin could not believe that Truman thought the Soviet Union was either.[60]

The Soviets' response to Truman's message came as no surprise to the staff officers in the Pentagon. Neither Leahy, who wrote the first draft, nor Byrnes, who added the controversial request for landing rights, had thought to consult the JCS before replying to Stalin.[61] When they saw how the message was worded, General Hull and Admiral Cooke predicted that the Soviets would reject it. Cooke thought that Truman should have agreed to Stalin's request to put the Kuriles in the Soviet zone with the stipulation that the islands below Etorofu would be considered adjacent islands which the Japanese would keep. The Soviets would receive the islands north of Etorofu, which Cooke thought they were entitled to, and Etorofu itself would become an international trusteeship with landing rights provided for the United States.[62]

After receiving Stalin's reply on August 22, Dunn called the War and Navy Departments for their opinions. He let it be known, however, that "the feeling in the higher levels of the State Department was that this matter should be dropped unless there was good reason why the military should secure such rights for the period of occupation."[63] By this time Hull and Cooke believed the matter was not worth persuing. "The State Department muffed this whole thing," complained Hull. "As a matter of fact," he added, "I don't personally think that it's too important." "I don't either," agreed Cooke, "and I don't believe in throwing something more to them and having them say no."[64]

Byrnes took responsibility for drafting the reply to Stalin's second message. Choosing to ignore Stalin's disappointment about Hokkaido, Byrnes explained that the United States was seeking emergency landing rights to facilitate the flow of air traffic into Japan during the occupation. He let the matter drop by offering to defer discussion of the question until a later date.[65]

The Russians were not the only ones to take exception to the General Order. As might be expected, the leadership of the Chinese Communists did not welcome the news that they were being denied a role in the surrender. The Communists were prepared for this eventuality, however, and under orders from General Chu Teh, CCP forces moved forward to disarm the Japanese. Chiang ordered them to stay at their posts but without result. By August 24 the Communist *New China Daily* reported that CCP troops were closing in on Peking. Communist troops were also reported to be fighting Japanese in the streets of Tientsin while other units had surrounded Tsingtao.[66]

The United States also encountered difficulties in arranging for the surrender of Hong Kong. When they first learned that the State Department had approved British plans to reoccupy Hong Kong, General Hull and Admiral Cooke predicted problems unless the General Order was modified to place Hong Kong in the British zone.[67] On August 16 the British notified the Chinese government that His Majesty's forces were preparing to occupy the colony. The British also explained that Japan's surrender made further negotiations over the operational boundaries in Indochina unnecessary. Instead it was suggested that British and Chinese assistance should be rendered for the purpose of restoring French control over the country.[68]

In passing a copy of this note to Washington, the Chinese government explained that it could not comply with British wishes. The Chinese justified their refusal by citing the clause in the General Order directing Japanese troops in the China theater to surrender to Chiang's representatives. Since the area of British responsibility outlined in the order did not include Hong Kong, it was assumed that the colony was still in the China theater. The Chinese government also pointed out that the General Order made no provision for restoring French control to Indochina.[69]

On August 18, while the Americans were still drafting a reply to Chiang, British Prime Minister Clement Attlee sent Truman a message requesting that the Japanese in Hong Kong be ordered to surrender to British troops.[70] That day the State Department's Office of Far Eastern Affairs drafted a reply to Attlee and sent an information copy to the War Department. The administration still hoped to avoid having to take sides in the dispute. Attlee was informed that the United States did not object to having British commanders take the surrender of Hong Kong, providing that full military coordination was effected between British and Chinese forces in the area. At the bottom of the message was a note intended for the War Department but which was mistakenly sent to London as well. It explained that Byrnes had met with T. V. Soong to inform him that the American decision "did not in any way represent U.S. views regarding the future of Hong Kong."[71]

Byrnes probably thought that his meeting with Soong settled the matter once and for all. Later on the eighteenth, however, Soong informed Byrnes that he still thought that Hong Kong should be surrendered to the Chinese. Soong further complicated matters by not reporting the American position, as described by Byrnes, to Chungking. The first Chiang heard of the American decision was on August 21 when the British sent Chungking a copy of Truman's reply to Attlee.[72] At this point the administration avoided any further confusion by directly notifying Chiang that the United States wanted the British to occupy Hong Kong.[73] After several days of negotiation the British and Chinese reached an agreement that allowed Chiang to save face while the British saved Hong Kong.[74]

By the end of August the final adjustments had been made in the assignment of Allied responsibilities for taking the surrender of Japanese forces. The General Order was issued on September 2, the day representatives of the Japanese government signed the official surrender documents aboard the USS *Missouri* in Tokyo Bay. In retrospect it seems clear that the process of drafting and gaining Allied approval of the General Order exposed many of the latent weaknesses in the Truman administration's postwar plans for East Asia. It can be argued that in effect there were two General Orders. The first reflected the administration's goals for the region. The second was determined by the military realities that existed at the time of Japan's surrender.

On August 15, the day Truman sent the General Order to the Allies, the administration's ambitions reached a high-water mark in Northeast Asia. At this point the United States was prepared to occupy a forward line that began in the Onekotan Straits in the Kuriles, ran down through the Soya Strait (between Hokkaido and Sakhalin), came ashore on the Korean peninsula at the thirty-eighth parallel, touched the Liaotung Peninsula at Dairen, and came ashore again on the Shantung Peninsula. Developed piecemeal on the recommendations of influential advisers such as Harriman, Forrestal, Byrnes, and McCloy, this belated attempt to block, or at least control, the flow of Soviet power into Northeast Asia was entirely consistent with the Truman administration's assessment of American interests in the region.

But while Truman and his advisers were attempting to stem the Soviet advance in Northeast Asia, the Joint Chiefs were concentrating on the problem of ending the war with Japan. As early as July the JCS's preparations for the sudden collapse of Japanese resistance had placed supreme importance on the rapid occupation of Japan's main islands. In deciding to forgo negotiations with the Russians at Potsdam and in choosing to deploy American troops on the mainland, Truman placed an unexpected burden on American forces in the Pacific. The Joint Chiefs were clearly dismayed by the disparity between MacArthur's resources and the re- quirements of his ever-expanding mission. Following Japan's surrender the JCS criticized their British colleagues for instructing Mountbatten to "show the flag" in Chinese ports at a time when troops and ships were needed for the "main effort" in Japan and Korea.[75] Having recently been denied any meaningful role in the preparations for Japan's invasion, the British must have found this rebuke especially galling. In reply to this request for assistance, the British chiefs surprised their "cousins" by explaining that since nothing about Korea had been settled, they had not made plans to send troops to the peninsula.[76] In postponing discussions on Korea, Truman had failed to secure a British commitment to the trusteeship plan. Now, American forces would have to assume full re- sponsibility for Korea below the thirty-eighth parallel.

The British were no doubt also perturbed by the provisions in the General Order that dealt with Hong Kong and Indochina. Here again the administration's handling of these two areas was consistent with the post- war policies that had been adopted during the summer of 1945. In treating the surrender of Japanese forces in Hong Kong and Indochina as a purely military matter, American officials continued to hope that a European restoration could be achieved in Southeast Asia without the direct support of the United States.

The administration's miscalculations readily became apparent once the General Order was dispatched to the Allies. Stalin, not Truman, deter- mined the scope of American influence in Northeast Asia. Even in the Kuriles, the one area where it was within the power of the United States to prevent a Soviet occupation, the United States acquiesced in Stalin's demands, rather than provide him with a justification for rejecting the surrender line in Korea. Chiang's response to the General Order also undermined Truman's plans by exposing the superficiality of the admin- istration's policy of noninterference in colonial affairs. In asserting his right under the General Order to reoccupy Hong Kong, Chiang made certain that the United States would not be able to hold the door open for the returning Europeans without bearing some of the stigma for supporting colonialism. It may have been to avoid any further association with colo- nialism and to placate Chiang after the Hong Kong incident that, despite

British and French protests, Truman agreed to leave northern Indochina in the China theater.[77] Finally, the administration's reliance on Japanese troops to temporarily hold north China offers perhaps the most revealing example of how American plans were upset by Japan's surrender.

The situation in East Asia at the end of August 1945 bore little resemblance to that which American policymakers hoped to see emerge from the war. Korea was divided and no trusteeship agreement had been made. China was on the verge of civil war, with only Japanese troops standing in the way of a Communist takeover in the north. The Soviet Union, firmly entrenched in Manchuria and north Korea, had it within its power to thwart American plans in China and Korea. Finally, despite American support for a French restoration in Indochina, the United States had acquiesced in the occupation of that country by an anticolonial power.

Nevertheless, the picture was not totally dark. Japan had been defeated and occupied, and American power in the Pacific was at its zenith. The situation on the mainland remained extremely volatile and somewhat out of focus. Did the events surrounding Japan's surrender reveal the inherent frailties of American postwar plans, or did the attendant chaos represent a momentary setback, an aberration of sorts? Should the United States continue to pursue its wartime policies, or should it reassess those policies in light of recent developments? Specifically, did Stalin's apparent restraint in Korea indicate that it was still possible to cooperate with the Soviet Union in a way that would protect American interests in the region? In the immediate postwar period these questions were at the center of a new debate over American East Asian policy.

6

The Residue of a Larger Plan

What, concretely, are we willing to do to help China become the stabilizing influence in the Far East? (Assistant Secretary of the Navy Artemus Gates)[1]

EVER SINCE TAKING office in April, Truman had been unable to keep pace with events. The defeat of Germany, the successful test of an atomic bomb, and the sudden collapse of Japanese resistance made for an atmosphere of almost unrelieved crisis during the first months of his presidency. The end of the war brought with it little relief, however, for Truman was suddenly compelled to deal with a multitude of other important postwar issues.

Heading the list of presidential problems was the need to define a postwar policy on atomic weapons and nuclear power. Truman also made passage of a universal military training bill a high priority. On the domestic side, politically sensitive questions on pricing policy, rationing, labor relations, and housing and full employment legislation required special attention.[2] Under these circumstances Truman was relieved to be able to turn over much of the responsibility for foreign policy to his new Secretary of State. Byrnes' performance at Potsdam had pleased Truman, and the President remained confident that his first cabinet appointment had been a wise one.

But Byrnes, like Truman, had little time for East Asian problems. Instead, Byrnes was preoccupied with preparations for the coming London Foreign Ministers conference where he would be dealing with European issues. After his return from Potsdam, Byrnes spent less than four weeks in Washington before leaving for London. Ultimately, he would spend nearly half his tenure as Secretary of State attending conferences outside the United States.

While Truman and Byrnes were distracted by other problems, events in East Asia were taking on a dynamic of their own. The arrival of American troops in China and Korea and the entry of Chinese and British forces into Indochina failed to produce the stabilizing effect that their presence was intended to create. Indeed, their arrival seemed to add to the existing turmoil on the mainland. Confronted by a new set of problems in the aftermath of Japan's surrender and lacking strong leadership from either Truman or Byrnes, American officials entered into what was to become a vigorous and often bitter debate over the role of the United States in postwar East Asia.

In the brief period between the end of the war and the beginning of the London conference, James Byrnes tried to assemble his own team within the State Department. In general, Byrnes' tenure as Secretary was characterized by only a superficial interest in the operations of the department. His frequent trips abroad helped account for this lack of interest, but Byrnes was by nature a practitioner of personal diplomacy. In his long government experience he had always worked with a small staff. When he took office, the new Secretary of State allowed the committee system created by Stettinius to atrophy. Byrnes' penchant for personal diplomacy and his frequent trips abroad inspired observers to quip that "the State Department fiddles while Byrnes roams."[3]

Byrnes' interest in the selection of department officers did not extend beyond the assistant secretary level. After choosing two associates, Ben Cohen and Donald Russell, for the posts of department counselor and assistant secretary for administration respectively, Byrnes decided to name James Dunn as Under Secretary. Both Cohen and Russell argued that Dunn was too conservative to hold such an important post, especially since Dunn would become Acting Secretary in Byrnes' absence. Instead they recommended Dean Acheson for the job. Dunn, however, as he had done so often before, had endeared himself to his new boss. When Acheson offered to resign as Assistant Secretary of State, Byrnes accepted. Several days later Byrnes called Acheson to say it had all been a mistake. Byrnes explained that he had been so caught up in his work that he neglected to tell Acheson how much he wanted him to be the new Under Secretary. After some hesitation Acheson accepted.[4]

Byrnes' explanation notwithstanding, it appears likely that the Acheson appointment was pushed on him by the President. Apparently Truman's friend and former senatorial colleague Fred Vinson recommended Acheson for the job. Vinson, it seems, had been greatly impressed by Acheson's abilities as the State Department's congressional liaison. Vinson met frequently with Truman, and he may have used one of those sessions to speak on Acheson's behalf. Acheson believed this to be the case. "I always thought Fred Vinson got in there," he recalled. "I saw his hand."[5]

The Acheson appointment had implications that went beyond the obvious one of saddling Byrnes with an Under Secretary he did not want. The selection of Acheson over Dunn deeply affected the balance of power within the department's Office of Far Eastern Affairs. If Dunn had been chosen, the Japan hands would have retained control of FE. In general the Japanese specialists were unenthusiastic about undertaking a major reconstruction of Japanese society. Politically conservative, they scoffed at the idea of having hordes of inexperienced New Dealers tinker with Japan's social system. In addition, the Japan hands were unsympathetic toward the aspirations of Asian Nationalists and openly hostile toward the Soviet Union.[6]

Although he was not a fervid New Dealer, Acheson was committed to a thorough reform program for Japan. As the person to oversee this occupation policy, Acheson chose John Carter Vincent, a liberal China hand, to head FE. The older Japanese specialists, especially Dooman and Joseph Ballantine, realizing that they would have limited influence under Acheson and Vincent, left the foreign service.[7] Liberal commentators rejoiced at this sudden setback for their opponents. Some even thought that the conservative bent of the entire department was about to be reversed.[8] Certainly the changes within FE were significant. It remained to be seen, however, what role the State Department would play in the development and execution of American policy in East Asia.

While this reorganization was taking place in Washington, the Army's XXIV Corps and the Marines' Third Amphibious Corps (IIIAC), in pursuance of the decisions made before Japan's surrender, took up their positions in Korea and north China respectively. With these landings, the total number of American troops on the mainland grew to more than double the wartime force in China. In Indochina, British forces occupied the southern half of that country in early September. Later that month a Chinese occupation force under General Lu Han entered the north. Although American troops did not take responsibility for a separate zone, they were involved in the occupation, particularly in the north. There a Military Assistance Advisory Group (MAAG) under Brigadier General

Philip Gallagher was attached to Lu Han's headquarters with instructions to aid the Chinese in disarming and repatriating Japanese forces.[9]

When Vincent took over in FE, the decisions to send American troops onto the mainland and to temporarily partition Korea and Indochina had already been made. Thus, he assumed his new responsibilities at a time when the pattern of American involvement was well established. As a foreign service officer with a total of fourteen years experience in China, Vincent had developed strongly held views on the proper American role in East Asia. He had witnessed the outbreak of antiforeign violence in China in the early 1920s, and watched as the Kuomintang, led by Chiang Kai-shek, purged its Communist members and marched north to unify the country. He had also been in Mukden in 1931 when the Japanese began their conquest of Manchuria, and he had served in the embassy at Chungking, Chiang's wartime capital deep in China's interior.

A soft-spoken Southerner (he was raised in Georgia), Vincent's personnel file contained numerous references to his "poise" and "sound common sense." As a young man, John Carter had been attracted to Woodrow Wilson's internationalism, and later he was drawn to what he termed the "economic democracy" of Franklin Roosevelt's New Deal. While serving in Chungking, he grew frustrated with Chiang's apparent unwillingness to prosecute the war against Japan. Vincent hoped to see a democratic China emerge from the war, but he doubted that such an event was likely if the United States continued its present policy. During the war, he had warned repeatedly that unless the United States pressured Chiang into making significant reforms, the CCP would inherit the Mandate of Heaven. In the immediate postwar period, as the United States attempted to bring order out of the chaos of Japan's surrender, Vincent became the leading advocate of an alternative postwar policy for East Asia.[10]

On August 10 General Wedemeyer received instructions from the Joint Chiefs to assist in the movement of Nationalist forces into central and north China for the purpose of taking the surrender of Japanese troops. Wedemeyer's directive, which had been hastily drafted in the Pentagon and approved by the State Department, also enjoined him to avoid aiding the Nationalists in a fratricidal war with the Communists.[11] As Wedemeyer's staff prepared for what was to be one of the largest troop movements in history, the general questioned the soundness of this part of his instructions. Wedemeyer realized that by moving Nationalist forces into the north to disarm the Japanese, the United States would be giving the central government an enormous lift in its struggle against the CCP.

Faced with an apparent conflict in his orders, Wedemeyer decided to transport the KMT troops while preventing as much as possible any direct contact between the Marines and CCP forces.[12] The JCS and the President quickly approved Wedemeyer's decision. Early in September, at the request of T. V. Soong, Truman agreed to provide American shipping, when it became available, to move KMT troops into Manchuria. Truman also agreed to continue equipping a total of thirty-nine Nationalist divisions in partial fulfillment of FDR's wartime pledge to arm ninety divisions. Finally, Truman also accepted Wedemeyer's and Chiang's recommendation to establish a Military Assistance Group in China.[13]

During September and October the first of the Chinese armies began arriving in the north. Ultimately close to 500,000 troops were transported. The Marines also took up their positions at this time, landing at Tientsin, Tsingtao, and Chefoo on the Shantung Peninsula. Most of the arriving troops were either flown into airfields held by the Americans, or ferried into ports that were also under Marine control.[14] Originally Wedemeyer's and Nimitz's staff officers had planned to make Shanghai the Marines' first priority. After Truman accepted McCloy's suggestion to land troops in north China, their destination was changed to the Shantung Peninsula.[15] Wedemeyer took command of the Marines once they came ashore. The ostensible purpose for transporting the Chinese into the north was so they could disarm the Japanese. As soon as they landed, however, the bulk of the KMT troops moved inland in pursuit of the CCP, leaving the Marines to protect the important communications centers in the region.[16]

In Washington, Vincent was greatly concerned by what he perceived as a deepening American involvement in China's internal affairs. His experience in China had convinced him that Chiang would be encouraged by these signs of American support to abandon political negotiations in favor of a military solution to the Communist problem. Vincent began his tenure as director of FE by attempting to restrict American military support to the Nationalists.

Through a curious set of circumstances Vincent did not learn of the decision to land Marines in China until he read about it in the newspaper. On August 14 the Army's liaison officer with the State Department discussed the impending operations with Dunn and Ballantine. Both men told the officer that they considered the areas in north China to be more important than Shanghai. There is no indication, however, as to why they thought this was the case.[17] The same day, Vincent met with Colonel Bonesteel and several other officers from OPD to discuss the China situation in connection with the surrender of Japan. According to a War Department memorandum, although the problems of disposing of Japanese arms and maintaining and feeding the surrendered Japanese were discussed, no mention was made of the pending Marine occupation of north China.[18] Following these meetings neither Dunn nor Ballantine discussed the prospective landings with Vincent, who, being the head of CA, might have been expected to have some interest in the proposed operations.

When he first learned that Marines might be arriving in China, Vincent was concerned that the Leathernecks would be used to put down civil disorder or keep the Communists out of the major cities in the north. In bringing the subject to Acheson's attention, Vincent recommended that the United States avoid any direct involvement in north China by flying in KMT troops. He also asked Acheson to find out from McCloy exactly what the Army planned to do with the Marines once they landed.[19]

Several days later, after a meeting with Army officers in the White House Map Room, Vincent's worst fears were confirmed. Preparations were already under way to put the Marines ashore on the mainland. Once again Vincent recommended flying KMT troops into the area as an alternative to placing American soldiers in a situation where they might have to use force against Chinese civilians or Communist troops. Noting that Wedemeyer had just arrived in Washington, Vincent also suggested that Truman be informed of the dangers posed by the use of American troops so that he could discuss the subject with the general. Unless there were "overriding military reasons" for undertaking these operations, Vincent could see no reason why the Marine occupation could not be abandoned in favor of using Chinese troops.[20]

On September 28 Acheson responded to Vincent's memorandum. Acheson explained that he had twice spoken to McCloy about the Marines. At first McCloy said that he thought the landings were "part of the residue of a larger plan in which it was contemplated that American troops would occupy several ports, including those now occupied by Soviet troops."[21] McCloy could not see any reason for carrying out the remainder of the plan, and he thought the operation should be scrapped. The "larger plan" to which McCloy referred was the failed attempt to occupy Dairen. McCloy, it will be recalled, had recommended landings at a port on the China coast not already in the Soviet zone, as a means of making the occupation of Dairen "less pointed." According to this scheme, the Soviets were to be told that the United States was seizing these areas for the purpose of preventing Japanese sabotage of vital port facilities.

Following this first discussion, McCloy called Acheson with some new information. After consulting Wedemeyer, McCloy reported that the Marines would be used to hold the north China ports so that an estimated four million Japanese in Manchuria, two million of whom were armed, could be evacuated in an orderly fashion. McCloy added that Wedemeyer said the ports in question were those "in the neighborhood of which trouble was most likely to start between the Government troops and the others [CCP] and that therefore the presence of American troops would strengthen the position of the National Government, help prevent any disorders from starting, and was desired by the Generalissimo."[22]

This was not the answer Vincent was looking for. As these conversations illustrate, the confusion that occasioned the initial decision to send the Marines into China continued to grow. The JCS's original plans called for emergency landings on the China coast to repatriate the Japanese. Wedemeyer, however, had wanted American troops to prevent the spread of Communist power in central and north China. For his part, McCloy had envisioned the occupation of the north China ports as part of a larger operation to limit Soviet expansion. This confusion over the origins of the Marines' occupation persisted well into November. At that time Byrnes told reporters that the decision to land the Marines in north China had been made by the War Department. This explanation did not conform with General Lincoln's understanding of the situation. In a memorandum to General Hull, Lincoln wrote that "prior to 15 August, at Mr. Byrnes' request, Dairen was included in the occupation plan for U.S. troops. When it was pointed out to Mr. Byrnes that Dairen was in the Russians' area, he then requested the Chief of Staff to pick out some other points on the China coast (I do not recall just what procedure was used in pointing out to Mr. Byrnes the situation as to Dairen)."[23]

It had been McCloy, of course, who told Byrnes about Dairen, and it had been McCloy who recommended occupying the China ports. Thus Byrnes was technically correct when he said the Marine occupation was a War Department decision. Nevertheless, the staff officers in OPD continued to believe the State Department was responsible for initiating the Marines' mission.

For his part, Wedemeyer must have thought that the Marines were being sent in answer to his requests. Although he had listed Shanghai as his first priority, the general was able to put the Marines to use when they arrived in north China. As McCloy's second conversation with Acheson indicated, the Marines were now performing two roles. First, they were aiding in the repatriation of Japanese troops. Second, they were lending support to Chiang, the exact nature of which was undefined. Eventually, as the KMT's outlook worsened, the Marines would assume a third role, that of a symbolic reminder to the Soviets of American interests in China. Given the changing roles of the Marines, the confusion surrounding the origins of their mission, and the controversial nature of the tasks they were performing, it is little wonder that the Truman administration was never able to provide a satisfactory public explanation for their presence in north China.

For Vincent, the decision to proceed with the Marine landings was a major setback. He believed that in addition to encouraging Chiang to forgo negotiations, the growing American military presence in China increased the potential for friction with the Soviet Union. With American troops about to arrive in China, the question of military aid to Chiang's government assumed new importance. As mentioned, the President had agreed to the JCS request to extend Lend Lease aid to China after Japan's surrender. Truman had also agreed to help move Nationalist troops into Manchuria and to send a military aid mission to China. The terms of the Lend Lease aid and the size of the military mission still had to be worked out by the two governments.

The question of postwar aid to China had first been brought before SWNCC in May 1945. At that time the State Department had decided to defer discussion of postwar military assistance until the internal situation in China settled down. At the end of August, however, McCloy reintroduced the subject. He maintained that the Army needed guidance as to the basic policy of the United States toward China and the terms on which any aid, if contemplated, would be extended.[24] Truman's decision to aid China still left it to SWNCC to determine how such aid would be administered. During the next two months the State Department's representatives battled with the War and Navy members over the terms on which aid would be given. The diplomats, led by Vincent, wanted to make aid contingent on Chiang's progress in reforming his government and settling the dispute with the CCP. The War and Navy departments argued that it was unreasonable to expect Chiang to establish a democratic regime anytime soon. In the meantime, the KMT would be deprived of much-needed aid, civil war would break out in China, and the ensuing turmoil would give the Soviets the justification they needed to intervene in the dispute.[25]

As a result of these discussions, SWNCC approved a vaguely worded compromise on October 22. The policy statement began by explaining that the success of American policy in East Asia depended on the development of a "friendly unified, independent [China] with a stable government resting insofar as practicable on the freely expressed support [of] the Chinese people."[26] Toward this end the United States would advise and aid China in the development of a modern army, navy, and air force. These forces would be developed to allow China to maintain its internal security, and fulfill its obligations in the occupation of Japan and Korea. The SWNCC statement also stipulated that all aid would cease if these forces were used to support a government that was not in conformity with American policies or if these forces were used to engage in civil war.[27]

Under the terms of the agreement, aid was permissible in the present circumstances. In this sense the policy statement represented another defeat for Vincent. Although the SWNCC paper afforded some consolation in that the continuation of aid would be subject to periodic review, the point at which aid would be cut off was not clearly defined. In noting this ambiguity Navy Secretary Forrestal wondered, "How do you draw a line between internal security and internal war?" Artemus Gates, the Navy's member on SWNCC, did not know. "That," suggested Admiral King, "is done arbitrarily."[28]

The SWNCC agreement of October 22 also provided for the establishment of a Military Advisor Group (MAG) in China. The terms of the mission were to be negotiated by the State Department through normal diplomatic channels. When he first heard of it in early September, Vincent did not oppose the idea of establishing an advisory group in China, providing the officers were no longer on the active lists of the American armed services.[29] When he read the JCS proposal, however, he changed his mind. The proposal looked too much like a bureaucratic ploy to expand the postwar mission of the armed services. In arguing for the program, the JCS justified the MAG on the grounds that if the United States did not send a mission to China someone else would. Vincent questioned whether this kind of reasoning would produce a military mission that was in the best interests of the United States. More important, he thought that the mission as described by the JCS, totaling 4,000 officers and men, would lead to an armaments race with the Soviets in Northeast Asia. The entire project caused him to wonder if the United States was not about to embark on the establishment of a "de facto colonial army" in China.[30] In this instance Vincent was able to reduce the size of the mission to 900 officers and men, a figure that Truman eventually approved.[31]

During the fall of 1945 Vincent became the department's "chief producing scribe" on China policy.[32] As head of FE, however, he was responsible for overseeing the formulation of American policy for all of East Asia. These larger responsibilities encouraged him to think more broadly about the historic changes that were taking place in the wake of Japan's defeat. Briefly put, Vincent concluded that a sound American policy would be one that enabled the United States to cooperate with the two most potent forces on the mainland—revolutionary nationalism and the Soviet Union. In the fall of 1945 the power of these forces was plainly in evidence on the Korean peninsula.

Responsibility for the occupation of Korea belonged to Lt. Gen. John R. Hodge, a combat-seasoned soldier's soldier with virtually no experience in civil affairs. Selected on the basis of availability (his outfit was closest to Korea when the war ended), Hodge was not the Army's first choice. That honor had gone to Chiang's former chief of staff and current nemesis, General Joseph Stilwell, but the generalissimo's strenuous objections canceled those plans.[33]

Hodge received only the vaguest instructions before arriving in Korea on September 8. He knew that the United States wanted to create a trusteeship for Korea and that his men were being rushed onto the peninsula to block the Soviet advance. As a stranger sent to govern a people about whom he knew almost nothing, Hodge was baffled by the activities of the numerous Korean political parties and factions. When he first arrived in the south a Korean People's Republic claiming strong support in the countryside was already in existence. In keeping with the American objective of creating a four-power trusteeship, Hodge received instructions not to recognize any self-proclaimed government of Korea.[34] Nevertheless, Hodge soon needed assistance in maintaining the basic services in the south. Rather than turn to the People's Republic, which was dominated by the Left, Hodge made the conscious decision to seek advice and assistance from the ultra-conservative leaders of the Korean Democratic Party (KDP). In doing so, he shunned the assistance of the most active of the wartime resistance groups in favor of a party largely comprised of collaborators.[35]

The leaders of the Right quickly fastened themselves to the American occupation government and thereby secured control of the efficient colonial bureaucracy bequeathed by the Japanese. Feeding Hodge's suspicions, KDP leaders described the People's Republic as a submissive tool of the Soviet forces to the north. Hodge and his State Department adviser, H. Merle Benninghoff, were both inclined to associate all left-wing activity with Soviet subversion, and they accepted the KDP's line almost without qualification.

In the first months of the occupation, despite its strong support in the countryside, the People's Republic played little part in the military government. During this time the KDP became ensconced in power, through the bureaucratic apparatus of the Japanese Government-General. The Right dominated the ranks of the national police and controlled the judicial system. In Korea, in contrast to Japan, the highly centralized government bureaucracy was maintained even though Americans understood that it had been created by the Japanese as a tool of oppression.[36]

In early October, the military government established a Korean advisory council. Although the KDP could claim only minimal support outside of the capital city of Seoul, nine of the council's eleven seats went to the members of the Right. By this time, Hodge and Benninghoff had begun to call for the return to Korea of the Korean Provisional Government, an exile group that had spent the war years in Chungking. The Provisional Government had been largely ignored by the State Department, since it had existed outside of Korea for its entire history. Nevertheless, the leaders of the Provisional Government had been vigorous champions of Korean independence, although at a distance. For this reason the KDP urged Hodge to recommend the Provisional Government's return. Evidently the Right hoped that the returning exiles would provide their movement with a leadership that was not tainted by any association with the Japanese. Both the military government and the Right also favored the return of Dr. Syngman Rhee, an elderly exile living in the United States.[37]

In the meantime, communications across the thirty-eighth parallel were almost nonexistent. To the north the Soviets left most of the local committees of the People's Republic intact. Instead they chose to exercise their authority through less formal means than a military government.[38] Although the Left was encouraged to believe that unification was still possible, the Soviets gave every indication that they were settling in for a long stay. In Washington, Truman still sought a four-power trusteeship leading to Korean independence. In Korea, however, American officers were being told that they had been sent to aid in the development of an "anti-communist bulwark" in the south.[39]

When Vincent turned his attention to the problems in Korea he once again found himself going against the grain in official Washington. Vincent feared that Hodge's heavy reliance on former Japanese collaborators and the military government's sponsorship of former Korean exiles such as Kim Koo, the head of the Provisional Government, and Syngman Rhee would create the impression that the United States was grooming a government to dominate Korean politics in the post-trusteeship period.[40] Vincent wanted Hodge to keep these men at arm's length, and he explicitly instructed the military government to purge the police of former collaborators.[41]

These criticisms concerning Hodge's use of former exile leaders did not go unchallenged. John McCloy, having just returned from a trip to the Far East, argued against placing unreasonable restrictions on Hodge. Speaking to officers in the War Department, McCloy likened the thirty-eighth parallel to a "reproduction of the situation in Germany with a complete lack of cooperation between zones."[42] To Dean Acheson, McCloy explained that Hodge faced a serious problem with Communists in the south. This subversion, he argued, endangered the prospects for free elections there. McCloy believed that Hodge should be allowed to build a "respectable government or group of advisors which [would] be able under General Hodge to bring some order out of the political, social, and economic chaos that now exists south of the thirty-eighth parallel and so provide the basis for, at some later date, a really free and uncoerced election by the people."[43]

Furthermore, McCloy thought it was foolish to refuse the assistance of Korean exiles while the Russians continued to rule the north through Soviet-trained proxies. McCloy favored giving Hodge wide discretion in this matter. He warned that if the United States refused to work with the exiles, and if the Soviets refused to cooperate while they sent agents into the south, the administration might discover "what Stalin meant when he agreed to the idea of a trusteeship for Korea with the delicate proviso, 'if necessary.' "[44]

In replying to McCloy, Vincent said that he did not object to Hodge's use of former exiles providing the general made it understood that such cooperation did not imply American recognition of any Korean government.[45] It is not clear how Vincent thought such cooperation could take place without providing the Koreans who were selected with at least tacit recognition. As McCloy's memorandum suggests, that was an underlying objective of his proposal. Vincent may have been willing to concede this point in part because he realized that Hodge was in a very difficult position. Moreover, Hodge had the full support of the State Department's political adviser in Korea. Vincent may also have thought that the period of military government in Korea was about to end. In early November it appeared that progress was being made in opening communications across the thirty-eighth parallel, and talks were scheduled to begin shortly on the development of the trusteeship machinery.

During the fall of 1945 Vincent's efforts to change the course of American policy in Korea and China frequently met with opposition from officials in the War and Navy departments. His efforts to develop a postwar policy for colonial Southeast Asia differed in this respect in that his most vigorous opponents could be found in the State Department's Office of European Affairs. The Europeanists, of course, were responsible for the administration's policy of "noninterference" in colonial affairs. This policy had been predicated on the assumption that the French, Dutch, and British could reassert their authority in their former possessions without American assistance. Such a policy appeared to offer the United States the best of two worlds. It served American interests by providing stability in Southeast Asia, while at the same time it allowed the administration to explain that it was not supporting imperialism. In the immediate postwar period the efficacy of this policy was being sorely tested in Indochina.

In late August, after Japan's surrender, the Vietminh (a coalition of Vietnamese parties dominated by the Communists) moved quickly to fill the void created by Japan's sudden collapse. On August 24, after having established control over most of Tonkin province in the north and parts of Annam and Cochin China in the south, the Vietminh announced the creation of the Democratic People's Republic of Vietnam.[46] The so-called "August Revolution" provided the clearest possible indication that the returning French authorities would meet with stiff resistance. In early September OSS and State Department officials sent repeated warnings to Washington that the Vietminh were determined to maintain their independence "even at the cost of lives."[47] Although these reports heightened the private misgivings of the Asian specialists in the State Department, the administration's first priority was to try to disassociate the United States from the activities of the British-controlled Southeast Asian Command. The department's officers were concerned that the public would perceive American representation on the SEAC staff as proof of the United States' support for the policy of the Allied commanders in that theater.[48]

Of particular concern to the State Department were the activities of the British officer sent to occupy Indochina. On September 13 Indian troops under the command of Major General Douglas Gracey entered Saigon, the capital of Cochin China. Shortly after his arrival Gracey announced that he intended to turn over responsibility for maintaining law and order to the French as quickly as possible.[49] In the meantime, Gracey tried to use the available Japanese troops to preserve order. On September 22 recurring anti-French violence and apparent Japanese apathy convinced him that he should arm approximately 1,400 French troops who had been interned by the Japanese during the war. That night the French seized all the public buildings in Saigon. Following the coup the Vietnamese retaliated by attacking French positions. Although they were driven back, anti-French violence escalated. On the night of September 24 at least 200 French civilians, mostly women and children, were massacred in a Saigon suburb.[50]

In the following days the Japanese cooperated more closely with the British and French. This multinational force began to secure the rest of the city. In October French reinforcements began arriving in the south. Armed with American weapons and wearing American-made uniforms, the French began to reoccupy Cochin China and Annam.[51] Although the French had acquired American supplies through Lend Lease intended for use in Europe, and through the British in SEAC, the Vietnamese were bound to conclude, as did General Lincoln, that any contribution of weapons to the French constituted aid against the Vietnamese, "regardless of whether those exact arms are used or not in the shooting."[52]

Although the French were making headway in reoccupying the south, they fared much worse in the north. There the Vietnamese cause received inestimable assistance as a result of the Chinese refusal to allow French troops to enter the area. In general the Chinese were more concerned with exploiting the region's resources than with facilitating Vietnamese independence. Nevertheless, the Vietminh were able to use this protection to extend their control throughout the countryside. On one occasion dubbed "gold week," the Chinese turned over 40,000 captured Japanese weapons to the Vietminh in exchange for large quantities of gold and Vietnamese piasters.[53]

The French wasted little time in complaining to American officials in Washington, Chungking, and Hanoi. Immediately after Japan's surrender the French had warned that the Chinese would pursue their own objectives in the north. The British likewise were unhappy with the prospect of a dual occupation. Early in September Byrnes belatedly suggested extending British control over the entire country if the Chinese agreed. The Chinese government replied, however, that preparations for entering Indochina "in full accordance with General Order No. 1" had advanced too far to be reversed.[54]

In the years to come numerous French officials, including de Gaulle, would accuse the United States of deliberately obstructing their return to Indochina. Some charged that the Americans had tried to compensate the Chinese for the loss of the Manchurian ports by allowing them to plunder north Indochina.[55] In attributing Machiavellian intentions to the United States, the French credited the Truman administration's Indochina policy with a clarity of purpose it did not possess. Simply put, the decision to assign northern Indochina to the Chinese was a mistake, the full scope of which was not realized until the occupation was under way. Although officials in Washington hoped for a peaceful French restoration, American officials in China were primarily concerned with the problem of maintaining order long enough to repatriate the Japanese. Toward this end the American representative on the Chinese Combat Command advised Nationalist commanders that it might be necessary to disarm French soldiers to preserve order during the occupation.[56] "The Americans in China," commended one French official, "have right along been playing the Chinese game, although unwittingly."[57]

In response to French complaints, the United States did try to get the Chinese to cooperate with French officials in Indochina.[58] Beyond that the administration did little to meliorate the effects of the Chinese occupation. In September the Americans refused French requests for assistance in negotiating a civil affairs agreement with the Chinese.[59] Throughout the fall the Chinese followed a policy of keeping the French and Vietminh at "sword's point" to advance their own cause.[60]

The American policy of noninterference was failing on both sides of the sixteenth parallel. The military operation then under way in the south convinced Vincent that the French were not serious about reforming the old regime in Indochina. This, he believed, would be a mistake. Vincent did not think the French could restore control without a bloodbath. Even then he did not think they would be successful. As an alternative to standing aside while French soldiers armed with American weapons reconquered the south, Vincent called for international mediation of the dispute. This suggestion was coldly received in EUR. The Europeanists dismissed reports about anti-French resistance as alarmist and predicted an early return to peace in the country. They viewed mediation as the first step toward ejecting the French from Indochina and warned that the Soviets would demand to participate in any international conference.[61]

Because of the bureaucratic arrangements in the State Department, Vincent could not make any progress on the mediation proposal without the Europeanists' approval. Stiffled by his colleagues, Vincent decided to take a modified version of the mediation plan before the public. In an address on East Asian policy to the Foreign Policy Association, Vincent explained that although the United States did not question French sovereignty in Indochina, it was not the government's intention to "assist or participate in forceful measures for the imposition of control by the territorial sovereign."[62] He added, however, that the United States would be prepared to "lend assistance, if requested to do so, in efforts to reach peaceful agreements."[63] The French declined to take Vincent up on this offer.[64]

In the immediate postwar period Vincent found himself frequently at odds with the members of the Office of European Affairs and the War and Navy departments. For Vincent, China held the key to a successful American policy in East Asia. "China," he told the Foreign Policy Association, "is in a position to form a buffer or a bridge in our relations with the Soviet Union in the Far East."[65] Clearly he preferred to see China in the latter role. In the same speech he reiterated the American promise to work for a unified and cooperative China "with a government based on democratic principles and popular sovereignty." But Vincent also indicated his desire to hurry the Marines out of China by noting that even Chiang had agreed that the Americans should leave north China as soon as they could be replaced by Chinese troops. "The process of relief," he declared, "is now in progress."[66]

In Korea Vincent supported the announced American policy of creating a trusteeship. His distance from the scene impaired his ability to understand how strongly all Koreans opposed the trusteeship plan. Still, Vincent thought that international cooperation would prevent a scramble for influence in Korea. At the same time, he sought to satisfy the demands of Korean Nationalists by offering them independence after a brief period of assistance and supervision. Vincent did not see the trusteeship as an end in itself. Rather he thought of it as a means of avoiding a conflict between the great powers.

International cooperation and gradual progress toward independence were also Vincent's answers to the Indochina problem. To him, the administration's decision to handle Indochina as a European problem was a mistake. Asian nationalism was a potent force that had to be reckoned with on its own terms. While the French tried to turn back the flood, Vincent attempted to direct the revolutionary current into more manageable channels.

Sizing up the situation in East Asia after Japan's surrender, Vincent believed that the United States was not in a position to impose its will on the mainland. The region's problems were too deeply rooted and Soviet power too firmly entrenched to suppose the United States could exert much influence from its small footholds on the mainland. Even with American assistance the Nationalists would not be able to subdue the Communists. Vincent believed that Chiang could best help himself by reforming his regime. He was unlikely to undertake this difficult task, however, as long as the United States assisted the Nationalists against the CCP. As a consequence, Vincent believed that the United States had to pressure Chiang by withholding aid from the Nationalists. Most important, he believed that the United States had to seek accommodation with the Soviets.

Neither of these views was likely to be accepted by the administration in the fall of 1945. To begin with, Vincent's recommendation to withhold aid from the Nationalists was politically dangerous. In effect, he was asking Truman to endorse a policy that might enhance the position of the Communists and possibly topple Chiang. Although most Americans realized that the Nationalists were in serious trouble, few thought the situation called for the drastic policy changes Vincent recommended.[67]

Now that Japan had been defeated it was possible for the military to devote greater attention to China. The JCS, however, were not wildly optimistic about Chiang's ability to unify the country. Intelligence assessments of Chinese Communist strength emphasized the present military weakness of the CCP, but predicted that the outbreak of civil war would lead to an eventual Communist victory. Colonel Ivan Yeaton, the leader of the Dixie mission at the end of the war, and a communist specialist in the Army's intelligence staff, reported that "the red army does not have the military strength to seriously oppose the KMT in position warfare but in a period of an occupational capacity the KMT will be a far-gone long-range loser even with United States help of occupation."[68] During a tour of the China theater in August, Colonel Laurence J. Lincoln, brother of George Lincoln and head of the Asiatic section of OPD, made a similar report to Washington. After noting the present military weakness of the CCP, he added that "this does not mean that the Communists will lose ground in a political sense, their appeal is very strong and it will spread, but not through force of arms for the time being."[69] Concern over the long-range political picture in China was counterbalanced by a growing confidence in Chinese military prowess at the end of the war. Brigadier General Paul Caraway, Wedemeyer's deputy chief of staff, wrote that the KMT troops had "learned a great deal in the past nine months and are managing some of their movements with considerable skill. If the Chinese soldier is ever really trained and given excellent officers he will be a real fighting machine."[70]

When Wedemeyer returned to Washington for a short stay in October, he told a meeting of the Joint Staff Planners that "the Generalissimo has sufficient power to cope with the Chinese Communists provided they do not receive increased aid from Russia. . . . the strength of the Communists in China has been overrated in this country and there is no need to fear them unless the Russians give them support beyond the present scale."[71] Clearly, Wedemeyer's assessment went beyond either Lincoln's or Yeaton's reports. The general's comments are especially surprising given that he had hand-picked Yeaton because he trusted his expertise and because he knew that the strongly anticommunist Yeaton would not be susceptible to CCP propaganda.[72]

Nevertheless, as strictly military evaluations of the *current* situation in China, the reports of all three officers were similar. All emphasized the present military weakness of the Chinese Communists. Of the three,

Wedemeyer's was the least cautious, but he could always blame any setback to the KMT on increased Soviet assistance to the Communists. Although Yeaton's and Lincoln's analyses were hedged against the possibility of a CCP victory, no one advocated a complete American withdrawal. Instead, Wedemeyer and his staff favored the creation of a military advisory group to replace the China theater headquarters, but only after Chiang's troops had reoccupied the north and the Marines were withdrawn. By deactivating the China theater they hoped to reduce American responsibility for KMT actions and at the same time provide important support and training for Nationalist forces. [73]

In part the military's recommendations tended to be bureaucratically self-serving, especially where the Air Force and Navy were concerned. Military assistance to China offered attractive possibilities for servicemen in search of a postwar mission. General Caraway complained that "the whole damn mission was a worse pyramidal setup than we had in China during the war. Everybody wants to be a General apparently."[74] Some officers, however, viewed even the growing interservice rivalry in China as being in American interests. Colonel Lincoln reported that "some of the Army are becoming a little alarmed at the Navy tentacles reaching into China. However, they may save the U.S. position and policy here so I am all for it."[75] From the information provided by Lincoln and Wedemeyer, the JCS concluded that in the short run the CCP did not pose a threat to Chiang. The longer a civil war could be avoided, the more assistance Chiang could receive, the better his chances for survival would become. After the Nationalists established control over most of China, Chiang could undertake the much-needed government reforms that would weaken the appeal of the CCP. As long as it seemed possible that a policy of timely assistance to the Nationalists and limited involvement on the mainland would be enough to sustain Chiang, there was little chance of Truman adopting the harsher measures advocated by Vincent.

Administration officials were also unlikely to share Vincent's attitude toward accommodation with the Soviet Union. From the point of view of Truman and other key officials, the Soviet Union was the major source of turmoil in Northeast Asia. As McCloy's remarks suggested, he believed that Hodge's control over the south was being challenged by Soviet-sponsored Korean infiltrators. Having agreed to an American occupation of Korea below the thirty-eighth parallel, Stalin now appeared to be trying to take by stealth what he had refrained from taking by force. Although the United States lacked any clear evidence proving that the Communists in Korea and China were manipulated from Moscow, they also lacked conclusive proof of their independence. Circumstantial evidence tended to support those who viewed the Chinese and Korean revolutionaries as the vanguard of Soviet influence in Asia. Intelligence reports indicated that the Soviets were turning over captured Japanese arms to the Chinese Communists, and the existence of Soviet-trained Koreans above the thirty-eighth parallel was well known. In late October the Russians added to Chiang's troubles by prohibiting Nationalist troops from landing at Dairen. Instead the Chinese had to land at Chinwangtao south of the Manchurian border. From there they would have to undertake a difficult march through Communist-held territory.[76]

For administration officials, Soviet behavior in East Asia seemed to fit too closely the pattern of Russian conduct in Eastern Europe. Concerning Soviet intentions in China, Wedemeyer warned that the Russians were "determined to penetrate North China and set up a buffer area there similar to what they have done in Europe, regardless of the thirty years treaty with China."[77] After Wedemeyer met with Truman in late October, the general wrote that the President had informed him that "U.S. policy in the Far East will include continued and full support of Chiang Kai Shek and the Nationalists," and that "a stiffening policy with regard to the Russians will be undertaken in the Far East."[78]

In the first two months of the postwar era American policy in East Asia was being determined by decisions made in haste at the time of Japan's surrender. Up to this point Vincent's efforts to change the direction of American policy had met with little success. If Vincent's recommendations had continued to go unheeded they would not warrant much attention beyond noting that they amounted to another road not taken by the United States in East Asia. But in early November Vincent's policies gained a new advocate, one with influence, or so it seemed, and an ability to make policy. In early November James Byrnes reentered the debate over East Asian policy.

7

Into the Cold War

The President wishes to keep America's promise and support the Central Government of China. Mr. Byrnes insists upon taking the so-called Chinese Communists into our camp. (Admiral Leahy, December 1945)[1]

By EARLY NOVEMBER, John Carter Vincent was growing tired of having to defend FE's policies almost single-handedly against the criticisms of the War and Navy departments. Vincent hoped that the Secretary of State would pay more attention to China policy. He conceded, however, that Byrnes had "so many Russian problems" that he barely had time for anything else.[2] At the time, this was an accurate assessment of the situation. Preoccupied by the London meeting of the Council of Foreign Ministers, Byrnes had given little attention to East Asian problems in the two months after Japan's surrender. This condition began to change, however, once Byrnes perceived that a connection existed between his Russian problems and East Asian policy.

One reason for the Secretary's renewed interest in Asian problems could be found in the sudden worsening of the situation in China. Almost overnight, the China problem became a top priority for the administration. Following Japan's surrender the incidence of clashes between the Nationalists and the Communists increased as both sides attempted to extend their influence into the areas previously occupied by Japanese forces. The line between helping the Nationalists repatriate the Japanese and aiding them against the Communists quickly became blurred. For some officials, who viewed the CCP as a tool of the Soviets, this distinction no longer mattered. Others, however, began to question the administration's commitment to Chiang. How far should the United States go to achieve its postwar goal of a united China under Chiang Kai-shek? To a great extent, the answer to that question depended on one's perception of Soviet activity in Northeast Asia.

At the time of Japan's surrender, Byrnes' assessment of Stalin's goals in the region had been unmistakably clear. The Secretary had supported the President's decision to occupy north China and Korea in an attempt to counter Russian influence on the mainland. Following the first meeting of the Council of Foreign Ministers, however, Byrnes' own perception of Soviet behavior changed significantly.

To Byrnes' dismay, Molotov had forced a breakup of the London conference in early October over a procedural dispute. To the Russians, who viewed the first postwar gathering as an exploratory meeting, the poor publicity resulting from the conference's failure mattered less than the information they acquired concerning American intentions.[3] Byrnes, however, emerged from the conference with his confidence badly shaken. By far the most stunning outcome of the meeting had been the Soviets' apparent indifference to the American atomic monopoly. The Secretary had arrived in London fully expecting that this "gun behind the door" would allow him to take charge of the conference. To Byrnes' surprise, Molotov remained unimpressed by this implied threat. Instead the Russian proceeded to joke about members of the American delegation carrying atomic bombs in their pockets. To say the least, the Americans were not prepared for this kind of behavior from the usually businesslike Molotov.[4]

The conference was deadlocked almost from the start. In keeping with the State Department's interpretation of the Yalta Declaration on Liberated Europe, Byrnes refused to recognize the Soviet-backed regimes in Eastern Europe until those countries held free elections. Molotov countered by citing American unilateral action in Japan and similar behavior by the British in Greece. Inasmuch as neither side was willing to compromise, there was no reason to continue. Seizing on a procedural question concerning the seating of the Chinese delegation, the Soviets forced an adjournment of the conference.[5]

Byrnes regarded the breakup of the meeting as a personal disaster. After losing the vice-presidential nomination in 1944, and then seeing Truman succeed FDR, Byrnes had decided that if the presidency was beyond his reach he could still fashion a fitting end to his long public career by creating a lasting peace out of the war's wreckage. Having donned the mantle of peacemaker, he knew that after London he would have to find some way to revive negotiations with the Soviets.[6]

Shortly after returning to Washington, Byrnes began to talk of the need to compromise with the Russians. In particular he thought some agreement might be possible concerning Bulgaria and Rumania. On October 10 he dispatched an independent commission headed by Mark Ethridge, a Louisville newspaper publisher, to investigate conditions in those countries. Byrnes mistrusted the reporting of the division of Eastern European affairs, which he regarded as anti-Soviet, and he hoped Ethridge would return with a more favorable report on Russian activities in the area.[7] A week later Byrnes told the Committee of Three that despite the current difficulties with the Soviets he was not pessimistic over the future of Russian-American relations.[8]

Despite his desire to reduce tensions between the two great powers, Byrnes was at first unwilling to consider Soviet objections concerning the American occupation of Japan. While at London, the Russians had protested American unilateral control of the occupation, suggesting that American policy made a resurgent Japan likely. To drive home this point Molotov recommended that the United States and the Soviet Union enter into an anti-Japanese defense pact.[9]

Ideally, Molotov wanted an Allied four-power Control Council, such as existed in Germany, to precede the formation of the American-supported Far Eastern Advisory Commission. But a Control Council that copied the German model would give Moscow a veto over American policy in Japan. In contrast, the Americans designed the Advisory Commission to be little more than a debating club with no authority to enforce its decisions. Byrnes, of course, could never agree to Molotov's request. Even as he searched for some way to resume the postwar negotiations, Byrnes continued to ignore Soviet appeals on this issue. The Russians responded by threatening to boycott the meetings of the Advisory Commission. Speaking to the Committee of Three, Byrnes explained that he was not sure that the Soviets would attend the first meeting of the commission, but he thought they would be in a weak position if they did not.[10] When the delegates assembled for the first session on October 23, the Russians were not present.

Faced with yet another public display of Allied dissension, Byrnes became even more anxious to smooth over the differences between the two powers. Two days later, on October 25, Byrnes received an important telegram from the American embassy in Moscow. Earlier that month he had asked Harriman to deliver a message from Truman to Stalin explaining the American decision to withhold recognition from Bulgaria and Rumania. When Harriman finally met with the Russian leader in the latter's retreat in the Caucasus, he found that Stalin was primarily concerned about American occupation policy in Japan. Harriman then wired Byrnes with the news that Stalin believed that the "control of Japan [was] the first question requiring settlement."[11]

Harriman's message had a clear impact on the Secretary of State. During a November 6 Committee of Three meeting, Byrnes argued against allowing other Allied troops to participate in the occupation of Japan until the Soviets agreed to send a contingent. Byrnes rejected Secretary of War Robert Patterson's recommendation to accept the forces of other Allies and leave "the Russians out if they don't want to come." The trouble with that step, Byrnes argued, was that it would be "merely making for two worlds and preparing the course for another war."[12] Byrnes added later that Stalin felt he had "been ignored on the question of Japan."[13]

By early November Byrnes was beginning to develop a new formula for future negotiations with the Russians. In response to Moscow's protests over the control of Japan, Byrnes abandoned his compartmentalized approach to the outstanding issues in favor of a grander, all-embracing plan. The firmness of Byrnes' negotiating posture also underwent a change at this time. Whereas before he had expected the American atomic monopoly to overawe the Soviets, he now thought some compromises were necessary. In adopting this new approach to Soviet policy, Byrnes began to distance himself from the leading members of the administration. At the same time, however, he became more receptive to Vincent's arguments on two areas of potential Soviet-American discord, Korea and China. Thus, early in November, after having failed for nearly two months to get Byrnes to take a sustained look at East Asian problems, Vincent suddenly found most of his recommendations being accepted by the Secretary. This was especially the case with regard to China, where Byrnes relied heavily on Vincent's expertise.

The Secretary's heightened awareness of Chinese affairs was directly attributable to a series of urgent messages issuing from Wedemeyer's headquarters in early November. On November 5, shortly after returning to China, the general informed the War Department that he had just refused a request by Chiang to transport more KMT troops north. Citing his directive of August 10, Wedemeyer explained that "dissident elements, not Japanese, are the cause of the present serious trouble and therefore the move of additional troops is not within the scope of my mission."[14] Having completed his assignment as defined by his August 10 directive, Wedemeyer told Marshall that he expected to begin withdrawing the Marines by November 15.

Although he still believed that the United States should continue to aid Chiang, Wedemeyer was increasingly concerned that the Marines might begin to clash with the Communists in north China. During their first month of occupation duty the Marines had been unmolested by the CCP. By the end of October, however, KMT troops began arriving in Chin-wangtao, after being turned away from Manchurian ports by the Soviets. As the Nationalists came ashore on beaches protected by the Marines, the Communists began to harass the Americans. Incidents involving Marine patrols increased, although no actual fighting was reported. On November 1 the head of the American observer group in Yenan reported that the Communists welcomed an "American-communist incident as soon as possible in order to flare U.S. and world public opinion and thereby stop American participation [in the conflict]."[15] Given these conditions, it seemed doubtful that Wedemeyer would be able to obey the injunction in his directive to avoid involvement in a "fratricidal war." The problem of Japan's surrender had now become hopelessly bound up with China's civil strife.

Wedemeyer's November 5 message touched off a month-long debate over China policy within the administration. Throughout November the Committee of Three and SWNCC reexamined the American position in China. Although the ostensible purpose of the Marines' occupation was to evacuate the Japanese and thus bring the war to a close, the War and Navy departments argued that the Leathernecks were needed to contain Soviet-CCP influence and strengthen Chiang's regime. Byrnes took a different tack. Influenced by his desire to reopen negotiations with Moscow, the Secretary revived Vincent's campaign to reduce American military involvement in China.

When the Committee of Three met on November 6, McCloy brought Wedemeyer's message to the group's attention. The administration, McCloy said, now had to make a basic decision as to how far it should back Chiang in his efforts to unify China. McCloy added that "wherever our flag flies, this is evidence of American support and greatly strengthens Chiang's prestige."[16] Byrnes then asked what effect a Marine withdrawal would have on the situation. "Chiang's prestige would suffer," thought

McCloy. He went on to say that the Marines were needed to control the Japanese who, being an undefeated army, were quite different from the troops encountered in Japan proper.[17] This last remark was part of the administration's public explanation for the Marine occupation. Yet the Japanese had shown no signs of being uncooperative. Indeed, they were actually sharing responsibility for protecting key areas in north China with the Marines.[18] The real problem, as Dean Acheson later explained, was that "if you told the Japs to throw their arms down on the ground and march to the seaboard, that entire country [north China] would be taken over by the Communists."[19] This was also McCloy's view. Asked by Byrnes how the United States could justify moving another army into the north, McCloy answered that "Chiang's real need of our aid is to increase his army's strength in North China against the Communists."[20]

No decisions were reached on Wedemeyer's orders during this meeting. Instead the general was told to delay any action on the Marine withdrawal until he received further instructions. Three days later Wedemeyer informed the War Department that he had refused Chiang's request to use American planes and personnel to move Nationalist troops into and within Manchuria. Citing his August 10 directive and General Order No. 1, Wedemeyer explained that he had no authority to aid in the recovery of Manchuria. That area, according to the General Order, was in the Red Army's sphere of responsibility. Therefore the recovery of Manchuria was an international problem to be resolved by direct negotiations between the Chinese and the Soviets.[21]

Wedemeyer's message coincided with an all-out effort by the Nationalists to take Shanhaikuan at the border of Manchuria. Beneath headlines heralding a "Struggle at the Gateway of Manchuria," the *New York Times* reported that heavy gunfire marked the first serious fighting in the "undeclared civil war."[22] The *Times* also reported that American military equipment located at Chinwangtao was said to be important to the Nationalists' chances of breaching the Great Wall.

With the siege of Shanhaikuan providing the backdrop, a working group of SWNCC's Far Eastern subcommittee met to discuss Wedemeyer's latest message. Little was resolved at this meeting, however, owing to what was described as a "wide divergence of views." According to a summary of the meeting (no minutes are available), "the State Department representative expressed the feeling that the U.S. should withdraw from military activity in China in order to avoid further complications, whereas the War Department representative took the opposite stand."[23]

Shortly after this meeting the committee received a memorandum from McCloy on the same subject. According to McCloy's count there were presently 450,000 Communists in north China as opposed to only 160,000 KMT troops and 60,000 Marines. In addition, there were still 4,000,000 Japanese soldiers and civilians in China. McCloy emphasized that the Chinese government was not in a position to effect the repatriation of the Japanese without continued American support. Yet Wedemeyer could not provide this assistance, because any additional troop movements were not "within the scope of his mission."[24] McCloy wanted the general's directive changed to permit the transfer of additional Chinese troops, even though it meant aiding the Nationalists in their struggle with the CCP. If the United States failed to render this much-needed assistance, McCloy warned, it might find that it had failed to achieve its wartime goal of a unified China or to maintain "the territorial integrity of China in accordance with international commitments and may have invited intervention by another power in Manchuria."[25] The JCS weighed in with similar predictions of "outside intervention." They also warned that without American assistance Chiang might try to employ Japanese troops to supress the Communists. "In either of these events," the Chiefs concluded, "the United States would be failing to capitalize upon the advantages gained in China during the war in which huge amounts of American money, resources and manpower were devoted."[26]

On November 20 the Far Eastern subcommittee met to discuss Wedemeyer's latest message together with the McCloy memorandum. During what appears to have been a heated discussion, the Army and Navy members sharply criticized the State Department's policy. The day before, the Navy had sent the State Department a proposal for an "agreed restatement of U.S. policy" that would permit continued aid to Chiang short of involving American forces directly in a fratricidal war.[27] Now, however, the Navy's representative declared that "until U.S. policy had changed, the Navy position was that the Marines should be taken out of Northern China."[28] Speaking for the Army, Colonel Bonesteel explained that "the Army desired only a clear statement of political policy in order to perform its job effectively."[29] No clarification was forthcoming, however, for the State Department's representative, James Penfield, simply noted that the Committee of Three was meeting that day to discuss the China problem. Any action on this subject would have to await the outcome of their meeting.[30]

Bonesteel's assertion that the Army desired "only a clear statement of policy" notwithstanding, the JCS and the civilian heads of the military were unanimous in their desire to continue supporting Chiang. In this respect Patterson, McCloy, Forrestal, and the JCS shared their subordinates' frustration with the State Department's policy. All agreed that the department's injunction to avoid aiding Chiang in a fratricidal war made the military's job unnecessarily difficult if not impossible. This is not to say that the military wanted to turn the Marines loose on the CCP or, as Michael Schaller has suggested, that they considered increasing the number of troops in China.[31] The military had become more interested in China following the defeat of Japan, but they still appreciated the dangers of becoming involved in a large land campaign on the mainland.[32] McCloy and the others wanted to continue the present form of assistance to China. This included moving additional troops into the north and leaving the Marines in China. Under the present policy this support would have to stop. Chiang already had enough men in the north to relieve the Americans and repatriate the Japanese. Any further aid would constitute direct support to the Nationalists in their struggle against the Communists. The solution, as McCloy and the others saw it, was to have the State Department revise the hastily written postwar directive to Wedemeyer.

Adding to the War and Navy departments' sense of frustration with the situation in China was the growing public dissatisfaction over the presence of the Marines in north China. Following the defeat of Japan, Americans on the homefront clamored for the return of the soldiers from overseas. Parents and wives of servicemen flooded Congress with appeals to hasten the already breakneck pace of the demobilization. Special offices that had been created to facilitate the mustering out of millions of servicemen were operating on a twenty-four-hour-a-day basis. Even then they could not keep pace with the work load.[33] As the public stepped up its calls to bring the boys back home, soldiers at bases in the Philippines and China added their voices to the chorus. In this highly charged atmosphere the Marines in China came in for special attention. Angry parents and disillusioned Marines condemned the American involvement in China's internal affairs. The occupation also aroused the ire of American liberals, many of whom already questioned Truman's fitness as a successor to FDR. All wanted to know why Americans and Japanese were being used to guard Chiang's communications if the Marines were in China to repatriate the Japanese.[34]

In response to the mounting public protest over the occupation, administration officials privately lashed out at their critics in and out of the government. In a revealing example of the developing Cold War mentality in Washington, the administration's critics were denounced as Communist sympathizers. Forrestal condemned what he called the "left wing boys" and "a certain group of columnists," and listened approvingly to Hurley's description of Communist supporters in the State Department.[35] In the War Department, Generals Hull and Embick blamed much of Wedemeyer's problems on an anonymous "leftist" in the State Department. In addition, members of the general staff, including Colonel Lincoln, referred to Vincent as a "fellow traveler," and refused to show him certain classified material.[36] Admiral Leahy also referred to "pinkies" in the State Department.[37]

Publicly, the administration took more conventional steps to silence its opponents. In early October two of Truman's staff members recommended that it would be a "good idea politically" for Truman to let the press know that he was requesting daily reports on the progress of demobilization from the Pentagon.[38] This would assure the public that the President was doing everything possible to bring the boys back home. Truman also tried his hand at drafting a public message on the role of the Marines in China. Although his staff supported the idea of releasing a statement, they disagreed with Truman's description of wartime events in China. In assessing the respective roles of the Nationalists and the CCP, Truman wrote that the "Central Government of China under Generalissimo Chiang Kai-shek has been deeply and helpfully involved in our common war against Japan while the Chinese forces now in opposition to the Central Government contributed nothing to our war effort."[39] In his notes for this draft Truman wrote that "we have reason to believe that the so-called Commies in China not only did not help us but on occasion helped the Japs. We are not mixing in China's internal affairs."[40] It is unclear whether Truman believed this to be the case or whether he was just venting his frustration as he did from time to time. In any case his staff convinced him that it might be best to let the War Department try its hand at a public statement.

In the meantime, on November 10, the Navy Department issued a press release explaining that the Marines were protecting the communications in north China for "the purpose, and the purpose only, of assisting the Nationalist Government to effect the surrender of Japanese forces in North China and to carry out the terms of the surrender in accordance with international agreements. The Marines are not in China for any purpose connected with the conflict between the Nationalists and the Communist elements in China."[41]

Two days later, Secretary of War Patterson issued a similar statement in which he explained that the Marines were in China to help the Nationalists take the surrender of the one million Japanese troops then under arms.[42] This estimate of Japanese strength was, however, grossly inflated. What is more, Patterson knew this to be the case. American intelligence placed the number of Japanese troops under arms in north China at no more than 203,000. An additional 158,000 Japanese still had not been disarmed in south and east China. Another 238,000 soldiers were still armed on Formosa. Together this brought the total to 599,000, or a little over half of Patterson's figure.[43]

Originally, the War Department had put the figure at one and a half million. After discovering that this was a mistake, officers in the Operation and Plans Division contacted Patterson and gave him the correct numbers. The Secretary told them not to worry about it. Because the statement was then at the White House for approval, the officers were not sure whether Patterson wanted them to make the corrections when it came back, or whether he wanted them to let the erroneous estimates stand. One of Patterson's staff thought the latter was the case. In any event, Patterson saw the statement once more before it was released. At that time he reduced the estimate from one and a half million to a million. The message was then issued to the press.[44] Figuratively speaking, Patterson could have disarmed another 400,000 Japanese soldiers. His own figures showed that there were about 600,000 armed imperial troops in China. For that matter he could have explained that only 203,000 soldiers remained under arms in the area controlled by the Marines. One million was a more imposing figure, however, and it seems that the Secretary was more concerned with silencing the administration's critics than with explaining the Marines' complicated mission in north China.

While the administration debated China policy and attempted to quiet the public's fears about being drawn into China's civil conflict, the Marines were coming under fire from the Communists. On November 16 Wedemeyer reported that a train en route to Chinwangtao had been attacked by Communist guerrillas. A Marine patrol had also been fired on in the same area. To prevent any more incidents the Marines planned to issue a warning to the CCP. If this failed they would strafe the village from which the fire had been reported. Before approving this plan Wedemeyer ordered that special precautions be taken to ensure the safety of civilians. In his report to Washington, the general concluded that the Marines would inevitably be drawn into more serious fighting, and he recommended an immediate evacuation of the entire contingent.[45]

Lest anyone think that evacuating the Marines would be an easy way out of the China tangle, Wedemeyer appended to his report a brief summary of what he believed would be the likely consequences of such a withdrawal. "The Chinese Communists," Wedemeyer predicted, "will interpret removal of U.S. forces as a complete success in their program of intimidation and propaganda."[46] Removal of the Marines would also expose vital communications to Communist attack. In particular, coal shipments to Shanghai would be interrupted, causing "suffering and chaos" in an area of vital political, economic, and psychological importance to the generalissimo. Wedemeyer also warned that open civil war might follow from the Marines' withdrawal. He added, however, that civil war might erupt even if the Marines remained.[47]

Wedemeyer's reports were received in the Pentagon as further evidence of the need to continue aiding the Nationalists. To recall the Marines now would seriously weaken Chiang's position in north China. Byrnes, however, saw things differently. While Wedemeyer's superiors were building their fire under the State Department, Byrnes was in the process of developing a new policy that called for an end to American military involvement in China. This new policy was, of course, nothing more than Vincent's old policy revived.

On November 19 Vincent completed a memorandum entitled "Our Military Position in China," which presented a series of four policy options together with a discussion of their pros and cons. The first three choices were (a) an immediate evacuation of the Marines, (b) a continuation of the status quo, (c) an increase in American military aid to the Nationalists. Each of these options appeared to contain serious weaknesses. If the Marines withdrew, Chiang might begin to use the Japanese as mercenaries against the Communists. On the other hand, enlarging Wedemeyer's mission and increasing aid to Chiang would arouse Soviet suspicions, incite public opinion, and prolong a civil war. Maintenance of the status quo was unacceptable. Under the present policy nothing was being done to repatriate the Japanese or prevent an outbreak of more serious fighting.

The fourth option, Vincent's preference, called for a more concerted effort on the part of the United States to repatriate the Japanese and negotiate an end to the internal conflict. To implement this policy Vincent explained that it would be necessary to establish a truce in north China. The Nationalists and Communists were expected to use this time to negotiate a "firm and realistic agreement providing for fair representation of all political elements in the Chinese Government and for cessation of hostilities."[48] While this truce lasted, the United States, after notifying the Soviet Union, would repatriate the Japanese soldiers and civilians in north China. The Marines would be withdrawn once their mission was completed in the hope that an agreement, if not already achieved, would be quickly forthcoming. To ensure that the Nationalists would negotiate in good faith the United States would threaten to withdraw the Marines and cancel all postwar aid to China until the conflict was resolved.[49]

On November 19, the same day Vincent's memo was completed, Byrnes met with Patterson to discuss the China situation. That evening the War Department sent Wedemeyer a summary of Byrnes' comments. The United States would not move any more Nationalist troops into the north. For the time being, however, the Marines would remain in China. This decision was based on the assumption that Chiang might need "considerable assistance and stimulation" to repatriate the Japanese.[50] Byrnes realized that a continuation of the occupation might "result in some collateral aid and prestige to the National Government."[51] Withdrawing the Marines, however, would undermine American long-range goals in China. As part of the same message, the War Department notified Wedemeyer that Byrnes wanted to know whether or not it was reasonable to say that the Marines were needed in north China to remove the Japanese. The Secretary also inquired into the long-range effects of an immediate withdrawal as opposed to a continuation of the occupation for an indefinite period.[52]

Some historians have interpreted Byrnes' query concerning the role of the Marines as evidence of "a wish to define the problem as a military rather than a political one."[53] It has also been suggested that Byrnes, like Patterson, Forrestal, and McCloy, was attempting to disguise the Marines' real mission, giving assistance to Chiang against the CCP, by explaining that the occupation was needed to repatriate the Japanese.[54] A third explanation of Byrnes' intentions seems possible.

Byrnes, I suggest, was beginning to consider the desirability of developing a new China policy along the lines recommended by Vincent. But first he needed to know whether it was necessary to keep the Marines in China. If the end result of a withdrawal of American forces was a conflict involving the Communists, Nationalists, and Japanese, they would have to stay. Vincent, it should be understood, advocated pulling the Marines out only *after* the Japanese were evacuated. Byrnes, like Vincent, opposed moving more Nationalist troops north, believing that such assistance would encourage Chiang to forgo negotiations with the Communists.

From this point on, Byrnes began to draw more heavily on Vincent's expertise. Of course once China became a pressing issue, Byrnes would have had to look for some guidance from the experienced personnel in the department. Nevertheless, he did not have to accept Vincent's recommendations. During this same period Everett Drumright, the head of the Division of Chinese Affairs, strongly favored increased aid to Chiang.[55] Vincent prevailed with the Secretary, it seems, because his recommendations fitted easily into the framework of Byrnes' new Soviet policy. Vincent's argument, that increasing aid to Chiang would lead to countermeasures by the Russians, could not fail to make an impression on Byrnes. Determined to make progress in his negotiations with the Kremlin, the Secretary was wary of increasing American military involvement in China. Once the Japanese were removed and the Marines withdrawn, it would be possible to work toward a settlement in China without risking further military intervention by the great powers.

Byrnes continued to develop his new policy during the next two meetings of the Committee of Three. The first meeting, on November 20, began with Byrnes reading aloud from Vincent's memorandum. Byrnes also emphasized the importance of keeping the Marines in China to repatriate the Japanese. Forrestal, in reference to remarks concerning the risks of leaving the Marines in China, commented that he did not want to see the Americans withdrawn "as a result of Russian pressure."[56] Inasmuch as Byrnes was still waiting for a reply from Wedemeyer, the meeting concluded without any final decisions being made on what to do about the Marines.

Before the committee met again on November 27, Wedemeyer sent three reports to Washington. Two replied to Byrnes' queries, a third provided a résumé of the situation in China. In his summary, the general's tone was pessimistic. Chiang's ability to recover Manchuria depended on Soviet cooperation and a satisfactory settlement with the Communists, neither of which seemed likely. Wedemeyer warned that Soviet actions in "Korea, Manchuria, Outer Mongolia, Inner Mongolia, Jehol, Chahar, and Sinkiang provinces suggest the pattern for the Far East where she may create conditions similar to those now existing on her western frontiers in Europe."[57] He added that the Russians were "creating favorable conditions for the realization of Chinese Communist and possibly their own plans in North China and Manchuria."[58]

In his two-part reply to Byrnes' questions, Wedemeyer said that the Marines were definitely needed to effect the repatriation of the Japanese.

He predicted, however, that Chiang would not be able to regain control of north China and Manchuria for months, possibly years in the case of the latter. Wedemeyer added that if the administration decided to keep the Marines in China to evacuate the Japanese, their orders would have to be changed to allow for the possibility that the Americans would become involved in a fratricidal war.[59]

Wedemeyer's warnings of possible Soviet encroachment in Manchuria and north China were received by officials in the Pentagon as proof of the need to continue aid to Chiang.[60] In a long and somewhat discursive report produced in S&P and signed by Forrestal and Patterson, the War and Navy departments recommended that Wedemeyer's directive be ammended to permit continued support of the Nationalists. The report also called on the State Department to clarify American short-range policy and to produce a long-range "definitive policy" for China.[61] The report concluded with a warning, added by Patterson, concerning Soviet activity in the region. In speaking to the possibility that the region might "pass to Soviet control or separate states under its domination," the paper stated that the "impact of such piecemeal action, uncoordinated internationally, on the U.S. and the world at large would, in the long run, probably be as grave militarily as any situation likely to arise due to continued U.S. support of the Nationalists Government, also uncoordinated internationally."[62]

Clearly the War and Navy departments viewed the Soviets as the major source of trouble in the region. In reviewing the study, Patterson explained that "the communist problem in China was minor to an understanding with the Russians."[63] That is to say Patterson thought that if the Communists were deprived of Soviet support, they would not pose a serious problem to the Nationalists. American intelligence summaries appeared to support this analysis. Basing their views on the field reports from the observer group in Yenan during the war, Colonel Lincoln and other staff officers believed that the Communists were capable of mounting only harassing raids against well-trained and supplied conventional forces.[64] Army intelligence in Washington put CCP strength at about 880,000 troops, half of whom were north of the Yellow River. Of these, 80 percent were believed to possess light equipment and little training, making them unsuitable for orthodox military operations. The intelligence summary concluded that "rapid and effective occupation of Communist held or controlled areas by Nationalist troops can be expected materially to reduce

Communist capabilities."[65] Events in China seemed to bear out this assessment. Referring to the highly publicized battle for Shanhaikuan, the War Department dismissed it as nothing more than "the passage of the Great Wall by a National Government Army without any Communist resistance worthy of the name."[66]

When the civilian heads of the armed services met with Byrnes on November 27, they continued to stress the Soviet factor in East Asia. During the discussion Forrestal sounded the now familiar refrain that the United States could not "yank the Marines out of North China now."[67] He went on to say that part of the administration's problem was that the public did not understand the China situation. Forrestal also suggested that the United States "talk the matter over realistically with the Russians." Failing that the administration should try to bring the United Nations organization into the picture.[68]

Byrnes replied that the Soviets were already on record as supporting the Nationalists. He also dismissed UN participation as impractical, since the first scheduled meeting of that organization was still months away. Instead Byrnes suggested that the United States "assume Soviet good faith in the matter, determine our policy, and tell the Soviet Government."[69] To reduce the possibility of American involvement in the civil war while the Marines repatriated the Japanese, Byrnes suggested trying to force the opposing sides to "get together on a compromise basis, perhaps telling the Generalissimo Chiang Kai-shek that we will stop the aid to his government unless he goes along with us."[70]

After the session ended, the Secretaries made their way over to the White House for a luncheon meeting of the cabinet. As the cabinet officers arranged themselves around the table, Truman entered the room holding a White House teletype sheet in his hand. "See what a son-of-a-bitch did to me," he exclaimed.[71] Passing the page around the room, Truman explained that Patrick Hurley had just resigned as ambassador to China. In announcing his resignation Hurley had issued a statement charging that American foreign service officers were sabotaging American policy by supporting the CCP. Hurley concluded that the government's China policy could be set right only after there had been a thorough housecleaning in the State Department.[72]

Hurley's resignation stunned Truman. Only the day before, the ambassador had told the President that he was returning to China. After making his opening remarks, Truman shifted the focus of the discussion to the current situation in China. Reading a message from Edwin Pauley, the head of the United States reparations commission, Truman reported that the Red Army had stripped most of the factories in Manchuria and north Korea of their machinery.[73] This was too much. Unless the United States took a strong stand in China, Truman declared, the Russians would take the place of the Japanese in East Asia. Byrnes commented that the Chinese ambassador had accused the Soviets of arming the Communists. Later in the meeting, however, Byrnes spoke of the need to disarm and evacuate the Japanese. Once this operation was completed, Byrnes thought that the United States should "stand pat and not give Chiang Kai-shek anything whatsoever until he agreed to come to terms with the Chinese Communists and give them some places in a combination cabinet."[74]

When the discussion came around again to the problem of Hurley's resignation, Agriculture Secretary Clinton Anderson suggested that Truman send General Marshall on a fact-finding mission to China. Anderson thought that a dramatic appointment would "steal thunder" away from Hurley's resignation.[75] That afternoon Truman phoned Marshall. Although he had just begun his retirement, the general dutifully agreed to undertake the mission. In solving one problem for Truman, the Marshall appointment created another for Byrnes and Vincent. A proponent of continued aid to the Nationalists, Marshall would now play a central role in the formulation of China policy. Consequently, the confrontation between the military and the diplomats over that policy was transformed into a battle over what instructions the general would carry with him to China.

Hurley's resignation could not have come at a less opportune time for Byrnes. Only days before, Byrnes had sprung a surprise of his own, much to the chagrin of British Foreign Minister Ernest Bevin. On November 23 Byrnes sent an urgent message to Moscow asking Molotov to host a meeting of the Big Three Foreign Ministers. Byrnes reminded Molotov that arrangements for periodic meetings of the Conference of Foreign Ministers (United States, Great Britain, and the Soviet Union) had been made at Yalta and confirmed at Potsdam. The Chinese and French, both members of the *Council* of Foreign Ministers, would not be invited.[76] After notifying Molotov, Byrnes wired Bevin. Angered by Byrnes' unilateral action, Bevin initially refused to attend. He finally relented, although he feared that Byrnes' insistence on holding the conference in December would leave the Allies too little time to prepare.[77]

In calling the conference, Byrnes was putting into action the new strategy that he had been developing since the breakup of the London meetings. By excluding the Chinese and French he hoped to turn the Moscow meeting, as much as possible, into direct negotiations with the Russians. Byrnes prepared an agenda for the talks and sent it to Bevin on November 29. Heading the list of nine subjects was a proposal for the creation of a United Nations–sponsored commission to consider the control of atomic energy. Byrnes was playing his trump card first. The talks would also cover the Japanese occupation, the establishment of an independent Korean government, the repatriation of Japanese in China, the transfer of Manchurian control to the Nationalists, recognition of the governments of Bulgaria and Rumania, and the removal of Allied troops from Iran. This last referred to the continuing presence of Soviet troops in northern Iran, where they supported a separatist movement.[78]

Byrnes' proposal for the conference agenda reflected his years of experience in the Senate as a promoter of compromises. The negotiations would begin with the Secretary offering to start the process of establishing controls on atomic energy. This offer would also include measures for the eventual exchange of scientific information. Byrnes hoped that by opening the conference with a discussion of atomic energy he could allay Soviet fears of the American monopoly. The United States would then recognize the Soviet-backed regimes in Rumania and Bulgaria in return for Russian acceptance of American unilateral control over Japan. The Chinese and Iranian problems were more difficult to pair. Byrnes believed that the Marines had to remain in China until the Japanese were evacuated. This he would try to make clear to the Soviets in the hope that they would recognize the limited role the Marines were going to play in China and reciprocate with a withdrawal from Iran.[79]

On Byrnes' agenda, Korea stood alone as a unique challenge to American-Soviet cooperation. Despite the strong recommendations from William Langdon, Hodge's political adviser, that the trusteeship idea should be scrapped; Vincent and most of his staff in FE continued to view the trusteeship as the best way to prevent a great power struggle over Korea. Vincent thought that if the United States eliminated this intermediate step and created a governing commission as Langdon suggested, the peninsula would be divided between the Left in the north and the Right in the south.[80] As an alternative, Vincent favored temporary American-Soviet supervision to ensure that a nationally representative government acceptable to both parties emerged. Vincent conceded that this supervision did not necessarily have to take the shape of a formal trusteeship, providing the United States and the Soviet Union could agree on an alternate first.[81]

Like his recommendations on China policy, Vincent's views on Korean policy fitted into the larger scheme of Byrnes' great power diplomacy. Conversely, Langdon's plan for an American-sponsored Korean governing commission was incompatible with Byrnes' desire to ease Soviet anxiety over American unilateral action in Japan. Byrnes decided to keep to the original trusteeship proposal until a Soviet-American agreement could be reached.

By late November Byrnes had incorporated two important elements of Vincent's East Asian policy into his overall approach to Soviet-American relations. Vincent had won Byrnes to his side on the China and Korea questions primarily because both of these issues constituted potential sources of friction between Moscow and Washington. The third component of Vincent's East Asian policy, Southeast Asian colonial affairs, did not directly involve the Soviets. For this reason Byrnes exhibited less interest in Vincent's proposal to mediate the deepening conflict in Indochina. As a result, the administration maintained its "hands off" policy toward the French possession.

To Vietnamese and other Asian Nationalists, the return of thousands of French troops armed and equipped with American Lend Lease supplies and carried on American ships seemed proof of the Truman administration's support of European imperialism. That fall, cables from American embassies and consulates in the region carried reports of Asian disillusionment with American colonial policy.[82] In an effort to disassociate the United States from the European conquest, American officials informed the British that the United States would be severing its ties to SEAC on November 1. At the request of the British, however, the JCS agreed not to publicize this move until December 31.[83] This decision had the same effect as postponing the withdrawal for two months.[84]

The administration's efforts to prevent the French from using Lend Lease supplies in Indochina were also ineffectual. During a news conference on October 25 Byrnes explained that the United States had requested that the Allies remove the American insignia from all Lend Lease items. He conceded, however, that the United States was not prepared to demand the recall of Lend Lease goods.[85] The United States would not pressure the French into negotiating with the Vietnamese. Without

Byrnes' support, Vincent had no chance of defeating his opponents in the Office of European Affairs.

The demands of the coming Moscow conference and the need to prepare Marshall's instructions left Vincent little time to battle his departmental foes. In particular, the debate over Marshall's instructions consumed much of his time. Here Byrnes and Vincent once again engaged the War Department over the future of American China policy. This process began on November 28 with Vincent submitting to the War Department an "Outline of Suggested Course of Action in China."[86] Based on the fourth alternative of his previous memorandum to Byrnes, this plan made a truce and the convocation of a national political convention preconditions for American assistance in moving Chinese troops into the north.

Marshall found Vincent's outline inadequate in several respects. The general believed that as a statement of policy Vincent's plan was too vague to serve as the basis of a new directive for Wedemeyer. Moreover, Marshall thought that the Communists would simply block the negotiations, since any delay in the movement of Chiang's troops would work to their advantage. In addition, Marshall believed that a halt in the movement of Nationalist troops would play into the hands of the Soviets, who, he feared, were preparing to take advantage of the chaotic situation in China. Consequently, Marshall reversed Vincent's proposed course of action, making a truce and political negotiations secondary to the air and sea lift of Nationalist troops into the north.[87]

Marshall's objections were incorporated into a revision of Vincent's memorandum. Originally the officers in OPD wanted to write an entirely new memorandum that would make it unequivocally clear that the United States would continue to support Chiang against the Communists. Marshall restrained them, however, telling them that they were only permitted to edit the State Department's policy statement.[88]

On receiving this revision of his memorandum, Vincent amended it by including a clause calling for a moratorium on KMT troop transfers if it appeared they endangered the success of political negotiations.[89] Citing the possible benefits to the Communists of any delay in moving the Nationalists, the War Department rejected Vincent's amendment. Relations between the two departments were fast becoming strained. In a strongly worded memo to Marshall, Lieutenant General Hull warned that the success of the entire mission depended on the creation of a "firm and unequivocal policy." "Otherwise," Hull predicted, "You, the JCS and the

War and Navy Departments may continue to be hamstrung by the vague, indecisive, delaying tactics which have characterized U.S. policy toward China since the Japanese capitulation."[90]

The continuing disagreements between the War and State departments eventually led to a series of meetings on December 9, 11, and 14, the latter two attended by Truman, during which Marshall's instructions were finally approved. Both sides agreed to a compromise proposal drafted by Vincent. Wedemeyer would be instructed to assist in the transfer of KMT troops to replace the departing Soviet forces in Manchuria and to prepare for the movement of additional troops into north China. The latter movement would be delayed, however, until Marshall was certain that it could be carried out "consistently with his negotiations," or until it became clear that the negotiations had failed.[91] Wedemeyer's preparations for these movements were to remain a secret so as to use that uncertainty "for the purpose of bringing influence to bear on the Generalissimo and the Communist leaders towards concluding a successful negotiation."[92]

During one meeting the question arose as to what should be done if because of Chiang's stubbornness the talks collapsed. Byrnes and Vincent had previously discussed this very point. Vincent argued that under those circumstances it would be necessary to evacuate the Japanese and Marines as quickly as possible even though it would open the region to a Communist takeover.[93] Byrnes took this position during his meeting with Marshall. Two days later in a meeting attended by Truman and Leahy, Marshall raised the question again. This time, according to Marshall's notes, Truman and Byrnes both agreed that the United States would, in Marshall's words, "swallow its pride" and move Chiang's troops into the north to complete the Japanese repatriation.[94]

Byrnes' reversal on this point is difficult to explain, but it appears Truman's presence was decisive. Although Marshall's notes show only that Byrnes and Truman agreed on the need to move the troops north, there may have been some initial disagreement among the conferees. The following day, December 12, Admiral Leahy recorded in his diary that "this morning the President expressed to me surprise and displeasure at the attitude of Secretary Byrnes expressed yesterday toward the Central Government of China."[95]

Although Byrnes would have been startled by these comments, the President's remarks were only the most recent indication of Truman's growing dissatisfaction with his Secretary of State. Two weeks earlier

Truman had directed Leahy to draft a statement on China policy. Leahy told George Elsey that although this was a State Department job, the President knew that he could not count on the diplomats to draft a clear and concise message. "The President's all right," Leahy explained, "he's behind Chiang. But those pinkies in the State Department can't be trusted."[96] Leahy did not include Byrnes among the "pinkies," but on another occasion he concluded that Byrnes was not "immune to the communisticaly [*sic*] inclined advisers in his Department."[97]

Byrnes probably knew that he had one potential enemy in the White House. The Byrnes-Leahy rivalry had been simmering ever since their encounter over the Japanese surrender. For his part, Leahy believed that Byrnes acted too independently and that he did not show Truman the deference he deserved as President.[98] Truman, however, was also beginning to express his displeasure with Byrnes' freewheeling style. The "grand thing" about Hurley's resignation, Truman told Henry Wallace, was that it would "give him a chance to get inside the State Department and straighten it out."[99] Another time Truman asked budget director Harold Smith, "I would have a pretty good government don't you think if I had a good Labor Department and a good State Department?"[100]

Byrnes seems to have been oblivious to the trouble brewing in Washington. As Robert Donovan has observed, Truman evidently made no effort to communicate his dissatisfaction directly to Byrnes.[101] Without knowing it, Byrnes had become isolated from the other major policymakers in the administration. Whereas Byrnes believed that he could smooth over differences between the United States and the Soviet Union, Truman did not. The events of the last two months had given Truman an entirely different perception of Soviet conduct. Truman saw the Soviets' violations of the Yalta agreements in Eastern Europe and their subversion in Iran as evidence of the need to take a stronger stand at the upcoming conference.

For Truman, Soviet activity in East Asia seemed to be merely part of the larger pattern of Russian expansionism. At every turn it seemed as though the Soviets were obstructing the administration's policies and profiting from the ensuing turmoil. They had kept the Nationalists out of Manchuria and allowed the Communists in. They had turned over captured arms to the CCP and plundered Manchuria and Korea. Despite Stalin's promise to allow the Nationalists to establish the civil administration in Manchuria, the Russians had restricted the movement of KMT officials and otherwise hampered their work.[102] In Korea they had blocked off the north, driven thousands of inhabitants into exile in the south, and brought in their own specially trained Korean agents. Given these circumstances the explanation for the failure of American policy seemed clear.

Four months after Japan's surrender, the United States seemed no closer to achieving its postwar goals in China and Korea. In attempting to deal with this situation Byrnes accepted Vincent's approach to problems in Northeast Asia and the recognition of the limited means available to the United States which it implied. Truman, however, was not yet ready to abandon his postwar goals. Byrnes would have to be brought back into line.

Inasmuch as Truman had checked Byrnes' initiative on China policy when Marshall's instructions were being written, there was little to be accomplished concerning China at the Moscow conference. The meeting did yield an agreement on Korea, however. This provided for a joint commission comprised of Soviet and American occupation forces. The commission would assist in the creation of a provisional government in cooperation with Korea's democratic parties and associations. These two bodies would then work to establish a progressive regime for Korea. The proposals of the joint commission and the provisional government would be subject to the approval of a four-power trusteeship which would last no longer than five years.

Regarding the rest of the conference, one student of Byrnes' diplomacy has described it this way: Byrnes "traded the Russians token concessions in Japan for token concessions in the Balkans, and American troops stayed in China while Soviet troops remained in Iran."[103] The main accomplishment of the conference was that it prevented a breach between the great powers and allowed the diplomatic process of treaty making to continue.

Truman, however, was no longer interested in making compromises on what he believed to be the legitimate interests of the United States. The President was supported in this view by Leahy, who described the Moscow communiqué as "an appeasement document which gives to the Soviet [sic] everything they want and preserves to America nothing," and by Senator Vandenberg, who thought Byrnes was giving away America's "trading stock" in the area of atomic information and technology.[104]

Following the conference Truman prepared a list of his grievances against Byrnes and the Russians and addressed it to the "Hon. Jas. F. Byrnes, Secretary of State." Truman claimed that he read the memorandum to Byrnes, but this appears doubtful.[105] Nevertheless, most historians agree that Truman's "Dear Jim" letter was an accurate reflection of the President's thoughts and not just another letter he wrote to let off steam.[106]

"There is no doubt in my mind," read the letter, "that Russia intends an invasion of Turkey and the seizure of the Black Sea straits in the Mediterranean. Unless Russia is faced with an iron fist and strong language war is in the making."[107] Truman opposed recognizing Bulgaria and Rumania until the Soviets held free elections. He also thought the United States should tell the Russians its position on Iran "in no uncertain terms." Regarding East Asia, Truman wrote that "we should maintain complete control of Japan. We should rehabilitate China and create a strong central government there. We should do the same for Korea." In a parting shot at Byrnes' labors at Moscow, Truman concluded the letter by announcing, "I'm tired [of] babying the Soviets."[108]

American control of Japan, strong and friendly central governments in China and Korea: this was simply a reiteration of the postwar agenda that Truman had been trying to secure since taking office. Nearly nine months later, Korea remained divided by a tangle of barbed wire and roadblocks, and the United States was deeply enmeshed in China's internal conflict. Frustration over the failure of American policy gave way to a growing feeling within the administration that the Soviet Union and its fellow travelers were responsible for thwarting Truman's postwar plans. By January 1946 the President himself was describing the critics of his China policy as "those people in this country who are more loyal to the Russian government than they are to their own."[109] The Cold War had begun in Asia.

Conclusion

If we had the transportation and troops available, we would have prevented them from doing what was done in Korea and Manchuria, but we had no transportation. Chiang Kai-shek was supposed to meet the situation, but he didn't get there. . . . We just didn't have the means. (Harry Truman, November 1953)[1]

THE AMERICAN POSITION in East Asia at the end of 1945 was the end result of an interconnected series of unexpected events, improvised responses, and unintended consequences. In his first months in office, Truman had grappled with the near impossible task of tying together the disparate strands of Roosevelt's policies. Before Potsdam he hoped to maintain the Grand Alliance, defeat Japan quickly, protect the Open Door, and promote free and friendly regimes in Korea and China. The tension between these goals proved too great, however, and by mid-July he dropped the first to grasp the remainder.

In forgoing cooperation with the Soviet Union, Truman was influenced by his advisers and by the logic of the State Department's plans for East Asia. Gradually, these postwar plans were transformed by the growing concern over Russian expansionism. In the face of this new threat, the need for allies in Europe took precedence over anticolonialism, and plans for the liberation and promotion of pro-American governments in China and Korea took on the added purpose of producing bulwarks against the spread of Soviet-sponsored communism.

Truman was receptive to this advice because it conformed with what he knew about Roosevelt's postwar plans. But although he accepted the State Department's recommendations concerning the Open Door, Chinese sovereignty over Manchuria, and the Korean trusteeship, he did not immediately resolve all of the conflicts in American policy. Necessity held him to the alliance with Russia, and American military strategy remained unchanged. Thus, when Truman raised the State Department's recommendations to the level of official policy, he committed the United States to a degree of involvement on the mainland that the military was not prepared to undertake.

At Potsdam, evidence of Soviet intransigence during the Stalin-Soong negotiations and the apparent unwillingness of the Japanese to meet Truman's surrender terms increased the possibility that the war might drag on while Soviet troops swept across Northeast Asia. Once he learned of the awesome success of the atomic bomb, Truman was encouraged to believe that he had found a solution to his East Asian problems. At that point he seems to have hoped that he would not have to make concessions to either the Japanese or the Soviets. American objectives suddenly must have seemed tantalizingly within reach. The war could be ended quickly and China and Korea might be spared Soviet occupation. When the Russians and Japanese quickly upset these calculations, Truman was forced to improvise. Faced with Japanese obduracy, he publicly agreed to what he had privately accepted, that Japan could keep the emperor. The problem of containing Soviet expansion proved more difficult.

In devising their postwar plans for East Asia, American officials had made several key assumptions about American power and the mutuality of U.S., British, and Chinese interests in the face of the Russian threat. These articles of faith were sorely tested in the final days of the war. The President had deferred discussion of the Manchurian, Korean, and Kuriles issues in the hope that the United States would be in a better position to bargain after Japan surrendered. When this gambit failed, Truman was besieged by contradictory advice. The President's civilian advisers, worried about Russian intentions, urged an early occupation of Korea, Dairen, and north China. The JCS, concerned about Japanese opposition and aware of the limited resources available to American commanders in the Pacific, cautioned against any adventures on the mainland until Japan was securely occupied. Truman approved the recommendations of his political advisers but left the ultimate decisions concerning surrender operations to the military. As a consequence, the Dairen operation, which amounted to a direct confrontation with Soviet power, never received serious consideration.

In the midst of all the confusion created by Japan's surrender, American officials counted on receiving more cooperation from their British and

Chinese allies than they should have expected. During the summer the new administration made it clear to Britain and France that the United States would not challenge their sovereignty over Indochina and Hong Kong. Despite indications that the Chinese would oppose a return to the status quo antebellum, the Truman administration failed to inform Chiang's government of its position on colonial policy. The Americans further confused the situation when they left Hong Kong and north Indochina in the Chinese occupation zone. Preoccupied with problems in Northeast Asia, administration officials hoped that somehow the British, French, and Chinese would work out their differences in a manner consistent with American interests in the region. This attempt to treat the surrender of Japanese forces as a purely military problem amounted to wishful thinking on the part of the Americans.

To prevent the Hong Kong dispute from developing into a more serious confrontation, Truman finally was forced to intervene. In settling the Hong Kong question in favor of the British, Truman disappointed the Chinese and placed the United States openly on the side of European imperialism. The administration's desire to avoid any further decisions of this nature helps to explain why the United States permitted the Chinese to occupy north Indochina, even though American policy favored the restoration of French sovereignty over the whole country. The absence of French military power in the region greatly simplified this decision. Unlike the British, the French were in no position to oppose the Chinese. In this way, the Truman administration indirectly and unwittingly contributed to the survival and growth of the Vietminh at a crucial moment in its struggle against French rule.[2]

In the course of settling the Hong Kong dispute, the United States was presented with yet another surprise when the British announced that they had no plans to participate in the occupation of Korea. As with the surrender of Hong Kong, Truman incorrectly assumed that an identity of interests existed between London and Washington. Despite American assertions that the occupation of Japan and Korea constituted the "main effort," Britain placed greater emphasis on securing its former colonies in Southeast Asia. This divergence of views on the importance of Korea would be a recurring theme in postwar Anglo-American relations. Britain's refusal to send troops to the peninsula also placed a greater burden on American resources, a problem that was compounded by Chiang's subsequent decision to focus on troubles closer to home. As a result, the anticipated four-power occupation of Korea became more clearly a contest between the United States and the Soviet Union.

In light of the confusion that attended Japan's surrender, the movement of large numbers of American troops onto the mainland by the end of September was an impressive military achievement. There was, however, a deceptive quality to this show of force. The American victory over Japan had been won by superior naval and air power, both of which were of limited utility in dealing with the problems of the immediate postwar period. Unlike the Soviet Union, the American presence was confined to the periphery of the Asian mainland. Truman and his advisers had ordered American troops into Korea and China in the hope that they would help stabilize the region and bring American objectives closer within reach. But the revolutionary events on the mainland were not so easily controlled. When American troops came ashore they encountered unexpectedly volatile situations, to which they added an additional element of uncertainty. Operating under hastily written instructions that no longer fitted the situations they confronted, Generals Hodge and Wedemeyer were quick to call for new orders from Washington.

Wedemeyer's reports, in particular, seemed both to reflect and contribute to the confusion in Washington. Alternately he disparaged CCP strength and then predicted a catastrophe whatever approach the United States attempted. At the time of Japan's surrender he requested eight divisions for China. Two months later he urged that the Marines be withdrawn only to clarify this recommendation within days by calling for a phased withdrawal in conjunction with the KMT's reoccupation of north China.

The very presence of the Marines in north China provided ample evidence of the disarray in Washington. The decision to send the Leathernecks onto the mainland was not an automatic consequence of American wartime support for Chiang Kai-shek. Although the proposed landings were supported by a variety of people for different reasons, the final decision to send in the Marines was more the product of afterthought than any clearly defined national policy. Only after the Marines took up their stations in China and the seriousness of the CCP challenge became clearer did a consensus form in Washington as to their mission. As Communist propaganda illustrated, CCP officials were sensitive to the changing role of the Marines in north China. Communist bitterness over this direct intervention in Chinese affairs would linger, long after the Americans were withdrawn.

Although Wedemeyer seemed uncertain about what role the Marines should play in China, he pushed consistently for continued military assistance providing that the administration was prepared to take responsibility for its actions. These requests, no doubt influenced by the general's belief that Chiang was the "benevolent dictator" that China needed, found a sympathetic audience in the Pentagon.[3]

Before Japan's defeat, the JCS seemed ready to accept the fact of Russian dominance in Manchuria, and possibly north China. These plans had been based on the expectation that the war would last another year, and that Russian troops would penetrate deeply into China proper. The sudden and unanticipated surrender of Japan altered the Chiefs' thinking dramatically. As bleak as the conditions on the mainland looked in August 1945, they were an improvement over what the JCS expected to see at the war's end. With China finally accessible to American aid, the Chiefs were ready to make a greater commitment to building up Chiang's forces than they had been when preparations for the invasion of Japan had dominated their thinking. Compared with what was at stake, the risks of limited involvement seemed minimal.

The decision to continue supporting the KMT was reinforced by several secondary arguments which were less clearly stated in the JCS's position papers. The competition for a postwar mission and the cautious optimism of officers who served in China at the end of the war produced recommendations for a military advisory group that even some officers thought was too bloated. It is difficult to determine the extent to which officers like Colonel Lincoln and General Caraway formed a network of mid-level staff officers in Washington and Chungking that mutually reinforced the decision to aid Chiang. It is clear, however, that they corresponded with each other officially and unofficially and that they drafted the papers used by McCloy, Marshall, and Wedemeyer. Largely hidden from the view of historians, the activities of these pick and shovel men may help to explain the consistency of the military's efforts to aid the Nationalists in the postwar era.

The policy of limited intervention was one of two alternatives being presented in the fall of 1945. The second was the Vincent-Byrnes proposal for gradual disengagement and compromise. The emergence of Vincent

as head of FE, and the subsequent departure of the Japan hands, made
for almost a complete reversal in the positions of the JCS and the State
Department. In retrospect, it seems clear that neither Vincent nor Byrnes
had much chance of engineering an abrupt change in American policy.
John Carter Vincent showed a greater awareness of the local sources of
the conflict in Asia, but at a time when the other offices in the department
were recommending a tougher policy toward the Russians in Europe and
the Middle East, he could not even claim full support from within his
branch. Lacking the guile required to quietly build support within the
bureaucracy, Vincent became a lightning rod for the pro-Nationalist critics
of the State Department.

In the case of Byrnes, it is considerably more surprising that as seasoned
a veteran of Washington's infighting as the Secretary of State would likewise leave himself so exposed. No doubt Byrnes mistakenly counted on
Truman's support to help him carry the day. But the Secretary's ambition
and his desire to play the role of peacemaker also blinded him to the
growing anticommunist consensus in Washington. Although he adopted
Vincent's recommendations, Byrnes' proposal that Chiang take a few Communists into his cabinet suggests that his understanding of China's internal
problems was no more sophisticated than Truman's. Secretive, erratic,
and at times even devious, Byrnes had managed to alienate most of official
Washington by the time of the Moscow conference.

The decision to send Marshall to China with instructions to support
Chiang signaled Truman's rejection of the Byrnes-Vincent demarche in
favor of one last effort to save his China policy. As Ernest May has
suggested, the Marshall mission was Truman's way of getting the China
problem off his desk.[4] But it also indicated that the President was still as
committed to seeing China unified under Chiang as he had been when he
first decided to send troops into north China and Dairen.

Truman was also unwilling to abandon his objective of a unified Korea
free of Russian influence. American troops had been rushed onto the
peninsula to prevent Korea from becoming the East Asian equivalent of
Poland. As late as January 1946, he was unwilling to see Korea permanently
partitioned. Given the developing Cold War between the two powers,
however, a divided Korea was almost a foregone conclusion. Here American officials in Korea were probably ahead of their colleagues in Washington. In urging the creation of a provisional government for the south,

Hodge and Langdon tacitly conceded the north to the Soviets. For them the thirty-eigth parallel had become a containment line.[5]

During the next two years the Truman administration remained consistent in its postwar objectives for China and Korea. By the end of 1947, however, it became clear that the administration's policy of limited intervention could not produce unified noncommunist states in either country. Gradually the United States withdrew its troops from the mainland. The ambitious plans of the immediate postwar period gave way to a more circumspect defensive strategy anchored on the island chains of the western Pacific. This defensive perimeter concept was part of an effort to develop a closer correspondence between ends and means in American East Asian policy.

Despite the apparent departure from previous policies that this strategy entailed, a degree of continuity existed between the immediate postwar period and the uncertain years of 1947–1950. The JCS continued to believe, as they had in 1945, that with the proper assistance and supervision the KMT could defeat their Communist adversary. Even after American troops withdrew from China and Korea, it became difficult to politically disengage the United States from the mainland. The extent to which the administration was committed to the KMT and south Korea was the subject of ongoing debate as late as June 1950.

In his seminal study of the Cold War in Asia, Akira Iriye has observed that prior to the Korean War the international setting in East Asia came very near to resembling the system envisioned in the Yalta agreements. In effect Iriye suggests that because the United States and the Soviet Union had protected their primary interests in the region, the Cold War developed more slowly in East Asia than it did in Europe and the Middle East.[6]

It is doubtful, however, that Truman would have agreed with this assessment. Truman perceived the postwar balance in East Asia as resulting from a "land grab stampede" in which the Soviets had beaten the United States off the mark. As his own comments on the subject suggest, Soviet transgressions in Northeast Asia disturbed Truman more than historians may have realized. By the end of 1945 most American officials saw Soviet meddling as the major cause of the administration's problems in East Asia, as well as in Europe and the Middle East. By that time, the Truman administration's response to the outstanding problems in Asia exhibited many of the features that would characterize American foreign policy in the Cold War. Minimizing the regional causes of the spreading strife in Asia, administration officials came to perceive nearly all Leftist revolutions on the mainland as Soviet inspired and controlled.[7] Negotiations and compromise were taken as a sign of weakness; criticism of American policy was seen as disloyalty or worse. A significant feature of American Cold War diplomacy, the militarization of foreign policy, was also under way by early 1946. Although a regional strategy for defending American interests was slow to develop, postwar military assistance to China and Korea had already begun. Indochina would not lag far behind.[8]

This is not to say that American involvement in the undeclared wars in Korea and Vietnam was predestined by the decisions made in 1945. There were numerous opportunities along the way to reassess American policy and choose another course. How and why the United States became involved in those conflicts will continue to be the subject of historical inquiry for years to come. Insofar as this book has been concerned primarily with beginnings, it has attempted to show only how the United States got started down that path. For the Truman administration, the Cold War did not emerge separately in East Asia; rather it grew out of a larger series of frustrations that began with the fall of the Japanese empire.

Notes

1. Weighing the Options: Truman and the Russians

1. 25 May 45, Eben Ayers Diary, Ayers Papers, Harry S. Truman Library, Independence, Mo. (hereafter cited as HST Library).
2. Robert J. Donovan, *Conflict and Crisis*, pp. 4–5.
3. Richard F. Haynes, *The Awesome Power*, p. 28; Robert Goralski, *World War II Almanac*, p. 397.
4. Robert Dallek, *Franklin D. Roosevelt and American Foreign Policy*, p. 534; John Lewis Gaddis, *The United States and the Origins of the Cold War*, p. 94. In contrast, Warren Kimball argues that despite the post-Yalta problems, FDR maintained his conciliatory approach toward the Russians. Kimball, "Naked Reverse Right, Roosevelt, Churchill, and Eastern Europe from TOLSTOY to Yalta—and a Little Beyond," *Diplomatic History* (Winter 1985), 9:22–23.
5. Robert Messer, *The End of an Alliance*, pp. 56–57, 80–84; Ralph B. Levering, *American Opinion and the Russian Alliance*, pp. 200–209.
6. Gaddis, *Origins of the Cold War*, pp. 163–164; Daniel Yergin, *Shattered Peace*, p. 63.
7. Gaddis, *Origins of the Cold War*, pp. 161–163; Dallek, *Franklin D. Roosevelt and American Foreign Policy*, pp. 513–516.
8. *United States Relations with China: With Special Reference to the Period 1944–1949*, pp. 113–114.
9. *Ibid.*
10. *Ibid.*
11. *Ibid.*
12. John J. Sbrega, *Anglo-American Relations and Colonialism in East Asia*, pp. 145–148; Christopher Thorne, *Allies of a Kind*, pp. 631–632.
13. James I. Matray, "An End to Indifference: American Korean Policy During World War II," *Diplomatic History* (Spring 1978), 2:181; William George Morris, "The Korean Trusteeship," pp. 69–77; Stephen Pelz, "U.S. Decisions on Korean Policy, 1943–1950: Some Hypotheses," in Bruce Cumings, ed., *Child of Conflict*, p. 99.

14. Roosevelt-Stalin Meeting, 8 Feb. 45, FRUS (Foreign Relations of the United States): Malta and Yalta, p. 770.

15. U.S. Department of Defense, The Entry of the Soviet Union Into the War Against Japan, p. 43.

16. Presumably, the other two "evils" were that the Russians might stay out of the war completely, not a likely possibility, or that they would wait until the American invasion of the home islands had progressed far enough to make the task of cleaning out Manchuria a relatively easy one. Robert William Love, Jr., "Ernest Joseph King," in Love, ed., The Chiefs of Naval Operations, pp. 176–177.

17. W. Averell Harriman and Elie Abel, Special Envoy to Churchill and Stalin, pp. 398–399.

18. Dorothy Borg and Waldo H. Heinrichs, Jr., Uncertain Years, pp. 4–6; Michael Schaller, The U.S. Crusade in China, p. 209.

19. Quoted in Gary May, China Scapegoat, p. 122. During the fall of 1944 Roosevelt had George Elsey, a White House aide, prepare a defense of the administration's China policy in case Chiang's government collapsed under the weight of the Japanese offensive. Dallek, Franklin D. Roosevelt and American Foreign Policy, pp. 500–501.

20. The most complete description of the State Department's planning apparatus can be found in Harley Notter, Postwar Foreign Policy Preparation. The changing committee structure and the evolution of postwar policy for Japan is analyzed in Hugh Borton, "American Presurrender Planning for Postwar Japan"; Marlene J. Mayo, "American Wartime Planning for Occupied Japan: The Role of Experts," in Robert J. Wolfe, ed., Americans as Proconsuls. Postwar planning for the Asian mainland is analyzed in Marc S. Gallicchio, "American East Asian Policy and the Fall of the Japanese Empire," Ph.D. dissertation, Temple University, Philadelphia, 1985, pp. 1–41.

21. "Outline of Long-Range Objectives and Policies of the U.S. with Respect to China" and "Unity of Anglo-American-Soviet Policy Toward China," in FRUS: Yalta, pp. 356–358, 352–354.

22. "Inter-Allied Consultation Regarding Korea," FRUS: Yalta, pp. 358–361; Matray, "An End to Indifference," pp. 193–195; Cumings, The Origins of the Korean War, pp. 114–115.

23. "Japan: Territorial Problems: The Kurile Islands," FRUS: Yalta, pp. 379–380.

24. Gaddis, Origins of the Cold War, pp. 86–87; Martin J. Sherwin, A World Destroyed, pp. 104–105.

25. Ernest R. May, "Lessons" of the Past, p. 20; Yergin, Shattered Peace, pp. 79, 86; Sherwin, A World Destroyed, p. 179.

26. Thomas Paterson notes the changes in diplomatic style between FDR and Truman in On Every Front, pp. 92–112; Yergin suggests that Truman's diplomacy was influenced by his perception of the Soviet Union as a "world bully" (Shattered Peace, p. 73). Messer views Truman's domestic political experience as the major influence on his diplomacy (The End of an Alliance, pp. 71–93). See also John Gaddis, "Harry S. Truman and the Origins of

Containment," in Frank T. Merli and Theodore A. Wilson, eds., *The Makers of American Diplomacy: Benjamin Franklin to Henry Kissinger,* pp. 493–522.

27. The idea for the Hopkins mission apparently originated with Harriman and Charles Bohlen, a Soviet specialist in the State Department. Donovan, *Conflict and Crisis,* p. 55; Charles Bohlen, *Witness to History,* pp. 215–216; Harriman and Abel, *Special Envoy,* p. 459. According to Truman, the idea of sending Hopkins to Moscow occurred to the President and Harriman at about the same time. Harry S. Truman, *Memoirs,* pp. 110, 329, 257–258. But as evidence for this assertion Truman used an incorrectly dated memo of a conversation with Davies. In his memoirs this memo is dated 30 Apr. 45 (p. 110), but the actual document is dated 22 May 45 in Truman's Longhand Notes, President's Secretary's Files, Truman Papers, HST Library. See also Robert Ferrell, *Off the Record,* pp. 31, 35; and Dwight William Tuttle, *Harry L. Hopkins and Anglo-American-Soviet Relations,* p. 275n. 26.

28. Hurley to Truman, 10 May 45, *FRUS 1945,* 7:865.

29. Harriman and Abel, *Special Envoy,* pp. 428–431, 447–450; Donovan, *Conflict and Crisis,* pp. 37–38; Lynn Etheridge Davis, *The Cold War Begins,* pp. 117–118.

30. Harriman and Abel, *Special Envoy,* pp. 461–462.

31. Memorandum between Joseph Grew and Edward Stettinius, 12 May 45, Joseph Grew papers, Harvard University, Cambridge, Mass.

32. On Grew's life and career, see Waldo H. Heinrichs, Jr., *American Ambassador.*

33. Joseph C. Grew, *Turbulent Era,* 2:1442.

34. Grew to Forrestal, 12 May 45, *FRUS 1945,* 7:869–870.

35. *Ibid.*

36. *Ibid.*

37. 14 and 15 May 45, Henry Stimson Diary (microfilm), Henry Lewis Stimson Papers, Yale University, New Haven, Conn. Minutes of the Committee of Three, 15 May 45, NNFD Reference File, Diplomatic Branch, National Archives, Washington, D.C. (hereafter cited as DB, NA). This is an artificial collection created by the archivists. There is no single complete set of Committee of Three minutes. Copies of the minutes have been taken from other collections and compiled in the Diplomatic Branch.

38. Henry L. Stimson and McGeorge Bundy, *On Active Service in Peace and War,* pp. 220–263; William Kamman, "Henry L. Stimson: Republican Internationalist," in Merli and Wilson, eds., *Makers of American Diplomacy,* pp. 103–126.

39. 14 May 45, Stimson Diary; Martin J. Sherwin, *A World Destroyed,* pp. 167–170, 188–192.

40. 16 May 45, Stimson Diary; Mark Paul, "Diplomacy Delayed: The Atomic Bomb and the Division of Korea," in Cumings, ed., *Child of Conflict,* pp. 73–74.

41. Paul, "Diplomacy Delayed," pp. 74–75.

42. Memorandum for the Acting Secretary of State, 21 May 45, ABC 336 Russia (22 Aug. 43), sec. 3, RG165, Records of the Army General and Special Staffs, Modern Military Records Branch, National Archives, Washington, D.C. (hereafter cited as MMRB, NA).

43. *Ibid.*

44. 18 May 45, James Forrestal Manuscript Diaries, Forrestal Papers, Princeton University Library, Princeton, N.J.

45. Memorandum for the Chief of Staff, 8 Mar.45, ABC 384 USSR (25–9–44), sec. 1-B, RG165, MMRB, NA.

46. Robert F. Sherwood, *Roosevelt and Hopkins,* pp. 887–916.

47. Gaddis, *Origins of the Cold War,* pp. 234–235.

48. Sherwood, *Roosevelt and Hopkins,* pp. 902–903; Harriman and Abel, *Special Envoy,* pp. 472–473; Harriman to Truman, 8 June 45, *FRUS: Potsdam,* pp. 61–62.

49. 1 June 45, Presidential Diaries, Henry Morganthau Papers, Franklin D. Roosevelt Library, Hyde Park, New York.

50. 6 and 7 June 45, Diary of Eben Ayers, Ayers Papers, HST Library.

51. 6 June 45, Stimson Diary.

52. *Ibid.*

53. *Ibid.*

54. 25 May 45, Ayers Diary, HST Library.

55. A copy of the Yalta agreements as described by Harriman was kept in a safe in the War Department. See "Yalta Agreement (Russia in the Far East)," ABC 336 Russia (22 Aug. 43), sec. 3, RG165, MMRB, NA; Minutes of the Committee of Three, 15 May 45, DB, NA.

56. Memorandum for the Secretary of War and the Secretary of the Navy, from John J. McCloy, 10 June 45, Forrestal Manuscript Diaries; 10 June 45, McCloy Diary, Copies in Rudolph Winnaker—Supporting Manuscripts for unpublished history of the Office of Secretary of War, RG319, MMRB, NA.

57. Ferrell, *Off the Record,* pp. 46–47.

58. Grace P. Hayes, *The History of the Joint Chiefs of Staff,* pp. 701–707; Russell F. Weigley, *The American Way of War,* p. 281.

59. Minutes of White House Conference, 18 June 45, *FRUS: Potsdam,* 1:903–910; Hayes, *The History of the Joint Chiefs of Staff,* p. 707. The Army Air Force's position is described in memorandum, 16 June–24 June 45, Trip to Pacific, box 272, Henry H. Arnold Papers, Library of Congress.

60. Minutes of the White House Conference, 18 June 45, *FRUS: Potsdam,* 1:903–910.

61. John J. McCloy interview with author, 2 Aug. 84.

62. *Ibid.* See also John J. McCloy, *The Challenge to American Foreign Policy,* p. 42; Millis, *The Forrestal Diaries,* p. 70; John J. McCloy, Oral History, John Foster Dulles Papers, Princeton.

63. Raymond G. O'Connor, *Diplomacy for Victory,* pp. 38, 49–53; Brian Villa, "The U.S. Army and Unconditional Surrender," pp. 69–70.

64. Mayo, "Wartime Planning for Japan," pp. 42–44; Villa, "The U.S. Army and Unconditional Surrender," pp. 70–72.

65. Japanese Reaction to German Defeat, 21 May 45, for COMINCH & CNO, SRH-075 (Special Research History), RG457, MMRB, NA. These SRH reports are based on deciphered Japanese communications.
66. Villa, "The U.S. Army and Unconditional Surrender," p. 78.
67. Mayo, "Wartime Planning for Japan," pp. 42–44; David S. McLellan and David C. Acheson, eds., *Among Friends*, p. 55. Opposition within the State Department to modifying unconditional surrender can be followed in the minutes of the Secretary's Staff Committee, especially 26, 28, and 29 May 45, RG353, Records of Interdepartmental and Intradepartmental Committees (State Department), DB, NA.
68. The President's message is reprinted in *Department of State Bulletin*, 13 May 45, p. 886.
69. Villa, "The U.S. Army and Unconditional Surrender," pp. 85–86.
70. McCloy did not share Stimson's view that the proclamation would have to be coupled with a demonstration of force to be effective. John J. McCloy interview with author, 2 Aug. 84.
71. Villa, "The U.S. Army and Unconditional Surrender," p. 87. Ultimately the United States suffered staggering losses in the fight for Okinawa. Over 4,900 sailors were killed or missing in action and 4,824 were wounded. The Army lost 7,613 killed and 31,807 wounded. A total of 36 ships were sunk and another 368 damaged. Samuel Eliot Morison, *History of United States Naval Operations in World War II*, 14:282.
72. Alan Brinkley, "Minister Without Portfolio."
73. *Ibid;* pp. 33–34. The quotation is from McCloy interview with author, 2 Aug. 1984.
74. Villa, "The U.S. Army and Unconditional Surrender," p. 68; Ray S. Cline, *Washington Command Post*, pp. 205–206.
75. Memorandum for Stimson from McCloy, 29 June 45, ABC 387 Japan (15 Feb. 45), sec. 1-B, RG165, MMRB, NA. In the same file, see also Memorandum for General Hull from Lincoln, 30 June 45; Colonel Bonesteel to Lincoln, 1 July 45, with attached draft proclamation.
76. Villa, "The U.S. Army and Unconditional Surrender," p. 87; Heinrichs, *American Ambassador*, p. 377.
77. Millis, *The Forrestal Diaries*, p. 73.

2. Ends and Means: Postwar Policy and Military Strategy on the Eve of Potsdam

1. JWPC 356/1/m, 23 May 45, CCS 092 Asia (5–11–45), RG218 (Records of the Combined Chiefs of Staff), MMRB, NA.
2. Dallek, *Franklin D. Roosevelt and American Foreign Policy*, pp. 499–502.
3. Truman's comment was made during an interview with Dean Acheson. Interviews with Dean Acheson, 17 Feb. 1955, Interviews with Associates, Post-Presidential Memoirs, HST Papers.
4. Ernest R. May, *The Truman Administration and China*, p. 6.

5. Hurley to Secretary of State, 9 June 45, *FRUS 1945*, 7:406–410.

6. *Ibid.*

7. May, *China Scapegoat*, pp. 126–127.

8. *Ibid.*, pp. 120–121.

9. Drumright to Joseph Ballantine, 16 June 45, 893.00/6–1645, RG59, DB, NA; and Drumright to Ballantine, 28 June 45, 893.00/6–2845, RG59, DB, NA.

10. Minutes of the Interdivisional Area Committee on the Far East (IDACFE), 31 May 45, Papers of the Policy and Planning Committee, Harley Notter Papers, RG59, DB, NA.

11. Grew to Truman, w/enclosure: Policy with Respect to China, 27 Apr. 45, Cabinet-State (Stettinius), PSF-Subject File, HST Papers.

12. *Ibid.* See also Thorne, *Allies of a Kind*, pp. 567–569.

13. Hurley to Secretary of State, 23 June 45, 893.00/6–2345, RG59, DB, NA.

14. Memorandum of Conversation, by the Acting Secretary of State, 9 June 45, *FRUS 1945*, 7:896.

15. Memorandum of Conversation, by the Acting Secretary of State, 11 June 45, *FRUS 1945*, 7:898–900.

16. Hurley to the Secretary of State, 15 June 45, *FRUS 1945*, 5:903–904; Russell D. Buhite, *Soviet-American Relations in Asia*, pp. 19–21.

17. Harriman to Truman and Grew, 1–3 July 45, *FRUS 1945*, 5:910–914.

18. Byrnes to Harriman, 4 July 45, *FRUS 1945*, 5, 914–915.

19. The presence in the United States of Korean exiles strongly opposed to any postwar arrangement other than immediate independence made it necessary to keep American plans secret. At the UN conference Stettinius stated that "the question of Korea was an extremely private matter and should not be mentioned outside the delegation." Minutes of the 5th meeting of the U.S. delegation, 30 May 45, *FRUS 1945*, 1:974–975. See also Charles Dobbs, *The Unwanted Symbol*, pp. 19–20; and Cumings, *The Origins of the Korean War*, p. 116.

20. Dobbs, *The Unwanted Symbol*, pp. 17–18.

21. Pelz, "U.S. Decisions on Korean Policy, 1943–1950: Some Hypotheses," in Cumings, ed., *Child of Conflict*, p. 111.

22. Kennan to Secretary of State, 17 Apr. 45, *FRUS 1945*, 6:1026–1027; Grew to Stimson, 28, June 45, w/enclosure, An Estimate of Conditions in Asia. . . . At the Close of the War . . . *FRUS 1945*, 6:563; Dobbs, *The Unwanted Symbol*, p. 23; Cumings, *The Origins of the Korean War*, pp. 116–117.

23. Colonel Donovan to the President, 23 June 45, OSS Reports to White House, Apr.–Sept. 1945, William Donovan Papers, Military History Institute, Carlisle Barracks, Carlisle, Pa. (hereafter cited as MHI).

24. Minutes of the Committee of Three, 15 May 45, Papers of the Committee of Three, DB, NA.

25. Quoted in James I. Matray, "Captive of the Cold War" 50:156.

26. Quoted in Thorne, *Allies of a Kind*, p. 599.

27. *Ibid.*

28. The departmental reorganization is described in *Department of State Bulletin*, 15 Jan. 44, 10:56. The differing views of the Asianists and European specialists are described in "Statement of Abott Low Moffat," U.S. Congress, Senate Committee on Foreign Relations, *Causes, Origins, and Consequences of the Vietnam War*, pp. 160–168; Martin Weil, *A Pretty Good Club*, pp. 148–149; and M. Hall to Grew, 30 May 44, 890.0146/5–3044, State Department Decimal Files, RG59, DB, NA.

29. Thorne, *Allies of a Kind*, pp. 630–631; Dallek, *Franklin D. Roosevelt and American Foreign Policy*, p. 512.

30. George C. Herring, "The Truman Administration and Indochina," 1:101–104.

31. Truman, *Memoirs*, pp. 14–15.

32. Grew to Ambassador in France, 9 May 45, *FRUS 1945*, 6:307.

33. Grew to Stimson, 28 June 45, w/enclosure, An Estimate of Conditions in Asia. . . . At the Close of the War . . . , *FRUS 1945*, 6:567–568.

34. During a SWNCC meeting H. Freeman Matthews, the State Department representative, raised the question of "whether it is politically wise to support their [French and Dutch troops] use for liberation." Matthews was concerned about having this objective explicitly written into a State Department memorandum to the JCS. Minutes of the 19th meeting of SWNCC, 18 June 45, SWNCC Minutes, SWNCC Papers (microfilm), DB, NA.

35. United States Postwar Military Policies with Respect to China, 3 Apr. 45, OPD 336.2, TS (29 May 45) fw. 24, case 24/3 (Top Secret files of the Operations and Plans Division), RG165, MMRB, NA; Thorne, *Allies of a Kind*, p. 549.

36. Thorne, *Allies of a Kind*, pp. 557–558.

37. Directive: Politico-Military Problems Far East: Treatment by U.S. Occupation Forces of Special Areas: Hong Kong, SWNCC 111/D, 14 May 45, Papers for SWNCC Far Eastern Subcommittee, SWNCC Papers (microfilm), DB, NA.

38. Grew to Hurley, 7 June 45, 851G.00/6–745, RG59, NA.

39. Report by the Special Assistant to the Assistant Secretary of State, SWNCC 111/1, 14 May 45; Draft Report by Far Eastern Subcommittee, 14 June 45; Report by the Joint Civil Affairs Committee, 2 July 45; all in CCS 092, Hong Kong–China (4–17–45), RG218 (Records of the Combined Chiefs of Staff), MMRB, NA.

40. Ferrell, *Off the Record*, p. 39.

41. Hayes, *The History of the Joint Chiefs of Staff*, p. 711; Charles F. Romanus and Riley Sunderland, *Time Runs Out in CBI*, pp. 360–363.

42. 16 May 45, Stimson Diary, Henry Lewis Stimson Papers, Yale University, New Haven, Conn.

43. Grew to Stimson, 22 May 45, w/enclosures, 890.01/5–2245, RG59, DB, NA; Grew to Stettinius, 18 May 45, *FRUS 1945*, 7:1485.

44. U.S. Post-War Military Policy in the Far East, n.d., OPD Executive Files, Exec. 5, Item 21a, RG165, MMRB, NA.

45. *Ibid*. This report was probably approved by Lincoln as it included a copy of a memo entitled "General Lincoln's 12 Points." This was a list of points for

postwar peace in East Asia. A copy can also be found in Japan folder, Stimson (Safe File), July 1940–September 1945, RG107 (Office of the Secretary of War), MMRB, NA.

46. Memorandum for Chief of Staff, n.d., CCS 334 Joint Chiefs of Staff (2–2–45), RG218, MMRB, NA.
47. Korea (Implications of Quadripartite Trusteeship), OPD Executive Files, Exec. 5, Item 21a, RG165, MMRB, NA.
48. *Ibid.*
49. Memorandum for General Lincoln, 6 July 45, w/enclosure, Control of Japan, OPD, 014.1, TS, sec. 3, case 47, RG165, MMRB, NA.
50. *Ibid.*
51. William Roger Louis, *Imperialism at Bay,* pp. 475–496.
52. U.S. Policy with Regard to Indo-China, OPD Executive Files, Exec. 5, Item 21a, RG165, MMRB, NA.
53. Herring, "The Truman Administration and Indochina," p. 109; Memorandum by the Acting Secretary of State to Truman, 16 May 45, *FRUS 1945,* 6:307–308. The JCS did not give their final approval on the use of French troops until the Potsdam conference.
54. Marcel Vigneras, *Rearming the French,* p. 398; Hayes, *The History of the Joint Chiefs of Staff,* pp. 716–717.
55. Ronald Spector, "Allied Intelligence and Indochina."
56. Vigneras, *Rearming the French,* p. 398; Sbrega, *Anglo-American Relations,* pp. 118–120.
57. Herring, "The Truman Administration and Indochina," p. 106.
58. James F. Schnabel, *The History of the Joint Chiefs of Staff: The JCS and National Policy,* p. 4.
59. Strategic Positions Selected for Occupation Upon Japanese Withdrawal, Collapse, or Surrender, JWPC 264/1, CCS 386.2 Japan (4–9–45), sec. 2, RG218, MMRB, NA.
60. Colonel Max Johnson to Chief, S&P, 23 May 45, ABC 384.1 Japan (22 Aug. 45), RG165, MMRB, NA.
61. *Ibid.*
62. Minutes of the 204th meeting of JSP, 30 May 45, CCS 386.2 Japan (4–9–45), sec. 2, RG218, MMRB, NA.
63. Occupation of Japan and Japanese Held Territory . . . , JWPC 375/2, 28 June 45, ABC 014 Japan (13 Apr. 44), sec. 16-A, RG165, MMRB, NA.
64. Discussion of JWPC 375/2 by J. E. Hull, ca. 6 July 45, ABC 387 Japan (15 Feb. 45), sec. 1-B, RG165, MMRB, NA.
65. Cline, *Washington Command Post,* p. 350; Lincoln's comments are in Minutes of the 208th meeting of JSP, 20 June 45, CCS 334 Joint Staff Planners (3–28–45), RG218, MMRB, NA.
66. Timing of Proposed Demand for Japanese Surrender, 29 June 45, ABC 387 Japan (15 Feb. 45), sec. 1-B, RG165, MMRB, NA.
67. *Ibid.*
68. *Ibid.*

69. Occupation of Strategic Areas of Japanese Empire, n.d., OPD Executive Files, Exec. 5, Item 21a, RG165, MMRB, NA.
70. U.S. Postwar Military Policy in the Far East, n.d., *ibid*.
71. *Ibid*.
72. *Ibid*.
73. Admiral Charles M. Cooke, "We Planned It That Way," (unpublished manuscript, n.d.), p. 23, Command File WWII, Navy History Center, Operational Archives, Washington, D.C.
74. 18 May 45, Forrestal Manuscript Diaries, Forrestal Papers, Princeton University Library, Princeton, N.J.
75. Memorandum for General Hull from Lincoln, 21 May 45, ABC 336 Russia (22 Aug. 43), sec. 3, RG165, MMRB, NA.
76. Schaller, *The U.S. Crusade in China*, pp. 231–250.
77. Lovett to McCloy, 5 Feb. 45, ASW 334.8, RG107 (Records of the Assistant Secretary of War—McCloy), MMRB, NA. "By planning to make readily available at very low prices airplanes and engines the United States can create a demand for these which will materially eliminate for some years construction of airplanes and engine factories in China, and forestall competition from other nations." Postwar Military Policy w/Respect to China, 25 Apr. 45, SWNCC 83/D, SWNCC Papers, DB, NA.
78. Colonel Gordon K. Pickler, "United States Aid to the Chinese Nationalist Air Force, 1931–1949," Ph.D. dissertation, Florida State University, 1971, pp. 281–285.

3. Potsdam: Truman Takes Charge

1. Robert Ferrell, ed., *Dear Bess: The Letters from Harry to Bess Truman, 1910–1959* (New York: 1983), p. 522.
2. Truman, *Memoirs*, p. 331.
3. Donovan, *Conflict and Crisis*, p. 72.
4. Ferrell, *Off the Record*, pp. 348–349.
5. Messer, *The End of an Alliance*, pp. 96–97; Bohlen, *Witness to History*, p. 226.
6. Henry D. Adams, *Witness to Power*, p. 59.
7. 25 June 44, 14 Aug. 45, 27 Oct. 45, Diary of William D. Leahy (microfilm), William D. Leahy Papers, Library of Congress, Washington, D.C.
8. Messer, *The End of an Alliance*, pp. 68–69.
9. Donovan, *Conflict and Crisis*, pp. 17–18.
10. "The President on His Way," *Time* (July 16, 1945), 50:3.
11. Messer, *The End of an Alliance*, pp. 68, 78–79.
12. *Ibid*., pp. 58–64.
13. George Elsey, interview with author, 8 Mar. 84. James F. Byrnes, *All in One Lifetime*, p. 268. See also Athan Theoharis, *The Yalta Myths* pp. 41–44.
14. For a different view, see Messer, *The End of an Alliance*, pp. 80, 101–103.

15. Martin Sherwin, *A World Destroyed*, p. 222.
16. 16 July 45, Joseph Davies Diary, Joseph Davies Papers, Library of Congress.
17. Sherwin, *A World Destroyed*, p. 223; Messer, *The End of an Alliance*, p. 86. Truman and Byrnes were concerned that the Manhattan Project would flop and they would have to explain the enormous expenditure of the taxpayers' money to an angry Congress.
18. Ferrell, *Off the Record*, p. 53.
19. 17 July 45, Stimson Diary, Yale University Library, New Haven, Conn.
20. Ferrell, *Dear Bess*, p. 519.
21. 17 July 45, Diary of William D. Leahy (microfilm), William D. Leahy Papers, Library of Congress, Washington, D.C.
22. Messer, *The End of an Alliance*, pp. 158–165.
23. Harriman to Truman and Byrnes, 9 July 45, *FRUS 1945*, 6:924–926.
24. 17, 18 July 45, Stimson Diary; Paul, "Diplomacy Delayed: The Atomic Bomb and the Division of Korea," in Cumings, ed., *The Child of Conflict*, pp. 81–82.
25. 18 July 45, Stimson Diary; Sherwin, *A World Destroyed*, pp. 222–223.
26. Ferrell, *Off the Record*, pp. 53–54.
27. Donovan, *Conflict and Crisis*, pp. 80–86; Davis, *The Cold War Begins*, pp. 288–298.
28. The full report appears in Sherwin, *A World Destroyed*, appendix P, pp. 308–314.
29. 21 July 45, Stimson Diary.
30. 22 July 45, Stimson Diary.
31. 23 July 45, Stimson Diary.
32. *Ibid*.
33. *Ibid*.
34. Ferrell, *Off the Record*, pp. 55–56.
35. John Ehrman, *Grand Strategy*, p. 255; John Terraine, *The Life and Times of Lord Mountbatten*, p. 125.
36. Matray, "Captive of the Cold War," p. 161.
37. Ferrell, *Off the Record*, p. 55.
38. *Ibid*., p. 56.
39. Matray, "Captive of the Cold War," p. 161.
40. This is also the view of Mark Paul, "Diplomacy Delayed," p. 83.
41. Truman to Hurley, 23 July 45, *FRUS 1945*, 7:950; Donovan, *Conflict and Crisis*, p. 94; Ehrman, *Grand Strategy*, p. 292.
42. 25 July 45, Walter Brown's Book, folder 602, James F. Byrnes Papers, Clemson University, Clemson, S.C.
43. Millis, *The Forrestal Diaries*, p. 78.
44. 26 July 45, Walter Brown's Book, Byrnes Papers; Donovan, *Conflict and Crisis*, p. 95.
45. Grew to Byrnes, 16 July 45, Grew Papers.
46. Memorandum of telephone conversation, 17 July 45, Grew Papers: Hull, *Memoirs*, 2:1593–1594.

47. 17 July 45, Stimson Diary.
48. Memorandum of telephone conversation, 17 July 45, Grew Papers.
49. Grew to Truman, Byrnes, and Leahy, 30 June 45, w/enclosures, *FRUS: Potsdam*, 1:198–199, 884.
50. *Ibid.*
51. 7, 9 July 45, Minutes of the Secretary's Staff Committee, *FRUS: Potsdam*, 1:900–902.
52. Matthias F. Correa to Forrestal, 4 July 45; and E. J. King to JCS, 6 July 45, both in file 331–21, Box 65, Forrestal–Secretary of the Navy, RG80 (General Correspondence Secretary of the Navy), Old Army and Navy Branch, NA (hereafter cited as OANB).
53. Military Aspects of Unconditional Surrender Formula, JCS 1275/6, 19 July 45, w/enclosure, ABC 387 Japan (15 Feb. 45), sec. 1-B, RG165, MMRB, NA.
54. *Ibid.*
55. Memorandum for General Handy from General Craig, 14 July 45, *Ibid.*; Mayo, "American Wartime Planning for Occupied Japan: The Role of Experts," in Wolfe, ed., *Americans as Proconsuls*, p. 44.
56. 17 July 45, JCS Minutes of Meeting, *FRUS: Potsdam*, 2:39.
57. Unpublished autobiography of Charles Donnelly, pp. 743–744, Charles H. Donnelly Papers, MHI. The navy's version of the minutes is in: Potsdam, "Terminal-Rough Notes," (F-07), Strategic Plans Division, box 69, series three, Navy Operational Archives, Naval History Center. It seems doubtful that the JSSC would have swayed Marshall had he been convined that the emperor question was vital to the success of the proclamation. The JSSC was not highly regarded by officers in the War Department. McCloy referred to it as "a planning group that didn't amount to much." Interview with author, 2 Aug. 84. See also Ernest R. May, "Writing Contemporary International History," *Diplomatic History* (Spring 1984), 8:111.
58. 17 July 45, JCS Minutes of Meeting, *FRUS: Potsdam*, 2:39.
59. Reports of the talks held on 10, 13, and 16 July are summarized in "Japanese Peace Talks in Berne," in MAGIC–Diplomatic Summaries, 23, 24 July 45, Intercepted Japanese Messages (Operation MAGIC), RG457, MMRB, NA (microfilm, reel 14). Some messages were sent immediately to Potsdam and thus could have been read before they appeared in the Diplomatic Summaries, although this is not certain. See Ronald Lewin, *The American MAGIC*, p. 282.
60. MAGIC—Diplomatic Summaries, 23, 24 July 45.
61. *Ibid.*
62. William Donovan to the White House, 18 July 45, OSS Reports to the White House, William Donovan Papers, MHI.
63. Summary of Message, 11 July 45, MAGIC–Diplomatic Summaries, Intercepted Japanese Messages (reel 14), RG457, MMRB, NA.
64. Summary of a message dated 5 June 45, in Proposed Peace Discussion in Berne, MAGIC–Diplomatic Summaries, Intercepted Japanese Messages (reel 14), RG457, MMRB, NA. Since Dulles was working through a third party it

is possible that he did not make the references to Russian entry into the war that were attributed to him in these reports. That is to say, either the third party or the Japanese may have embellished what was said. Dulles, of course, made no references to Russia in his reports to Washington.

65. Summary of message dated 22 July 45, in Japanese Navy Orders Berne Official to Withdraw from Peace Negotiations, MAGIC–Diplomatic Summaries, 28 July 45, Intercepted Messages (reel 14), RG457, MMRB, NA.

66. Ferrell, *Off the Record*, p. 53; Donovan, *Conflict and Crisis*, p. 92

67. John A. Harrison, "The USSR, Japan, and the End of the Great Pacific War," *Parameters* (Summer 1984), 14:82–84; Lewin, *The American MAGIC*, pp. 280–282.

68. "Big Three Asked To Tell Foe Price of Peace," *New York Times*, July 12, 1945, p. 3.

69. "Terms To End War Urged on Truman," *New York Times*, July 23, 1945.

70. McCloy says he was aware of Allen Dulles' activities in Berne. McCloy interview with author, 2 Aug. 45. See also Memorandum for Stimson from McCloy, 29 June 45, ABC 387 Japan (15 Feb. 45), sec. 1-B, RG165, MMRB, NA.

71. "Japan Warned To Give Up Soon," *New York Times*, July 22, 1945, p. 1.

72. "Truman Approved Warning to Japan," *New York Times*, July 23, 1945, p. 5. Grew doubted that the *Times'* story was correct. Grew to Dunn, 24 July 45, Grew Papers.

73. Forrestal to Assistant Secretary of the Navy, 28 July 45, General Correspondence, file 95–3–14; and E. S. Duffield to Edward Barrett, 24 July 45, General Correspondence, file 56–11–35; both in Forrestal-Secretary, RG80, OANB, NA.

74. Gabriel Kolko, *The Politics of War*, p. 564.

75. 23 July 45, Stimson Diary.

76. 24 July 45, Stimson Diary.

77. *Ibid.*

78. *Ibid.*

79. Proclamation Defining Terms for Japanese, *Department of State Bulletin*, 29 July 45, 13:137–138.

80. *Ibid.*

81. *Ibid.*

82. Robert J. C. Butow, *Japan's Decision to Surrender*, pp. 143–146.

83. *Ibid.*

84. *Ibid.*, p. 148.

85. *Ibid.*, p. 149.

86. Donovan, *Conflict and Crisis*, p. 96.

87. Gar Alperovitz, *Atomic Diplomacy: Hiroshima and Potsdam: The Use of the Atomic Bomb and the American Confrontation with Soviet Power* (New York: 1965), pp. 184–187, 239–240. Alperovitz repeats this argument in a new introduction to the revised edition of *Atomic Diplomacy*. See Alperovitz, *Atomic Diplomacy* (expanded and updated edition), pp. 52–53.

88. Lisle Rose, *Dubious Victory*, pp. 326–334; and Lisle Rose, *After Yalta* (New York: 1973), p. 82.

89. Kolko, *The Politics of War,* pp. 564–565.
90. McCloy to Stimson, 29 June 45, ABC 387 Japan (15 Feb. 45), sec. 1-B, RG165 MMRB, NA.
91. Summary of Message, Sato to Togo, 16 July 45, Intercepted Japanese Messages, MAGIC–Diplomatic Summaries (reel 14), RG457, MMRB, NA; Ronald Spector, *Eagle Against the Sun,* p. 549. Given this and other messages indicating confusion in Tokyo and the military's reluctance to accept an occupation of Japan, it is hard to credit Alperovitz's assertion that "it is very clear that well before atomic weapons were used, both the Japanese and U.S. governments had arrived at the same understanding of acceptable terms of surrender." Alperovitz, *Atomic Diplomacy* (expanded and updated edition), p. 30.
92. 26 July 45, Leahy Diary.
93. Ferrell, *Off the Record,* p. 56. It is also possible that Truman believed that with all the speculation and discussion taking place in the United States, and with Dulles' meetings at Berne, the Japanese would be able to read between the lines and understand that the emperor would not be harmed.
94. Matray, "Captive of the Cold War," pp. 156, 159–161; Paul, "Diplomacy Delayed," p. 84.
95. Grace P. Hayes, *The History of the Joint Chiefs of Staff,* pp. 720–721; John R. Deane, *Strange Alliance,* pp. 268–275.

4. Final Preparations

1. Robert J. Wood Oral History Interview, p. 29, Senior Officers Debriefing Program, MHI.
2. MacArthur expected to use 22 2/3 divisions to occupy Japan in force. MacArthur to War Department, 27 July 45, CCS 386.2 Japan (4–9–45), sec. 3, RG218, MMRB, NA.
3. Brief of BLACKLIST, 11 July 45, ABC 387 Japan (15 Feb. 45), sec. 1-B, RG165, MMRB, NA.
4. *Ibid.*
5. JCS to MacArthur and Nimitz [22 July 45], Terminal Messages, box 19, Double Zero 1941–1950, Chief of Naval Operations, NOA, NHC.
6. I have not found a copy in the Truman Papers, but Lincoln recalled that Marshall presented a similar paper at Truman at Potsdam. Lincoln to Charles Donnelly, n.d, "Comments on OPD Manuscripts," box 372, 2–3–7 Washington Command Post (Supporting Papers), RG319, MMRB, NA; and Lincoln to Colonel Roberts, w/enclosure, Memorandum for the President, 25 July 45, OPD Executive Files, Exec. File 2, Item 11, RG165, MMRB, NA.
7. *Ibid.*
8. *Ibid.*
9. *Ibid.*
10. *Ibid.*
11. *Ibid.*

12. *Ibid*.

13. JCS to MacArthur, Victory 295, 25 July 45, CCS 386.2 Japan (4–9–45), sec. 3, RG218, MMRB, NA.

14. *Ibid*.

15. JCS to MacArthur and Nimitz, Victory 357, 26 July 45, ABC 387 Japan (15 Feb. 45), sec. 3, RG165, MMRB, NA; Morison, *History of United States Naval Operations in World War II*, pp. 353–354; Paul Varg, *The Closing of the Door*, p. 208.

16. JCS to MacArthur and Nimitz, Victory 357, 26 July 45, ABC 387 Japan (15 Feb. 45), sec. 3, RG165, MMRB, NA.

17. Quoted in Morison, *History of United States Naval Operations in World War II*, p. 354. MacArthur's views were summarized in Memorandum for the Chief of Staff, 1 Aug. 45, OPD 014.1 TS, case 50/2, RG165 MMRB, NA. See also D. Clayton James, *The Years of MacArthur*, p. 771.

18. Marshall to General Handy, 29 July 45, ABC 387 Japan (15 Feb. 45), sec. 1-B, RG165, MMRB, NA.

19. *Ibid*. It is not clear whether these remarks were incldued in the message sent to MacArthur. Marshall's draft contained a request that General Handy, who was in Washington, edit the message in light of any information he might have received from the Pacific theater. In his oral history General Hull said that he often edited Marshall's messages to MacArthur to soften their tone. Handy may have done the same thing. See Hull, Oral History Interview, MHI.

20. *Ibid*., Marshall to Handy.

21. Quoted in Romanus and Sunderland, *Time Runs Out in CBI*, pp. 390–391.

22. *Ibid*., pp. 386–388.

23. *Ibid*., pp. 368–381.

24. *Ibid*., pp. 390–391.

25. William D. Leahy, *I Was There*, pp. 337–338.

26. Wedemeyer to War Department, 4 Aug. 45, OPD 336 TS, case 133, RG165, MMRB, NA.

27. Romanus and Sunderland, *Time Runs Out in CBI*, p. 395.

28. Lincoln to the Acting Chief of Staff, 28 Aug. 45, w/enclosure, Brief of Japanese Capitulation Plan Prepared in China Theater, OPD 014.1 TS, sec. 4, RG165, MMRB, NA.

29. *Ibid*.

30. Minutes of the CCS, 24 July 45, Rec.'s of the JCS, part I, Meetings of the JCS and CCS (reel 4), University Publications of America, Frederick, Md.

31. CCS 900/3, 24 July 45, *FRUS: Potsdam*, 2:1462–1473; S. Woodburn Kirby, *The War Against Japan*, pp. 224–225.

32. Kirby, *The Surrender of Japan*, pp. 224–225.

33. Hayes, *The History of the Joint Chiefs of Staff*, pp. 713–716.

34. Sbrega, *Anglo-American Relations*, p. 120.

35. Terraine, *Mountbatten*, p. 124.

36. Ehrman, *Grand Strategy*, p. 248.

37. Terraine, *Mountbatten*, p. 125.

38. Lewin, *The American MAGIC*, pp. 280–281.
39. George Lensen, *The Strange Neutrality*, pp. 156–158.
40. *Ibid.*; Lt. Col. David M. Glantz, *August Storm: The Soviet 1945 Strategic Offensive in Manchuria*, pp. 73, 185–186.
41. Harriman to Byrnes, 31 July 45, *FRUS 1945*, 7:953–954.
42. Byrnes to Harriman, 5 Aug. 45, *FRUS 1945*, 7:955–956.
43. Butow, *Japan's Decision to Surrender*, p. 151.
44. *Ibid.*, pp. 151–152.
45. *Ibid.*, pp. 153–154.
46. At the time of the Potsdam conference the JCS estimated that there were 930,000 Japanese troops in Manchuria and Korea, but these estimates said nothing about the possible readiness or quality of these units. Although the information on Korea was up-to-date, the latest intelligence on Manchuria dated from January 1945. See Plan for U.S. Occupation of Strategic Positions in the Far East in the Event of a Japanese Surrender, JWPC 264/6, 10 July 45, CCS 386.2 Japan (4–9–45), sec. 3, RG218; History of the Intelligence Group, Military Intelligence Service, part 2, p. 197, SRH-131, RG457, MMRB, NA; and Hull Oral History Interview, p. 9, MHI. On the weakness of the Kwantung army, see Louis Allen, *The End of the War in Asia*, pp. 194–195.
47. Lensen, *The Strange Neutrality*, pp. 159–161; Allen, *The End of the War in Asia*, p. 196.
48. Harriman to Byrnes, 8 Aug. 45, *FRUS 1945*, 7:958–959.
49. Byrnes to Harriman, 9 Aug. 45, *FRUS 1945*, 7:965–966.
50. Harriman to Byrnes, 10 Aug. 45, *FRUS 1945*, 7:967. In his message, Harriman recalled that at Potsdam the JCS had prepared contingency plans for emergency landings on the mainland. These plans were for use in the event that Japan surrendered *before* the Soviets entered the war. As will be seen, the JCS were not prepared to move American troops into what they perceived to be the Soviet area of operations. Estimate of U.S. Forces Required for Occupation of Strategic Positions Other Than in Japan in the Event of Sudden Collapse or Surrender, JWPC 264/5, CCS 386.2 Japan (4–9–45), sec. 3, RG218, MMRB, NA. Truman received a similar recommendation on August 11 from Edwin Pauley, American representative on the Allied Reparations Commission. Pauley, a California oil man and Democratic party fund-raiser, had been appointed by Truman. Matray, "Captive of the Cold War," p. 164.
51. Butow, *Japan's Decision to Surrender.* p. 174.
52. *Ibid.*, p. 176.
53. Wood says that Hull and Lincoln, both of whom knew about the bomb, did not believe that it would be powerful enough to end the war. Wood, Oral History Interview, p. 37, MHI.
54. Jay Luvaas, *Dear Miss Em*, p. 298.
55. *Ibid.*, pp. 298–299.
56. Bonesteel to Lincoln, 9 Aug. 45, ABC 387 Japan (15 Feb. 45), sec. 1-B, RG165, MMRB, NA.

57. *Ibid.*

58. Minutes of the IDACFE, 27 July 45, Records of the Policy and Planning Committees, Notter Papers, DB, NA; Memorandum Comparison of the Potsdam Proclamation of July 26, 1945, with the Policy of the Department of State [ca. 30 July 45], *FRUS: Potsdam*, 2:1284–1287.

59. Minutes of the IDACFE, 31 July and 1, 3 Aug. 45, Records of the Policy and Planning Committees, Notter Papers, DB, NA.

60. Bonesteel to Lincoln, 9 Aug. 45, ABC 387 Japan (15 Feb. 45), sec. 1-B, RG165, MMRB, NA.

5. Peace Breaks Out

1. Telephone conversation between Dunn and Lincoln, 17 Aug. 45, ABC 387 (15 Feb. 45), sec. 1-B.

2. Donovan, *Conflict and Crisis*, p. 99.

3. History of the United States Army Forces in Korea, HQ FE Command, unpublished ms., p. 1, formerly office of the Chief of Military History, now in MMRB, NA (hereafter cited as HUSAFIK).

4. Luvaas, *Dear Miss Em*, pp. 298–299.

5. For a thorough analysis of the internal debate over Japan's offer to surrrnder, see Barton J. Bernstein, "The Perils and Politics of Surrender"

6. John K. Emmerson, *The Japanese Thread*, pp. 237–238. The caution shown by the Japan specialists on the phrasing of the surrender agreement appears to have been justified. The Swedish official who passed the messages between the Americans and Japanese asked the Japanese representative in Stockholm if the phrase concerning the prerogatives of the emperor meant that there would be no change in the state's governing system or no change in the position of the emperor. Okamototo replied that he had no explanation of the matter, but he felt the "words include both interpretations." Japan's Surrender Maneuvers, p. 6, SRH-090, RG457, MMRB, NA.

7. John M. Blum, *The Price of Vision*, pp. 473–475.

8. *Ibid.*

9. Bernstein, "The Perils and Politics of Surrender," p. 8.

10. Dean Rusk to G. Bernard Noble, 12 July 50, *FRUS 1945*, 6:1039.

11. *Ibid.*; Lt. Paul McGrath, "U.S. Army in the Korean Conflict," unpublished ms., n.d., pp. 42–44, 46 (formerly Office of the Chief of Military History, now in MMRB, NA). McGrath interviewed a number of the participants in the August 10–11 meetings. See also General George A. Lincoln, 6 Nov. 45, Proceedings of the Board of Officers, OPD 210.52, sec. 7-A, case 49, RG165, MMRB, NA.

12. Matray errs in saying that Gardner "outlined Truman's desires" in proposing the thirty-ninth parallel. According to McGrath, Gardner made this proposal because Forrestal favored it. As will be seen, Truman never proposed changing the General Order so as to put Dairen in the American zone. Matray, "Captive of the Cold War," p. 165; McGrath, "U.S. Army in the Korean Conflict," p. 46.

13. Stimson to Byrnes, 11 Aug. 45, enclosing SWNCC 21/5, in SWNCC 21, Papers of the SWNCC (microfilm), DB, NA.

14. Lincoln to Charles Donnelly, JCS Historical Division, 18 July 49, Folder Comments on OPD Manuscripts, box 372, 2.3–7 Washington Command Post, CG5 Supporting Papers, MMRB, NA.

15. *Ibid.*

16. *Ibid.*

17. U.S. Position with Regard to General Soviet Intentions for Expansion, 6 July 45, ABC 092 USSR (15 Nov. 44), RG165, MMRB, NA.

18. Examination of Plans for the Immediate Occupation of Japan, JWPC 264/8, 10 Aug. 45, in CCS 386.2 Japan (4–9–43), sec. 4, RG218, MMRB, NA.

19. Deane, *Strange Alliance*, pp. 268–275.

20. Stimson to Byrnes, 11 Aug. 45, enclosing SWNCC 21/5, in SWNCC 21, Papers of SWNCC (microfilm), DB, NA; Transcript of telephone conversation, Hull and Admiral Charles M. Cooke, 11 Aug. 45, OPD Executive Files, Exec. 17, Item 35 (Telephone Conversations), RG165, MMRB, NA.

21. JCS to MacArthur, Nimitz, and Wedemeyer, WARX 47945, 11 Aug. 45, CCS 386.2 Japan (4–9–45), sec. 3, RG218, MMRB, NA.

22. JCS to MacArthur, Nimitz, and Wedemeyer, WARX 48004, 11 Aug. 45, *ibid.*

23. Mark Paul writes that Truman ordered the Dairen operation before he received the recommendations of the SWNCC or the JCS. This is technically correct in that these committees did not officially approve the General Order until August 14. The Stimson memorandum and the conversation between Hull and Cooke cited above indicate, however, that Byrnes *and* Leahy had a copy of the first draft of the order on the morning of August 11. It seems quite possible, therefore, that Truman reviewed the order before issuing the Dairen directive.

24. Transcript of telephone conversation, Hull and Cooke, 1340, 11 Aug. 45, OPD Executive Files, Exec. 17, Item 35 (Telephone Conversations), RG165, MMRB, NA.

25. Sbrega, *Anglo-American Relations*, pp. 178–182.

26. Action in the event of an early Japanese surrender, CCS 901/1, 11 Aug. 45, ABC 387 Japan (15 Feb. 45), sec. 1-B, RG165, MMRB, NA.

27. Memorandum of telephone conversation, McCloy and Byrnes, 5:45 P.M., 11 Aug. 45, files 385–387, McCloy–Assistant Secretary, RG107, MMRB, NA.

28. *Ibid.*

29. *Ibid.*

30. *Ibid.*

31. In proposing an American occupation of the Kuriles, McCloy may have been influenced by the JWPC's recommendation that the U.S. occupy several of the islands so as to "assist any negotiation for post-war airfield rights." JWPC 264/8, 10 Aug. 45, in CCS 386.2 Japan (4–9–45), sec. 4, RG218, MMRB, NA.

32. Minutes of the 21st meeting, 12 Aug. 45, SWNCC Minutes, SWNCC Papers (microfilm), DB, NA.

33. Report of Mr. Dunn at approximately 6:30 P.M., 12 Aug. 45, SWNCC 21, *ibid.*

34. Further Action as to the Immediate Occupation of Japan and Japanese Held Areas, JWPC 264/9, 13 Aug. 45, CCS 386.2 Japan (4–9–45), RG218, MMRB, NA.
35. Instruments for the Surrender of Japan, Report of the JSP, JCS 1467/1, 13 Aug. 45, w/enclosures, in SWNCC 21, SWNCC Papers (microfilm), DB, NA.
36. Mark Paul concludes that Truman saw the JCS memo but declined to notify Stalin of the impending operations. I have found no evidence to indicate that the JCS memo was sent to Truman. It appears that only the General Order went to the White House. Because the Chiefs did not plan to show Truman the drafted message until the American landings became imminent, it is safer to assume that the President never saw the memorandum. See Paul, "Diplomacy Delayed: The Atomic Bomb and the Division of Korea," in Cumings, ed., *The Child of Conflict*, p. 90.
37. This new provision was first discussed in the SWNCC meeting of August 14. Later that evening it was reviewed by Byrnes. Memorandum for SWNCC from Major Davidson Sommers, 15 Aug. 45, SWNCC 21/7, SWNCC Papers (microfilm), DB, NA; Transcript of telephone conversation, Hull and General McFarland, 1815, 14 Aug. 45, OPD Executive Files, Exec. 17, Item 35 (Telephone Conversations), RG165, MMRB, NA.
38. Herbert Feis did not regard this provision as effectively ruling out the possibility of surrenders being made to Communist commanders because it did not threaten to punish Japanese officers who gave up their arms to CCP representatives. Nevertheless, the new provision strengthened the General Order by forbidding the Japanese to surrender to anyone but the designated commanders. The Japanese apparently understood this aspect of the message, for they continued to resist CCP efforts to enter several cities in north China. Feis, *The China Tangle*, pp. 341–343.
39. Matray, "Captive of the Cold War," p. 163; JCS to Wedemeyer, 10 Aug. 45, *FRUS 1945*, 7:527–528.
40. Romanus and Sunderland, *Time Runs Out in CBI*, pp. 394–395.
41. Wedemeyer to War Department, 14 Aug. 45, China-India-Burma Folder, Chairman's Files (Admiral Leahy), RG218, MMRB, NA; MacArthur to War Department, 14 Aug. 45, ABC 387 Japan (15 Feb. 45), sec. 3, RG165, MMRB, NA; Hull to Wedemeyer, 14 Aug. 45, OPD 336 TS (case 133 only), RG165, MMRB, NA; Marshall to Wedemeyer, 14 Aug. 45, ABC 336 China (26 Jan. 42), sec. 1-B-3, RG165, MMRB, NA.
42. JCS to MacArthur, WARX 49334, 14 Aug. 45, in JCS 1331/8, CCS 386.2 Japan (4–9–45), sec. 4, RG218, MMRB, NA.
43. This transcript was filed in two separate locations. Hull showed the second page to Marshall on the same day. The two pages appear to belong together. A later conversation between Lincoln and Gardner suggests that Lincoln talked with Dunn only once. Hull to Marshall, 15 Aug. 45, enclosing memo of conversation between Dunn and Lincoln, OPD O14.1 TS, sec. 4, case 61/

7; Telephone conversation, Dunn and Lincoln, 15 Aug. 45, OPD 336 China, sec. 3, case 71 (entry 418–box 919); and Telephone conversation, Gardner and Lincoln, 15 Aug. 45, ABC 387 Japan (15 Feb. 45), sec. 1-B, all in RG165, MMRB, NA.

44. Transcript of telephone conversation, Gardner and Lincoln, 15 Aug. 45, ABC 387 Japan (15 Feb. 45), sec. 1-B, RG165, MMRB, NA.

45. Transcript of telephone conversation, Cooke and Hull, 15 Aug. 45, OPD Executive Files, Exec. 17, Item 35a, RG165, MMRB, NA.

46. JCS to MacArthur, Nimitz, and Wedemeyer, 15 Aug. 45, in CCS 386.2 Japan (4–9–45), sec. 4, RG218, MMRB, NA.

47. Lincoln to McFarland, 13 Aug. 45, enclosing JCS 1464, Action in the Event of an Early Japanese Surrender, OPD 014. TS, sec. 4, case 63, RG165, MMRB, NA.

48. Transcript of telephone conversation, Hull and Cooke, 15 Aug. 45, OPD Executive Files, Exec. 17, Item 35a (Telephoning Conversations), RG165, MMRB, NA.

49. Hurley to Byrnes, 13 Aug. 45, *FRUS 1945*, 7:1348.

50. Stalin to Truman, 16 Aug. 45, 740.00119 PW/8–1645, RG59, DB, NA.

51. *Ibid.*

52. Harriman to Byrnes, 11 Aug. 45; and Byrnes to Harriman, 11 Aug. 45, *FRUS 1945*, 6:630; Deane, *Strange Alliance*, p. 277.

53. Buhite, *Soviet-American Relations*, pp. 107–109; William Taubman, *Stalin's American Policy*, pp. 114–115.

54. JCS to SWNCC, 17 July 45, SWNCC 70, SWNCC Papers (microfilm), DB, NA.

55. Cumings, *The Origins of the Korean War*, p. 181; Dobbs, *The Unwanted Symbol*, p. 27; *The Reluctant Crusade*, p. 46.

56. Truman to Stalin, 17 Aug. 45, enclosed in General Craig to General Marshall, 18 Aug. 45, ABC 387 Japan (15 Feb. 45), sec. 1-B; and Colonel McCarthy to Marshall, 18 Aug. 45, ABC 387 Japan (15 Feb. 45), sec. 3, RG165, MMRB, NA.

57. Transcript of telephone conversation, Lincoln and Gardner, 18 Aug. 45, OPD Executive Files, Exec. 17, Item 35a (Telephone Conversations), RG165, MMRB, NA.

58. McCarthy to Marshall, 18 Aug. 45, ABC 387 Japan (15 Feb. 45), sec. 3 RG165, MMRB, NA. For a somewhat different account of these events, see Michael Sandusky's *America's Parallel*, especially pp. 250, 328.

59. Truman to Stalin, 18 Aug. 45, 740.00119 PW/8–1845, RG59, DB, NA.

60. Stalin to Truman, 22 Aug. 45, 740.00119 PW/8–2245, RG59, DB, NA.

61. Transcript of telephone conversation, Dunn and Lincoln, 17 Aug. 45, ABC 387 (15 Feb. 45), sec. 1-B, RG165, MMRB, NA. Memo for Chief of Staff from Craig, 18 Aug. 45, ABC 387 Japan (15 Feb. 45), sec. 1-B, RG165, MMRB, NA.

62. Transcript of telephone conversation, Hull and Cooke, 0823, 23 Aug. 45, OPD Executive Files, Exec. 17, Item 35a (Telephone Conversations), RG165, MMRB, NA.
63. Memorandum for Hull from Colonel Gerhardt, 23 Aug. 45, ABC 686 (6 Nov. 43), sec. 25, RG165, MMRB, NA.
64. Transcript of telephone conversation, Cooke and Hull, 1710, 23 Aug. 45, OPD Executive Files, Exec. 17, Item 35a (Telephone Conversations), RG165, NMRB, NA.
65. Byrnes to Truman, enclosing suggested message from Truman to Stalin, 25 Aug. 45, *FRUS 1945*, 6:692.
66. Hurley to Byrnes, no. 1335, 12 Aug. 45; Hurley to Byrnes, 1336, 12 Aug. 45; Hurley to Byrnes, 20 Aug. 45, in *FRUS 1945*, 7:514–516, 534–535; *New York Times*, August 24, 1945, p. 1.
67. Transcript of telephone conversation, Hull and Cooke, 15 Aug. 45, OPD Executive Files, Exec. 17, Item 35a (Telephone Conversations), RG165, MMRB, NA.
68. Hurley to Byrnes, 16 Aug. 45, *FRUS 1945*, 7:500–501.
69. *Ibid.*
70. Attlee to Truman, 18 Aug. 45, *FRUS 1945*, 7:504; Leahy to Byrnes, 18 Aug. 45, *FRUS 1945*, 7:505.
71. The following was written next to the closing paragraph of the memo: "Is this explanatory or did it go to London with the rest of memo. Let Mr. Vincent know." Further down it read: "Went to London." John Carter Vincent to Dunn, w/enclosure, 18 Aug. 45, 740.00119 PW/8–1845, RG59, DB, NA.
72. T. V. Soong to Byrnes, 18 Aug. 45, *FRUS 1945*, 7:503; Hurley to Byrnes, 21 Aug. 45, *FRUS 1945*, 7:507–508.
73. Byrnes to Hurley, enclosing Truman to Chiang, 21 Aug. 45, *FRUS 1945*, 7:509.
74. Kirby, *The Japanese Surrender*, p. 283.
75. British action upon Japanese surrender, Memo by U.S. Chiefs of Staff, appendix, JCS 1464/1, 16 Aug. 45, ABC 387 Japan (15 Feb. 45), sec. 1-B, RG165, MMRB, NA. An earlier draft of this memo admonished the British to make certain that "no element of imperialism is being added to other problems harassing the Chinese republic." Lincoln to JSP, Reference CCS901/4, enclosing JCS to British, 16 Aug. 45, ABC 387 Japan (15 Feb. 45), sec. 1-C, RG165, MMRB, NA.
76. CCS 901/11, 30 Aug. 45, ABC 387 Japan (15 Feb. 45), sec. 1-C, RG165, MMRB, NA.
77. The ostensible reason for leaving north Indochina in the China theater, so Chiang could protect his right flank during the coming offensive, disappeared when Japan surrendered. Chinese troops did use Haiphong as debarkation point for north China, but this does not appear to have been a factor in the American decision. The French learned that they would not be able to assume immediate control in Indochina from a Foreign Office announcement issued in London in late August. *Newsweek* (September 3, 1945), 26:24.

6. The Residue of a Larger Plan

1. Memorandum of the Assistant Secretary of the Navy, 19 Oct. 45, SWNCC 54, SWNCC-FE Subcommittee, SWNCC Papers (microfilm), DB, NA.
2. Donovan, *Conflict and Crisis*, pp. 108–115.
3. For Byrnes' relationship with the State Department, see Weil, *A Pretty Good Club*, pp. 228–250. Robert Messer emphasizes Byrnes' Senate background as an influence on his diplomacy in *The End of an Alliance*, pp. 96–100.
4. Dean Acheson, *Present at the Creation*, p. 119; Weil, *A Pretty Good Club*, pp. 236–237.
5. Acheson interview, 6 Feb. 55, Memoirs—Post-Presidential, HST Papers. David McClellan is probably mistaken in describing the Acheson appointment as Byrnes' idea. McClellan, *Dean Acheson*, p. 57.
6. Weil, *A Pretty Good Club*, pp. 237–238; John K. Emmerson, *The Japanese Thread*, p. 252.
7. Weil, *A Pretty Good Club*, pp. 237–238.
8. *Ibid*.
9. Edward Drachman, *U.S. Policy Towards Vietnam, 1940–1945*, p. 130.
10. May, *China Scapegoat*, pp. 55, 60, 120–124.
11. JCS to Wedemeyer, 10 Aug. 45, *FRUS 1945*, 7:527–528.
12. Schaller, *The U.S. Crusade in China*, pp. 262–264.
13. Memorandum of conversation by the Acting Secretary of State, 7 Sept. 45, *FRUS 1945*, 7:551–552; JCS to Wedemeyer, 18 Sept. 45, *FRUS 1945*, 7:565; Leahy to JCS, 15 Sept. 45, CCS 540 (9–13–45), RG218, MMRB, NA; Herbert Feis, *The China Tangle*, pp. 370–371.
14. Schaller, *The U.S. Crusade in China*, p. 265; Kenneth Chern, *Dilemma in China*, p. 118.
15. Memorandum to the Assistant Chief of Staff, OPD, Brief of BELEAGER, 19 Aug. 45, OPD 014 TS, sec. 4, RG165, MMRB, NA.
16. May, *China Scapegoat*, p. 134.
17. Memorandum for the Record, re: Occupational Priorities, 14 Aug. 45, ABC 387 Japan (15 Feb. 45), sec. 3, RG165, MMRB, NA.
18. Memorandum for S&P Record, 15 Aug. 45, ABC 387 Japan (15 Feb. 45), sec. 1-B, RG165, MMRB, NA.
19. Vincent to Acheson, 20 Sept. 45, *FRUS 1945*, 7:566–567.
20. Vincent to Acheson, 27 Sept. 45, *FRUS 1945*, 7:570–571.
21. Acheson to Vincent, 28 Sept. 45, *FRUS 1945*, 7:571.
22. *Ibid*.
23. Memorandum of Press Conference, 7 Nov. 45, no. 56, Office of the Special Assistant to the Secretary in Charge of Press Relations, Verbatim Reports of Press Conferences, p. 18, RG59, DB, NA; Lincoln to Hull, 8 Nov. 45, ABC 014 Japan (13 Apr. 44), sec. 18-B, RG165, MMRB, NA.
24. Politico-Military Problems in the Far East, SWNCC 16/6, n.d., SWNCC 16 series, SWNCC Papers, DB, NA; Feis, *The China Tangle*, pp. 294–295.
25. Feis, *The China Tangle*, p. 374; Memorandum for McCloy, re: U.S. Policy

Towards China, 11 Sept. 45, ABC 336 China (26 Jan. 42), sec. 1-B, RG165, MMRB, NA; Minutes of the JSP, 221st meeting, 10 Oct. 45, Joint Staff Planners (8–2–45), RG218, MMRB, NA.

26. SWNCC 83/6, 22 Oct. 45 *FRUS 1945*, 7:583–590.
27. Ibid.
28. Navy Department Top Policy Group, Minutes of the 39th meeting, 5 Nov. 45, RG80, OANB, NA.
29. Vincent to Acheson, 6 Sept. 45, *FRUS 1945*, 7:550–551.
30. Minutes of the SWNCC–Far Eastern Subcommittee, 11 Sept. 45, SWNCC-FE Subcommittee Minutes, SWNCC Papers, DB, NA.
31. Schnabel, *The JCS and National Policy*, p. 419.
32. May, *China Scapegoat*, p. 132.
33. Cumings, *The Origins of the Korean War*, pp. 122–126.
34. *Ibid.*, pp. 126–129.
35. *Ibid.*, pp. 141–151; William Whitney Stueck, Jr., *The Road to Confrontation*, p. 23.
36. Cumings, *The Origins of the Korean War*, pp. 151–169.
37. *Ibid.*, pp. 179–182.
38. Morris, "The Korean Trusteeship," p. 136; *History of the United States Army Forces in Korea*, part 2, p. 15, Office of the Chief of Military History, Historical Manuscript File, unpublished ms. (now in MMRB, NA).
39. Cumings, *The Origins of the Korean War*, p. 493 n. 6. Truman's statement is in *Department of State Bulletin* (hereafter cited as *DSB*) 23 Sept. 45, 13:326.
40. Vincent to Colonel Russell Vittrup, 7 Nov. 45, ABC 014 Japan (13 Apr. 44), sec. 17-A, RG165, MMRB, NA; Morris, "The Korean Trusteeship," p. 133.
41. Cumings, *The Origins of the Korean War*, p. 161.
42. War Council Minutes, 7 Nov. 45, box 23, Robert Patterson Papers, Library of Congress, Washington, D.C.
43. McCloy to Acheson, 13 Nov. 45, *FRUS 1945*, 6:1122–1124.
44. *Ibid.*
45. Vincent to Acheson, 16 Nov. 45, *FRUS 1945*, 6:1127–1128.
46. John T. McAlister, Jr., *Vietnam*, pp. 171–183; Drachman, *U.S. Policy Towards Vietnam*, pp. 128–129.
47. Ballantine to WE, 23 Aug. 45, 851G.oo/8–2345, and Oakes (Colombo) to Byrnes, 6 Sept. 45, 851G.oo/9–645, both in RG59, DB, NA; and Donovan to White House, 5, 6 Sept. 45, OSS Reports to White House, Apr.-Sept. 45, Donovan Papers, MHI.
48. Acheson to Yost (Dehli), 6 Sept. 45, 851G.oo/9–645, RG59, DB, NA.
49. F. C. Jones, Hugh Borton, and B. R. Pearn, *The Far East*, 8:260–261.
50. McAlister, *Vietnam*, pp. 193–194.
51. Herring, "The Truman Administration and Indochina," p. 119.
52. Lincoln to Policy Section, 15 Dec. 45, ABC 384 Indochina (16 Dec. 44), sec. 1-C, RG165, MMRB, NA.
53. McAlister, *Vietnam*, pp. 207–208; JCS Historical Division, "The History of

the Joint Chiefs of Staff: The History of the Indochina Incident, 1940–1954," unpublished ms., MMRB, NA; United States Congress, House, Committee on Armed Services, *United States–Vietnam Relations*, 1:B-42.

54. Byrnes to Hurley, 31 Aug. 45, and Hurley to Byrnes, 6 Sept. 45, *FRUS 1945*, 7:513–514.
55. Ronald H. Spector, *United States Army in Vietnam*, pp. 59–61; Charles de Gaulle, p. 928.
56. Notes on conference held between General McClure, General Gallagher, Mr. Miao, 2 Oct. 45; and Notes on conference between Generals Ho Ying Chin, Lu Han, McClure, and Gallagher, 3 Oct. 45, both in Commanders Conferences on the Surrender of the Japanese Forces in Northern French Indochina, supporting ms. for Romanus and Sunderland, *Time Runs Out in CBI* (formerly Center for Military History, now in MMRB, NA).
57. Memorandum for the President, 22 Aug. 45, OSS Reports to the White House, Donovan Papers, MHI.
58. Drachman, *U.S. Policy Towards Vietnam*, pp. 131–133.
59. Memorandum of conversation between François Lacoste, Minister Counselor of the French embassy, and Joseph Bonbright, 17 Sept. 45, 851G.00/9–1745, RG59, DB, NA; Drachman, *U.S. Policy Towards Vietnam*, pp. 135–137.
60. JCS Historical Division, "Indochina Incident," p. 94.
61. Herring, "The Truman Administration and Indochina," pp. 113–114.
62. The Postwar Period in the Far East, *DSB*, 21 Oct. 45, 13:644–648.
63. *Ibid*.
64. Drachman, *U.S. Policy Towards Vietnam*, p. 127.
65. The Postwar Period in the Far East, *DSB*, 13:644–648.
66. *Ibid*.
67. See Memorandum of the Chief of CA (Drumright), 10 Nov. 45, *FRUS 1945*, 7:629–634.
68. Col. Ivan Yeaton to Wedemeyer, 15 Aug. 45, Radios, Eyes Alone Book 5, China-India-Burma Theater, RG407, Federal Records Center, Suitland, Md.
69. Colonel H. A. Byrode, Acting CoS Asiatic Section, OPD, to General Hull, transmitting extracts of Colonel Lincoln's letters, 1 Sept. 45, OPD 336 China, sec. 3, RG165, MMRB, NA.
70. Brig. Gen. Paul Caraway to Col. John H. Hill, 29 Sept. 45; Caraway to Col. Devere Armstrong, 2 Sept. 45; Caraway to Col. William H. Bauhmer, 7 Sept. 45, all in Correspondence File, Paul Caraway Papers, MHI. The Air Force also believed that the Chinese made better pilots than the Japanese, if given the proper training. See Postwar Military Policies w/Respect to China, 25 Apr. 45, SWNCC, 83/D, SWNCC Papers, DB, NA.
71. Meeting of the JSP, 17 Oct. 45, 22nd meeting, CCS 334 Joint Staff Planners (8–2–45), RG218, MMRB, NA.
72. According to Harry Hopkins' biographer, in 1941 Yeaton was relieved of his post as military attaché to Moscow because Hopkins believed Yeaton's anti-communism had led him to underestimate the Soviet Union's ability to resist Hitler. Yeaton believed he was transferred because Hopkins was soft on

communism. See Sherwood, *Roosevelt and Hopkins,* pp. 395–396; Memoirs of Ivan D. Yeaton, USA (Ret.), 1919–1953, Hoover Institution on War, Revolution, and Peace, Stanford, Calif. (copy in Yeaton Papers, MHI), pp. 37–38, 97; Romanus and Sunderland, *Time Runs Out in CBI,* p. 384.

73. Caraway to Gen. Raymond Maddocks, 5 Nov. 45, Correspondence File, Caraway Papers, MHI. Byroade to Hull, transmitting extracts of Colonel Lincoln's letters, OPD 336 China, sec. 3, RG165, MMRB, NA.

74. Caraway to Maddocks, 5 Nov. 45, Correspondence File, Caraway Papers, MHI.

75. Byroade to Hull, transmitting Colonel Lincoln's letters, 1 Sept. 45, OPD 336, sec. 3, RG165, MMRB, NA.

76. William Whitney Stueck, Jr., *The Road to Confrontation,* p. 15; Buhite, *Soviet-American Relations,* pp. 28–29; Navy Dept. to State Dept., 16 Nov. 45, *FRUS 1945,* 7:634–635; Joint Intelligence Committee Weekly Summaries, 22 Nov. 45, file ASW 334.8, McCloy Papers, RG107, MMRB, NA.

77. Minutes of JSP, 222d meeting, 17 Oct. 45, CCS 334 Joint Staff Planners (8-2-45), RG218, MMRB, NA. Hodge was reaching a similar conclusion in Korea, HUSAFIK, p. 21.

78. Wedemeyer to Leahy, 27 Oct. 45, China Folder, Leahy Papers, RG218, MMRB, NA.

7. Into the Cold War

1. 11 Dec. 45, Leahy Diary, Leahy Papers, Library of Congress.
2. Yergin, *Shattered Peace,* p. 155.
3. Patricia Dawson Ward, *The Threat of Peace,* pp. 49–50.
4. Paterson, *On Every Front,* p. 164; Messer, *The End of an Alliance,* pp. 128–129.
5. Ward, *The Threat of Peace,* p. 48.
6. *Ibid.,* pp. 135–136; Yergin, *Shattered Peace,* p. 111.
7. Gaddis, *Origins of the Cold War,* p. 275; Yergin; *Shattered Peace,* p. 144.
8. Minutes of the Committee of Three, 10 Oct. 45, papers of the Committee of Three, DB, NA.
9. Memorandum of conversation between Byrnes and Molotov, 22 Sept. 45, 740.00119 PW/9–2245, RG59, DB, NA.
10. Minutes of the Committee of Three, 6 Oct. 45, Papers of the Committee of Three, DB, NA.
11. Harriman to Byrnes, 25 Oct. 45, *FRUS 1945,* 6:785–786.
12. Minutes of the Committee of Three, 6 Nov. 45, Papers of the Committee of Three, DB, NA.
13. *Ibid.*
14. Wedemeyer to Marshall, 5 Nov. 45, *FRUS 1945,* 7:603–605.
15. Quoted in James Reardon-Anderson, *Yenan and the Great Powers,* p. 117. See also Varg, *The Closing of the Door,* p. 223.
16. Minutes of the Committee of Three, 6 Nov. 45, Forrestal Manuscript Diaries, Forrestal Papers, Princeton University Library.

17. *Ibid.*
18. The authors of the official history of the occupation write that "when the routine of repatriation was settled, only one company of the 29th Marines plus a relatively few liaison officers and interpreters from division headquarters were needed to supervise and control the program." Frank and Shaw, *Victory and Occupation*, pp. 580–583.
19. Memoirs—Dean Acheson, Interviews with Associates, 17 Feb. 55, Post-Presidential Memoirs, HST Papers.
20. Minutes of the Committee of Three, 6 Nov. 45, Forrestal Manuscript Diaries.
21. Wedemeyer to Marshall, 9 Nov. 45, *FRUS 1945*, 7:611–613.
22. *New York Times*, November 11, 1945, p. 1.
23. Memorandum for Mr. Vincent from Lieutenant Farley, 19 Nov. 45, w/ enclosure, Draft Statement of Policy, SFE-series 150, SWNCC-FE Subcommittee Papers, DB, NA.
24. McCloy to SWNCC, ca. 11 Nov. 45, ABC 336 China (26 Jan. 42), 1-C, RG165, MMRB, NA.
25. *Ibid.*
26. H. Freeman Matthews to Byrnes, 13 Nov. 45, *FRUS 1945*, 7:619–624.
27. Memo for Vincent from Lieutenant Farley, SFE-series 150, SWNCC-FE Subcommittee Papers, DB, NA.
28. Extract from 52d meeting, SWNCC-FE Subcommittee, 20 Nov. 45, SFE-series 154, SWNCC-FE Subcommittee Papers, DB, NA.
29. *Ibid.*
30. *Ibid.*
31. Schaller, *The U.S. Crusade in China*, pp. 286–288.
32. Admiral Gardner thought the United States should limit aid to the Nationalists until the situation clarified. He added that the United States could not build up China's forces to withstand Soviet aggression and urged caution in this respect, since "any effort we might support in that direction would obviously be pointed at Russia." Gardner to Generals Lincoln and Cabell, 6 Oct. 45, ABC 336 China (26 Jan. 42), sec. 1-B; and Minutes of the JSP, 221st meeting, 10 Oct. 45, Joint Staff Planners (8–2–45), RG218, MMRB, NA.
33. Jack Stokes Ballard, *The Shock of Peace*, pp. 84–92.
34. Chern, *Dilemma in China*, pp. 130–138.
35. Transcript of telephone conversation between Forrestal and Vincent, 7 Nov. 45, file 7–6–8, Forrestal, General Correspondence, RG80, OANB, NA; 6 Nov. 45, Forrestal Manuscript Diaries.
36. Transcript of telephone conversation between Embick and Hull, 10 Nov. 45, ABC 336 China (26 Jan. 42), sec. 1-C, RG165, MMRB, NA; Laurence J. Lincoln, Oral History Interview, MHI; Gary May, *China Scapegoat*, p. 147.
37. Elsey memo, 30 Nov. 45, Historical Reports and Notes: China, George Elsey Papers, HST Library.
38. This was initialed by HST. Memorandum for the President, 2 Oct. 45, Cabinet-General, 1946–1951, PSF, Subject File, HST Papers.
39. 5 Nov. 45, Ayers Diary, Ayers Papers, HST Library; Royall to Hull, 10 Nov. 45, OPD 336 China, sec. 4, RG165, MMRB, NA.

40. Ferrell, *Off the Record*, p. 74.
41. Telephone transcript, Forrestal and Vincent, 7 Nov. 45, file 7–6–8, Forrestal General Correspondence, RG80, OANB, NA.
42. *New York Times*, November 12, 1945, p. 2.
43. Memorandum for the Record, 12 Nov. 45, OPD 336.2 Japan, sec. 3, case 39, RG165, MMRB, NA.
44. *Ibid.*
45. Wedemeyer to Marshall, 16 Nov. 45, *FRUS 1945*, 7:635–636; Reardon-Anderson, *Yenan and the Great Powers*, p. 118.
46. Wedemeyer to Marshall, 16 Nov. 45, *FRUS 1945*, 7:635–636.
47. *Ibid.*
48. Vincent memorandum, Our Military Position in China, 19 Nov. 45, *FRUS 1945*, 7:639–643.
49. *Ibid.* On Vincent's preference for the fourth option, see May, *China Scapegoat*, pp. 137–138.
50. Eisenhower to Wedemeyer, 20 [19] Nov. 45, *FRUS 1945*, 7:644–645.
51. *Ibid.*
52. *Ibid.*
53. Feis, *The China Tangle*, p. 398; Chern, *Dilemma in China*, p. 127. Chern notes that Byrnes subsequently rejected a military solution in China. Schaller also notes a change in Byrnes' attitude during the November 27 meeting of the Committee of Three, which he attributes to the bleak reports Wedemeyer sent to Washington toward the end of the month. As I argue here, Byrnes had already made up his mind by November 19, primarily because of his concern over the state of Soviet-American relations. Schaller, *The U.S. Crusade in China*, pp. 286–287.
54. Schaller, *The U.S. Crusade in China*, pp. 280–281.
55. Everett Drumright memorandum, Situation in China, *FRUS 1945*, 7:629–634.
56. Minutes of the Committee of Three, 20 Nov. 45, Papers of the Committee of Three, DB, NA.
57. Wedemeyer to Eisenhower, 20 Nov. 45, *FRUS 1945*, 7:650–660.
58. *Ibid.*
59. Wedemeyer to Eisenhower, 23, 25 Nov. 45, *FRUS 1945*, 7:662–667, 669–670.
60. Steven I. Levine, "A New Look at American Mediation in the Chinese Civil War," 3:351.
61. Memorandum by Patterson and Forrestal to Byrnes, 26 Nov. 45, *FRUS 1945*, 7:670–678.
62. *Ibid.* On Patterson's contribution, see Memo for the Record, 24 Nov. 45 ABC 336 China (26 Jan. 42), sec. 1-D, ABC Decimal File RG319, MMRB, NA.
63. Memo for the Record, 24 Nov. 45, *ibid.*
64. Lincoln Commentary on Professor Clyde's "China in War and Victory," n.d., ed. 1971, Lincoln Papers, MHI. Wedemeyer also deprecated the organiza-

tion and strength of the CCP. See Edwin Locke Oral History, p. 88, HST Papers.

65. Clayton Bissell to Chief, Strategy Section, 28 Nov. 45, ABC 336 China (26 Jan. 42), sec. 1-D, RG165, MMRB, NA.
66. Patterson and Forrestal to Byrnes, 26 Nov. 45, *FRUS 1945*, 7:670–678.
67. Minutes of the Committee of Three, 27 Nov. 45, *FRUS 1945*, 7:684–686.
68. *Ibid.*
69. *Ibid.*
70. *Ibid.*
71. Blum, *The Price of Vision*, pp. 519–522.
72. *Ibid.*; Hurley to Truman, 26 Nov. 45, *FRUS 1945*, 7:722–726.
73. Blum, *The Price of Vision*, pp. 519–522.
74. *Ibid.*
75. *Ibid.*; May, *China Scapegoat*, p. 140.
76. Byrnes to Harriman, 23 Nov. 45, *FRUS 1945*, 2:578–581; Byrnes *All in One Lifetime*, p. 326.
77. Byrnes to Bevin, 25 Nov. 45, Record of teletype conversation, Byrnes and Bevin, 27 Nov. 45, Bevin to Byrnes, 28 Nov. 45, all in *FRUS 1945*, 2:578–586; Ward, *The Threat of Peace*, pp. 53–54.
78. Byrnes to Bevin, *FRUS 1945*, 2:587. On the Iran question, see Bruce R. Kuniholm, *The Origins of the Cold War in the Near East*, especially pp. 270–282.
79. Buhite, *Soviet-American Relations*, p. 118; Messer, *The End of an Alliance*, pp. 137–141.
80. Langdon to Byrnes, 20 Nov. 45, *FRUS 1945*, 6:1130–1132; Dobbs, *The Unwanted Symbol*, p. 61.
81. Byrnes to Langdon, 29 Nov. 45, *FRUS 1945*, 6:1137–1138.
82. Byrnes to American Mission, New Dehli, 28 Nov. 45, 711.90/11–2845; R. D. Gatewood (Colombo) to Byrnes, 5 Dec. 45, 711.90/12–545, RG59, DB, NA.
83. JCS Historical Division, "Indochina Incident," p. 48.
84. Colonel Vittrup to Mr. Penfield, enclosing General Terry to War Department, 25 Dec. 45, 711.90/12–2645, RG59, DB, NA.
85. Drachman, *U.S. Policy Towards Vietnam, 1940–1945* 128–129.
86. Outline of Suggested Course of Action in China, 28 Nov. 45, *FRUS 1945*, 7:746–747.
87. Marshall to Leahy, 30 Nov. 45, w/enclosure U.S. Policy Towards China, *FRUS 1945*, 7:747–751. The preparation of Marshall's instructions are also described in May, *China Scapegoat*, pp. 140–142.
88. Lincoln Oral History Interview, Lincoln Papers, MHI.
89. U.S. Policy Towards China, 8 Dec. 45, *FRUS 1945*, 7:754–757.
90. Lieutenant General Hull to Marshall, 8 Dec. 45, *FRUS 1945*, 7:758–759.
91. Memorandum for the War Department, 9 Dec. 45; Memorandum of conversation, 10 Dec. 45; Notes on a meeting with Marshall, Truman, Leahy, and Byrnes, 11 Dec. 45, *FRUS 1945*, 7:760–763, 767–769.

92. Memorandum for the War Department, 9 Dec. 45, *FRUS 1945*, 7:760–761.
93. Vincent to Byrnes, 9 Dec. 45, *FRUS 1945*, 7:759–760.
94. Notes of a meeting w/Marshall et al., 11 Dec. 45, *FRUS 1945*, 7:767–769.
95. 12 Dec. 45, Leahy Diary.
96. Elsey memorandum, 30 Nov. 45, Historical Reports and Notes: China, Elsey Papers, HST Library.
97. 28 Nov. 45, Leahy Diary.
98. Weil, *A Pretty Good Club*, pp. 253–255; Donovan, *Conflict and Crisis*, pp. 155–159; Messer, *The End of an Alliance*, pp. 146–147.
99. Blum, *The Price of Vision*, p. 523.
100. Quoted in Donovan, *Conflict and Crisis*, p. 154; Yergin, *Shattered Peace*, pp. 156–157.
101. Donovan, *Conflict and Crisis*, p. 155.
102. *New York Times*, November 15, 1945, p. 1.
103. Ward, *The Threat of Peace*, pp. 76–77. See also Yergin, *Shattered Peace*, pp. 161–162. For a different view, see William Taubman, *Stalin's American Policy*, p. 127.
104. 28 Dec. 45, Leahy Diary; Gregg Herken, *The Winning Weapon*, pp. 77–81, 85–88.
105. Yergin, *Shattered Peace*, p. 160.
106. Robert Messer provides the best analysis of this episode in *The End of an Alliance*, pp. 158–165. See also Donovan, *Conflict and Crisis*, p. 161; Yergin, *Shattered Peace*, pp. 16–162.
107. Ferrell, *Off the Record*, pp. 78–80.
108. *Ibid.*
109. HST to Congressman Hugh DeLacy, 12 Jan. 46; and DeLacy to HST, 13 Feb. 46, China-1946, PSF-Subject File, HST Papers.

Conclusion

1. Truman interview, 3 Nov. 53, Memoirs—Foreign Policy, Yalta and Potsdam, Memoirs File, Post-Presidential, HST Papers.
2. On the importance of the Chinese occupation to the success of the Vietminh, see McAlister *Vietnam*, p. 251.
3. Wedemeyer to Marshall, 17 Aug. 45, Radios-Eyes Alone, Book 5, CIB-Wedemeyer Papers, Federal Records Center.
4. Quoted in Waldo Heinrichs, "Roosevelt and Truman: The Presidential Perspective," in Dorothy Borg and Waldo Heinrichs, eds. *Uncertain Years*, p. 10.
5. Bruce Cumings, "The Course of Korean American Relations, 1943–1950," in Cumings, ed., *Child of Conflict*, pp. 14–16.
6. Iriye, *The Cold War in Asia*, p. 160.
7. By early 1946 American officials were growing concerned over Ho Chi Minh's possible connection to the Soviet Union. Donovan, *Conflict and Crisis*, p. 252; Lisle A. Rose, *Roots of Tragedy*, p. 69.
8. Rose, *Roots of Tragedy*, pp. 70–71.

Bibliography

Primary Sources

Manuscripts and Archival Records

Library of Congress, Washington, D.C.
  Henry H. Arnold Papers
  Benjamin V. Cohen Papers
  Joseph Davies Papers
  Norman Davis Papers
  Herbert Feis Papers
  Cordell Hull Papers
  William D. Leahy Papers
  Robert Patterson Papers
Harvard University Library, Cambridge, Mass.
  Joseph Grew Papers
Military History Institute, Carlisle, Pa.
  Paul Caraway Papers
  Charles H. Donnelly Papers
  William Donovan Papers
  John E. Hull Papers
  Laurence J. Lincoln Papers
  Senior Officers Debriefing Program (Oral Histories)
National Archives, Washington, D.C.
  Diplomatic Branch:
  RG59: General Records of the Department of State, 1945
  RG353: Records of Interdepartmental and Intradepartmental Committees
  Modern Military Records Branch:
  RG107: Records of the Office of the Secretary of War
  RG165: Records of the Army General and Special Staffs
  RG218: Records of the Combined Chiefs of Staff

RG457: Special Research Histories
Cline, Ray S. *Washington Command Post*. Related Papers.
Far Eastern Command. "History of the Occupation of Korea." Unpublished manuscript. Historical Manuscript File. (Formerly in the Office of the Chief of Military History.)
Joint Chiefs of Staff. "History of the Indochina Incident, 1945–1954." Unpublished manuscript. Joint Chiefs of Staff Historical Division.
McGrath, Lt. Paul. "U.S. Army in the Korean Conflict." Unpublished manuscript. (Formerly in the Office of the Chief of Military History.)
Romanus, Charles and Riley Sunderland. *Time Runs Out in CBI*. Related Papers.
Old Army and Navy Branch:
RG80: Records of the Secretary of the Navy—Forrestal
Operational Archives, Naval Historical Center, Washington, D.C.
  Chief of Naval Operations Files, Double Zero, 1941–1950
  Command File, World War II
  Ernest J. King Papers
  William D. Leahy Papers
  Strategic Plans Division
Federal Records Center, Suitland, Md.
  China-India-Burma Theater (Wedemeyer) Papers
Princeton University Library, Princeton, N.J.
  John Foster Dulles Papers
  James Forrestal Papers
  Arthur Krock Papers
Franklin D. Roosevelt Library, Hyde Park, N.Y.
  Harry Hopkins Papers
  Franklin D. Roosevelt Papers: Map Room File, Official File, President's Secretary's File
  Charles Taussig Papers
Harry S. Truman Library, Independence, Mo.
  Eben Ayers Papers
  George Elsey Papers
  Edwin Locke Papers
  Harry S. Truman Papers: Central File, Confidential File, Map Room File, Official File, President's Secretary's File
Yale University Library, New Haven, Conn.
  Henry L. Stimson Diaries (Microfilm)

Interviews and Correspondence

  Hugh Borton, 7 January 1984 (Correspondence)
  George Elsey, 8 March 1984
  John J. McCloy, 2 August 1984
  Dean Rusk, 30 January 1984

Contemporary Newspapers and Magazines

Newsweek, 1945.
New York Times, 1945.
Time, 1945.

United States Government Publications

U.S. Congress. House. Committee on Armed Services. *United States–Vietnam Relations, 1945–1967*. 12 vols. Washington, D.C.: GPO, 1971.
U.S. Congress. Senate. Committee on Foreign Relations. *Causes, Origins, Lessons of the Vietnam War*. 92d Cong., 2d Sess. Washington, D.C.: GPO, 1972.
U.S. Department of Defense. *The Entry of the Soviet Union Into the War Against Japan*. Washington, D.C.: GPO, 1955.
U.S. Department of State. *Department of State Bulletin, 1944–1945*. Vols. 10–11.
U.S. Department of State. *United States Relations With China: With Special Reference to the Period 1944–1949*. Washington, D.C.: GPO, 1949.
U.S. Department of State. *FRUS (Foreign Relations of the United States)*.
   FRUS: The Conferences at Cairo and Tehran, 1943. Washington, D.C.: GPO, 1961.
   FRUS: The Conferences at Malta and Yalta, 1945. Washington, D.C.: GPO, 1955.
   FRUS, 1945, Vol. 1. *General: The United Nations*. Washington, D.C.: GPO, 1967.
   FRUS, 1945, Vol. 5. *Europe*. Washington, D.C.: GPO, 1967.
   FRUS 1945. Vol. 6. *The British Commonwealth; The Far East*. Washington, D.C.: GPO, 1969.
   FRUS 1945. Vol. 7. *The Far East: China*. Washington, D.C.: GPO, 1969.
   FRUS: The Conference of Berlin (Potsdam), 1945. 2 vols. Washington, D.C.: GPO, 1957.

Secondary Sources

Acheson, Dean. *Present at the Creation: My Years in the State Department*. New York: New American Library, 1970.
Adams, Henry D. *Witness to Power: The Life of Fleet Admiral William D. Leahy*. Annapolis: Naval Institute Press, 1985.
Allen, Louis. *The End of the War in Asia*. London: Hart Davis, MacGibbon, 1976.
Alperovitz, Gar. *Atomic Diplomacy: Hiroshima and Potsdam*. Expanded and updated edition. New York: Penguin, 1985.
Ballard, Jack S. *The Shock of Peace: Military and Economic Demobilization After World War II*. Washington, D.C.: University Press, 1983.

Bernstein, Barton J. "The Perils and Politics of Surrender: Ending the War with Japan and Avoiding a Third Atomic Bomb." *Pacific Historical Review* (February, 1977), 66:1–25.

Blum, John M., ed. *The Price of Vision: The Diary of Henry A. Wallace, 1942–1946*. Boston: Houghton Mifflin, 1973.

Bohlen, Charles. *Witness to History, 1929–1969*. New York: Norton, 1973.

Borton, Hugh. "American Presurrender Planning for Postwar Japan." *Occasional Papers of the East Asian Institute*. New York: Columbia University, East Asian Institute, 1967.

Borg, Dorothy and Waldo Heinrichs, eds. *Uncertain Years: Chinese American Relations, 1947–1950*. New York: Columbia University Press, 1980.

Brinkley, Alan. "Minister Without Portfolio: The Most Influential Private Citizen in America." *Harper's* (February 1983), 266:30–46.

Buhite, Russell D. "Major Interests: American Policy Toward China, Taiwan, Korea, 1945–1950." *Pacific Historical Review* (August 1978), 47:425–453.

Buhite, Russell D. *Patrick J. Hurley and American Foreign Policy*. Ithaca, N.Y.: Cornell University Press, 1973.

Buhite, Russell D. *Soviet-American Relations in Asia, 1945–1954*. Norman: University of Oklahoma Press, 1981.

Buhite, Russell D. *Decisions at Yalta: An Appraisal of Summit Diplomacy*. Wilmington: Scholarly Resources, 1986.

Burns, James MacGregor. *Roosevelt: The Soldier of Freedom*. New York: Harcourt Brace Jovanovich, 1970.

Butow, Robert J. C. *Japan's Decision to Surrender*. Stanford: Stanford University Press, 1954.

Byrnes, James F. *All in One Lifetime*. New York: Harper, 1958.

Byrnes, James F. *Speaking Frankly*. New York: Harper, 1947.

Campbell, Thomas M. and George C. Herring, eds. *The Diaries of Edward Stettinius, Jr., 1943–1946*. New York: New Viewpoints, 1975.

Chern, Kenneth. *Dilemma in China: America's Policy Debate, 1945*. Hamden, Conn.: Archon, 1980.

Clemens, Diane S. *Yalta*. New York: Oxford University Press, 1970.

Cline, Ray S. *Washington Command Post: The Operations Division (United States Army in World War II: The War Department)*. Washington, D.C.: Office of the Chief of Military History, 1951.

Cumings, Bruce. *The Origins of the Korean War: Liberation and the Emergence of Separate Regimes, 1945–1947*. Princeton: Princeton University Press, 1980.

Cumings, Bruce, ed. *Child of Conflict: The Korean-American Relationship, 1943–1953*. Seattle: University of Washington Press, 1983.

Dallek, Robert. *Franklin D. Roosevelt and American Foreign Policy, 1932–1945*. New York: Oxford University Press, 1979.

Davies, John Paton, Jr. *Dragon by the Tail: American, British, Japanese, and Russian Encounters with China and One Another*. New York: Norton, 1972.

Davis, Lynn Etheridge. *The Cold War Begins: Soviet-American Confrontation Over Eastern Europe*. Princeton: Princeton University Press, 1974.

Deane, John R. *Strange Alliance: The Story of Our Efforts at Wartime Co-Operation with Russia*. New York: Viking Press, 1947.

De Gaulle, Charles. *The Complete War Memoirs of Charles de Gaulle*. Jonathan Griffin, tr. New York: Simon and Schuster, 1964.

Dobbs, Charles. *The Unwanted Symbol: American Foreign Policy, the Cold War, and Korea, 1945–1950*. Kent: Kent State University Press, 1981.

Donovan, Robert J. *Conflict and Crisis: The Presidency of Harry S. Truman, 1945–1948*. New York: Norton, 1977.

Drachman, Edward. *U.S. Policy Toward Vietnam, 1940–1945*. Rutherford, N.J.: Farleigh Dickinson University Press, 1970.

Ehrman, John. *Grand Strategy. Vol. 6: October 1944–August 1945*. London: Her Majesty's Stationery Office, 1956.

Emmerson, John K. *The Japanese Thread: A Life in the U.S. Foreign Service*. New York: Holt, Rinehart and Winston, 1978.

Feaver, John Hansen. "The Truman Administration and China, 1945–1950: The Policy of Restrained Intervention." Ph.D. dissertation, University of Oklahoma, 1982.

Feis, Herbert. *Churchill, Roosevelt, Stalin: The War They Waged and the Peace They Sought*. Princeton: Princeton University Press, 1967.

Feis, Herbert. *The China Tangle: The American Effort in China from Pearl Harbor to the Marshall Mission*. Princeton: Princeton University Press, 1953.

Feis, Herbert. *Japan Subdued: The Atomic Bomb and the End of the War in the Pacific*. Princeton: Princeton University Press, 1961.

Ferrell, Robert, ed. *Dear Bess: The Letters of Harry to Bess Truman, 1910–1959*. New York: Norton, 1983.

Ferrell, Robert, ed. *Off the Record: The Private Papers of Harry S. Truman*. New York: Penguin, 1980.

Fetzer, James Alan. "Senator Vandenburg and the American Commitment to China." *The Historian* (February 1974), 36:283–303.

Frank, Benis M. and Henry I. Shaw, Jr. *Victory and Occupation. History of U.S. Marine Corps Operations in World War II*. Washington, D.C.: Historical Branch, Headquarters, Marine Corps, 1968.

Gaddis, John Lewis. *Strategies of Containment: A Critical Appraisal of Postwar American National Security Policy*. New York: Oxford University Press, 1982.

Gaddis, John Lewis. *The United States and the Origins of the Cold War, 1941–1947*. New York: Columbia University Press, 1972.

Glantz, Lt. Col. David M. *August Storm: The Soviet Strategic Offensive in Manchuria. Leavenworth Papers*. Fort Leavenworth, Kansas: Combat Studies Institute, 1983.

Gorlaski, Robert. *World War II Almanac, 1931–1945*. New York: Putnam, 1981.

Grew, Joseph C. *Turbulent Era: A Diplomatic Record of Forty Years (1904–1945)*. Vol. 2. Boston: Houghton Mifflin, 1952.

Hamby, Alonzo L. *Beyond the New Deal: Harry S. Truman and American Liberalism*. New York: Columbia University Press, 1973.

Hayes, Grace Person. *The History of the Joint Chiefs of Staff in World War II: The War Against Japan*. Annapolis: Naval Institute Press, 1982.

Harriman, W. Averell and Elie Abel. *Special Envoy to Churchill and Stalin, 1941–1946*. New York: Random House, 1975.

Haynes, Richard F. *The Awesome Power: Harry S. Truman as Commander in Chief*. Baton Rouge: Louisiana State University Press, 1973.

Heinrichs, Waldo H., Jr. *American Ambassador: Joseph C. Grew and the Development of the United States Diplomatic Tradition*. Boston: Little, Brown, 1966.

Herken, Gregg. *The Winning Weapon: The A-Bomb in the Cold War, 1945–1950*. New York: Knopf, 1980.

Hull, Cordell. *The Memoirs of Cordell Hull*. Vol. 2. New York: Macmillan, 1948.

Herring, George C. "The Truman Administration and the Restoration of French Sovereignty in Indochina." *Diplomatic History* (Spring 1977), 1:97–117.

Iriye, Akira. *Power and Culture: The Japanese-American War, 1941–1945*. Cambridge: Harvard University Press, 1981.

Iriye, Akira. *The Cold War in Asia: A Historical Introduction*. Englewood Cliffs, N.J.: Prentice Hall, 1974.

James, D. Clayton. *The Years of MacArthur. Vol. 2:1941–1945*. Boston: Houghton Mifflin, 1975.

Jones, F. C., Hugh Borton, and B. R. Pearn. *The Far East, 1942–1946*. Survey of International Affairs, 1939–1946. Arnold Toynbee, ed. London: Oxford University Press, 1955.

Kennan, George F. *Memoirs, 1925–1950*. Boston: Little, Brown, 1967.

Kirby, Stanley Woodburn. *The War Against Japan*. London: Her Majesty's Stationery Office, 1969.

Kolko, Gabriel. *The Politics of War: The World and United States Foreign Policy, 1943–1945*. New York: Random House, 1968.

Kuniholm, Bruce Robellet. *The Origins of the Cold War in the Near East: Great Power Conflict and Diplomacy in Iran, Turkey, and Greece*. Princeton: Princeton University Press, 1980.

Leahy, William D. *I Was There: The Personal Story of the Chief of Staff to Presidents Roosevelt and Truman*. New York: Whittlesey House, 1950.

Lensen, George A. *The Strange Neutrality: Soviet-Japanese Relations During the Second World War, 1941–1945*. Tallahassee: Diplomatic Press, 1972.

Levering, Ralph B. *American Opinion and the Russian Alliance, 1939–1945*. Chapel Hill: University of North Carolina Press, 1976.

Levine, Steven I. "A New Look at American Mediation in the Chinese Civil War: The Marshall Mission and Manchuria." *Diplomatic History* (Fall 1979), 3:349–375.

Lewin, Ronald. *The American MAGIC: Codes, Ciphers, and the Defeat of Japan*. New York: Farrar, Straus and Giroux, 1982.

Louis, William Roger. *Imperialism at Bay: The United States and the Decolonization of the British Empire, 1941–1945*. New York: Oxford University Press, 1978.

Love, Robert William, Jr., ed. *The Chiefs of Naval Operations*. Annapolis: Naval Institute Press, 1980.

Luvaas, Jay, ed. *Dear Miss Em: General Eichelberger's War in the Pacific, 1942–1945*. Westport, Conn.: Greenwood Press, 1972.

McAlister, John T., Jr. *Vietnam: The Origins of Revolution*. Garden City, N.Y.: Doubleday, 1971.

McCloy, John J. *The Challenge to American Foreign Policy*. Cambridge: Harvard University Press, 1953.

McLellan, David. *Dean Acheson: The State Department Years*. New York: Dodd, Mead, 1976.

McLellan, David S. and David C. Acheson, eds. *Among Friends Personal Letters of Dean Acheson*. New York: Dodd, Mead, 1980.

Matloff, Maurice. *Strategic Planning for Coalition Warfare, 1943–1944 (United States Army in World War II: The War Department)*. Washington, D.C.: Office of the Chief of Military History, 1959.

Matray, James I. "Captive of the Cold War: The Decision to Divide Korea at the 38th Parallel." *Pacific Historical Review* (May 1981), 50:145–168.

Matray, James I. *The Reluctant Crusade: American Foreign Policy in Korea, 1941–1950*. Honolulu: University of Hawaii Press, 1985.

May, Ernest R. *The "Lessons" of the Past: The Use and Misuse of History in American Foreign Policy*. New York: Oxford University Press, 1976.

May, Ernest R. *The Truman Administration and China, 1945–1949*. Philadelphia: Lippincott, 1975.

May, Gary. *China Scapegoat: The Diplomatic Ordeal of John Carter Vincent*. Prospect Heights, Ill.: Waveland Press, 1979.

Merli, Frank T. and Theodore Wilson, eds. *The Makers of American Diplomacy: Benjamin Franklin to Henry Kissinger*. New York: Scribner's, 1974.

Messer, Robert L. *The End of an Alliance: James F. Byrnes, Roosevelt, Truman, and the Origins of the Cold War*. Chapel Hill: University of North Carolina Press, 1982.

Millis, Walter, ed. *The Forrestal Diaries*. New York: Viking Press, 1951.

Morison, Samuel Eliot. *History of United States Naval Operations in World War II: Victory in the Pacific, 1945*. Boston: Little, Brown, 1961.

Morris, William George. "The Korean Trusteeship, 1941–1947: The United States, Russia, and the Cold War." Ph.D. dissertation, University of Texas at Austin, 1974.

Nagai, Yonosuke and Akira Iriye. *The Origins of the Cold War in Asia*. New York: Columbia University Press, 1977.

Notter, Harley. *Postwar Foreign Policy Preparation, 1939–1945*. Washington, D.C.: GPO, 1949.

O'Conner, Raymond G. *Diplomacy for Victory: FDR and Unconditional Surrender*. New York: Norton, 1971.

Paterson, Thomas. *On Every Front: The Making of the Cold War*. New York: Norton, 1979.

Pickler, Colonel Gordon K. "United States Aid to the Chinese Nationalist Air Force, 1931–1949." Ph.D. dissertation, Florida State University, 1971.

Pogue, Forrest. *George C. Marshall: Organizer of Victory.* New York: Viking Press, 1973.

Reardon-Anderson, James. *Yenan and the Great Powers: The Origins of Chinese Communist Foreign Policy, 1944–1946.* New York: Columbia University Press, 1980.

Romanus, Charles and Riley Sunderland. *Time Runs Out in CBI. United States Army in World War II: China Burma India Theater.* Washington, D.C.: Office of the Chief of Military History, 1959.

Rose, Lisle. *After Yalta.* New York: Scribner, 1973.

Rose, Lisle. *Dubious Victory: The United States and the End of World War II.* Kent: Kent State University Press, 1973.

Rose, Lisle A. *Roots of Tragedy: The United States and the Struggle for Asia, 1945–1953.* Westport, Conn.: Greenwood Press, 1976.

Sandusky, Michael C. *America's Parallel.* Alexandria: Old Dominion Press, 1983.

Sbrega, John J. *Anglo-American Relations and Colonialism in East Asia, 1941–1945.* New York: Garland, 1983.

Schaller, Michael. *The U.S. Crusade in China, 1938–1945.* New York: Columbia University Press, 1979.

Schnabel, James F. *The History of the Joint Chiefs of Staff: The JCS and National Policy, 1945–1947.* Wilmington, De.: M. Glazier, 1979.

Sherwin, Martin J. *A World Destroyed: The Atomic Bomb and the Grand Alliance.* New York: Vintage, 1977.

Sherwood, Robert E. *Roosevelt and Hopkins: An Intimate History.* New York: Harper, 1948.

Smith, Perry M. *The Air Force Plans for Peace, 1943–1945.* Baltimore: Johns Hopkins University Press, 1970.

Spector, Ronald. "Allied Intelligence and Indochina, 1943–1950." *Pacific Historical Review* (February 1982), 51:23–50.

Spector, Ronald. *Eagle Against the Sun: The American War with Japan.* New York: Free Press, 1985.

Spector, Ronald. *United States Army in Vietnam. Advice and Support: The Early Years, 1941–1960.* Washington, D.C.: Center of Military History, 1983.

Stephan, John J. *The Kurile Islands: Russo-Japanese Frontier in the Pacific.* Oxford: Clarendon Press, 1974.

Stimson, Henry L. and McGeorge Bundy. *On Active Service in Peace and War.* New York: Harper, 1947.

Stueck, William Whitney, Jr. *The Road to Confrontation: American Policy Toward China and Korea, 1947–1950.* Chapel Hill: University of North Carolina Press, 1981.

Taubman, William. *Stalin's American Policy: From Entente to Detente to Cold War.* New York: Norton, 1982.

Terraine, John. *The Life and Times of Lord Mountbatten.* London: Hutchinson, 1968.

Theoharis, Athan. *The Yalta Myths: An Issue in U.S. Politics.* Columbia: University of Missouri Press, 1970.

Thorne, Christopher. *Allies of a Kind: The United States, Britain, and the War Against Japan, 1941–1945*. New York: Oxford University Press, 1978.

Truman, Harry S. *Memoirs: Year of Decisions*. Garden City, N.Y.: Doubleday, 1955.

Tuchman, Barbara W. *Stilwell and the American Experience in China, 1911–1945*. New York: Bantam, 1972.

Tuttle, Dwight William. *Harry L. Hopkins and Anglo-American-Soviet Relations, 1941–1945*. New York: Garland, 1983.

Varg, Paul A. *The Closing of the Door: Sino-American Relations, 1936–1946*. East Lansing: Michigan State University Press, 1973.

Vigneras, Marcel. *Rearming the French (United States Army in World War II: Special Studies)*. Washington, D.C.: Office of the Chief of Military History, 1956.

Villa, Brian. "The U.S. Army, Unconditional Surrender, and the Potsdam Proclamation." *Journal of American History* (June 1976), 63:66–92.

Ward, Patricia Dawson. *The Threat of Peace: James F. Byrnes and the Council of Foreign Ministers, 1945–1946*. Kent: Kent State University Press, 1979.

Wedemeyer, Albert C. *Wedemeyer Reports!* New York: Holt, 1958.

Weigley, Russell F. *The American Way of War: A History of United States Military Strategy and Policy*. Bloomington: Indiana University Press, 1973.

Weil, Martin. *A Pretty Good Club: The Founding Fathers of the U.S. Foreign Service*. New York: Norton, 1978.

Wolfe, Robert, ed. *Americans as Proconsuls: United States Military Government in Germany and Japan, 1944–1952*. Carbondale: Southern Illinois University Press, 1984.

Yergin, Daniel. *Shattered Peace: The Origins of the Cold War and the National Security State*. Boston: Houghton Mifflin, 1978.

Zacharias, Capt. Ellis M. *Secret Missions: The Story of an Intelligence Officer*. New York: Putnam, 1946.

Index